THE PRESS GANG

THE PRESS GANG

Tales from the Glory Days of Irish Newspapers

Edited by David Kenny

NEW ISLAND

THE PRESS GANG: TALES FROM THE GLORY DAYS OF
IRISH NEWSPAPERS

First published in 2015
by
New Island Books
16 Priory Hall Office Park
Stillorgan
County Dublin
Republic of Ireland

www.newisland.ie

PRINT ISBN: 978-1-84840-478-6
EPUB ISBN: 978-1-84840-479-3
MOBI ISBN: 978-1-84840-480-9

British Library Cataloguing Data.
A CIP catalogue record for this book is available from the British Library.

Typeset by JVR Creative India
Cover design by Mariel Deegan.
Printed by ScandBook AB, Sweden.

10 9 8 7 6 5 4 3 2 1

*In memory of Michael Carwood,
and all our colleagues and friends who have met the
ultimate deadline.*

Contents

The News in Brief

Foreword

Tim Pat Coogan
(Editor, *Irish Press*, 1968–1987)

Like a lot of national treasures, the *Irish Press* has disappeared into the bog of history. It literally was a very Irish institution and, in its day, a valuable one.

It was born out of the fertile brain of Éamon de Valera, who, having spent most of the period of the Black and Tan War in America propagandising, returned to Ireland to take command of the emerging peace negotiations some months before the war ended, leaving millions of dollars, subscribed by Irish emigrants to the Irish cause, lying in New York banks.

During the 1920s a New York court, unable to decide between de Valera and the Free State government, both of whom claimed the money, returned the bonds to the original subscribers. De Valera had seen to it that the subscribers' names and addresses were kept on file. His lawyers had briefed him to expect the verdict, and he had letters prepared notifying the bondholders that he was founding a truly national newspaper. He included forms with this announcement that he invited the bondholders to fill in, deeding the bonds over to him so that he could use them as collateral to help found the *Irish Press*.

Many did so believing, like most of the early *Irish Press* staff who were employed by the paper when Padraig Pearse's mother pressed the button to start the presses in 1931, that they were still working for 'the cause'. The staff were mostly Republican, literate, loyal, and incredibly hard-working. It cannot be claimed that their loyalty was always rewarded by the paper's controllers, for in reality the staff were working not for 'the cause' but for a segment of the de Valera family. De Valera passed the papers on to his eldest son, Vivion, who in turn entrusted them to his son, Éamon.

An episode that occurred while I was editor (1968–87) says much about the attitude of employers to those employed. Paddy Clare, who had been a Sinn Féiner, supporting Arthur Griffith, later mounted the barricades on the Republican side during the Civil War, and subsequently joined the *Irish Press*, which to him was a part of the vision of Ireland for which he had risked his life.

Somehow, during all his working years, Paddy was never made a member of the staff. He was paid on a docket and worked for decades on a graveyard shift from well before midnight until after 6 o'clock the following morning. Having retired on a not-very-generous pension, he came to me one day telling me that: 'The lungs are bad and the doctor says I can't take the winters here any more; I need to go to Spain. Trouble is, the pension won't stretch. I need another fiver a week.'

Paddy never got the extra fiver. He died of emphysema.

Despite this, and many other stories of tight-fistedness toward staff that could be told, the Press Group had an extraordinary feeling of camaraderie about it. A great general manager, Jack Dempsey, helped to persuade the cautious de Valera senior (and Vivion) to add to the morning paper's income stream by founding the *Sunday Press* in 1949, and the logical result of this growth process was the *Evening Press*, an extraordinarily successful venture, which began under the editorship of Douglas Gageby in 1954, when I joined the company.

For several years thereafter, the Irish Press Building on Burgh Quay, Daniel O'Connell's Conciliation Hall, later the Tivoli Music Hall, was a place of youth, laughter, low pay and incredibly hard work. It was also the setting for some of the best journalism in the English-speaking world, motivated by something of 'the cause' feeling, although by now the ideals of 1916 were dimming, and in the *Irish Press* 'the cause' was represented by a dull, dutiful support of the machine politics of Fianna Fáil.

In fact, Fianna Fáil, and to a large extent the GAA, both owe a large proportion of their success to the *Irish Press*, which at the time went out of its way to promote their ideals. In the early 1930s the other papers regarded Fianna Fáil with marked hostility, and GAA games were hardly noticed by the Unionist *Irish Times* and the right-wing, business-oriented *Irish Independent*. But the obvious circulation gains of the *Irish Press* forced the other papers to follow its lead, from which the GAA benefited enormously.

The influence of the *Press* permeated Irish society in all sorts of unexpected ways. One of its many small columns read by devoted circles of niche readers was a historical snippet, 'Window on the Past', compiled by 'S. J. L.' S. J. L.'s son is today the highly respected author and financial journalist Pat Leahy, political editor of the *Sunday Business Post*, which in turn was founded by another *Irish Press* journalist, Damien Kiberd, whom I had the good fortune to hire.

One of those niche columns in the *Irish Press* nearly caused me serious grief. After internment was introduced in Northern Ireland in 1971, I wanted to see what conditions were like and had myself smuggled into Long Kesh under the assumed name of a prisoner's relative. Just as the Hiace van containing the real relatives and me drew up at the prison, a man sitting opposite me said in a loud voice: 'Hey, you're the editor of the *Irish Press*, Tim Pat Coogan! I'm a coin collector and the *Irish Press* is the only paper that gives the numismatists [coin collectors] a show. Congratulations!' Fortunately, the soldiers did not hear him.

Unfortunately, by 1968 the paper had become dull and unduly dutiful in its support of Fianna Fáil. Old, rural readers were dying, and no young city dwellers were being attracted to replace them. The diversion of resources to the *Sunday Press* and *Evening Press* from the flagship *Irish Press* meant that the paper was losing circulation at a rate of 20,000 copies a year. I was appointed with a promise that resources would be forthcoming both to stop the rot and to restore the paper to the position of influence it once held. For a time it did prove possible to halt the slide, even increasing the circulation.

However, at the same time, Vivion de Valera had embarked on an ambitious building programme that turned the Burgh Quay site into a version of the glass-covered Express Building in London's Fleet Street, where Vivion had been sent to serve a brief newspaper internship.

Thereafter, working amidst the sound of builders' drills and the sight of falling plaster, the spirit of the Tivoli rather than of Conciliation Hall permeated the place. I brought Harold Evans, the innovative editor of *The Sunday Times*, on a tour of the paper one evening, and the subeditors greeted us with a banner saying: 'Welcome to Short Kesh'.

The building took forever to complete, but when it was finally finished, no increased flow of capital for the *Irish Press* ensued. The company at the time was one of the big property owners of Dublin, and money could have been found for investment in the paper, but this was anathema to the de Valera philosophy of control. No dilution of control by bringing fresh money into the coffers and fresh faces into the boardroom could be contemplated. It is not true as some wiseacres maintained that Dublin was over-supplied with newspapers. The *Daily Mail* and its Sunday paper were able to come into Dublin with deep pockets and show what could be done.

If Tony O'Reilly had not diverted large sums from the Independent Group to subsidise the London *Independent* and to purchase an evening newspaper, the *Belfast Telegraph*, for some €400m, in order both to bolster his claim to be the biggest press baron in Ireland and England and to secure a knighthood, that powerful group could also have been considerably wealthier. Even the solitary *Irish Times* somehow continues to breast the waves, as does the *Irish Examiner*.

However, suffice it to say that no life-sustaining outside influences were brought into the *Irish Press*. The company danced to the tune of a tone-deaf ceili band, while outside its walls *Riverdance* sounded. The awful industrial-relations climate got worse, not better. The Irish Press Group was the only one to suffer a closure when it introduced new technologies and dispensed with hot metal. After publication resumed, the *Irish Press* was not brought back until weeks after the other papers had hit the street – a clear indication of where priorities lay in the group, now headed by Vivion's son. Moreover, when the *Irish Press* did resume, the manning agreement between the former printers and the management could not take the additional strain of the third paper, and there were many missed deadlines and lost sales.

A disastrous attempt to correct matters was made by turning the broadsheet *Irish Press* into a shoddy little tabloid. The size of the circulation soon resembled that of the paper.

Worse was to follow. A disastrous interlude of lawsuits and unpleasantness came in the wake of the catastrophic decision to bring Ralph Ingersoll into the management structure. Ingersoll's father had been a great journalist, but he had made his reputation as an asset stripper of existing newspapers in the United States.

He brought his people with him, but they did not gel with the group's traditions. There is a famous anecdote concerning an alleged passage of arms between one of his cost-cutters and the art editor who assigned photographers:

Art Editor: 'We're covering the climbing of Croagh Patrick next Sunday.'

Ingersoll representative: 'Why? I've checked the papers and you covered that last year!'

The Ingersoll/IP experiment ended in tears and expensive lawsuits. The always-unfortunate relationship between the management and the staff suggested by the Paddy Clare anecdote persisted and accelerated throughout the 1980s and 1990s, and the paper closed its doors in the midst of an industrial dispute in 1995, never to reopen.

The last, fatal row could only have occurred in the Irish Press Group. Colm Rapple, the leading financial journalist with the *Irish Press*, took part in an *Irish Times* series on newspapers in which he did some straight talking about the situation facing the Press Group. The industrial-relations situation in the group at the time was akin to a building in which large amounts of petrol have been spilled. In this climate, the *Press*'s management fired Rapple for 'disloyalty'. So much for freedom of speech. Predictably, the staff immediately ceased work. The upshot was that the paper closed its doors.

Newspapers are strange creations and attract strange people at managerial as well as at other levels. Vanity publishing costing hundreds of millions is not unique to Ireland, nor is the desire to retain control in the teeth of reality. The great general manager, Jack Dempsey, had not been followed by an outside replacement.

Dempsey had been succeeded by the loyal and patient Colm Traynor, who had formed a link with the great days of the paper's birth. His father was Oscar Traynor, whose Fianna Fáil and Republican credentials were such that he was the Fianna Fáil minister chosen to bell the cat by informing the aging Éamon de Valera the first that it was time for him to retire as Taoiseach, which he duly did, and instead became president. Colm told me himself that he didn't get on too well with 'your man', meaning Éamon, the grandson. However, as Colm began to grow disillusioned and lose patience with his situation, Éamon the lesser came to an unfortunate decision and an even more unfortunate choice. For some years the *Sunday Press* had been losing circulation. Éamon de Valera decided to remove the editor, Vincent Jennings, but to make of him the Jack Dempsey of the day. This happened in 1986. Many of the occurrences described above followed afterwards.

I left in 1987. By then the end was obviously near, and my advice on diversification and the bringing in of new expertise was unwelcome, or at least certainly unheeded. But I do remember the professionalism of my comrades over the decades with great affection, and in one or two areas with considerable pride. For some years after the Troubles erupted, the *Irish Press* coverage of Northern Ireland was amongst the best in the world. In 1976 the *Press* successfully campaigned against Conor Cruise O'Brien's attempts to restrict press coverage by extending to the print media the provision of the Broadcasting Acts forbidding interviews with Sinn Féin spokespersons and inhibiting discussion of the 'Northern issue'. Also, whether everyone would agree that it was an unmitigated blessing or not I don't know, but I unwittingly helped to bring feminism to Ireland! That is to say, in 1968 I appointed Mary Kenny as woman's editor. She did the rest with the people and the teams she drew around her.

I also remember with respect the author and *Evening Press* features editor Sean McCann, who one day in 1968 introduced me to David Marcus, who wanted to extend his career as an editor of literary magazines by devoting a full page in a national newspaper to new Irish writing each week. I thought the idea a brilliant one, and as a result, for twenty years, almost every Irish writer or poet of consequence had their first or subsequent writings published in the paper. I'd like to think that Sean's son, Colm, the novelist, forms part of that tradition.

Two colleagues who I cannot conclude without mentioning were Fintan Faulkner and John Garvey, both of whom worked with me as deputy editors. I could not have asked for more loyal or professional men at my elbow.

The end of the *Irish Press* was sad, recalling words spoken after the Battle of the Boyne: 'Change kings and we'll fight you again,' but in its day it made a real and valuable contribution to Irish life.

Editor's Note

David Kenny

A day may be a long time in politics, but it's an eternity in the newspaper business. What was influential, entertaining, annoying and – above all – newsworthy at breakfast, is cat litter by supper time. The print industry is built on immediacy, where hour by hour each edition makes its predecessor redundant and irrelevant.

The memory of each edition fades, but the memory of the *title* remains. This is the case with the legendary Irish Press Group. It is twenty years since its demise, but its readers still remember it. So do its employees. Many of those who worked for it are still active and thriving in the business, having learned their craft in the most inventive newspaper group this country (or *any* country) has ever produced. The *Press*'s influence lives on.

The group (Sunday, Irish and Evening) constantly floundered, and those half-drowned souls who manned the pumps did so because they loved it. Financial reward never came into the equation; to work for the *Press* meant being constantly broke. The rewards for being a journo are not tangible, and in the case of the *Press* they are only memories now. Memories of stories broken, deadlines met, mad characters sidestepped, bizarre work practices and monstrous hangovers. Memories of an age when a pen, a notebook and a public payphone were the laptops and Google of their day.

So why bother celebrating a failed business after all these years? The answer is that the *Press* was never a business to its readers or writers: it was a way of life. That way of life and news dissemination has vanished like the Linotype. In terms of influence, a single tweet can replace an entire day's labour by a footsore hack. This book is a collective memoir by sixty former papermen/women that aims to give an insight into the golden (or at least, pyrite-hued) pre-Twitter/internet age of newspapers. It shows how news was published the hard way: with boots on the ground and, occasionally, faces on the ground too, generally under a bar stool.

It started with a tentative post on the *Irish Press* journalists' Facebook page. 'I want to do a memoir,' I typed (hesitantly). 'Anyone interested in writing a piece?'

My brief was simple: write what you remember, and at all times be entertaining. And this book *is* entertaining, for anyone who has ever picked up, thrown down or cleaned themselves intimately with a newspaper. It was never intended to be just a dry academic tome for journalism students – although I humbly suggest that it should be required reading.

That said, there will be critics who will point out omissions. There are some household names missing, and I would have liked to have had more sport. Some former writers had put the past to bed and were unwilling or unable to document their experiences. This was a voluntary enterprise by its contributors; I could only gently cajole people and hope that most were aware of the project's existence. I couldn't contact all of the 600 'Pressers' who worked there in May 1995. If I had – and they had all agreed to write a piece – then this book would never have fitted through the door of your downstairs loo. Besides, many of them are dead.

I decided from the start that I would take a 'light-touch' sub-editing approach to this book. A number of strong personalities (Tim Pat Coogan, Gerry O'Hare, Dermot McIntyre, etc.) crop up in many of the stories. Descriptions, situations and work practices do too. I believe their reappearance creates its own narrative sub-thread. Each chapter stands alone and is deeply personal to its author. As editor, I didn't want to impose my own voice on my colleagues' work; they are old enough and skilled enough to tell their own stories without interference.

The book has a rough chronology, starting in the 1950s and ending in the 1990s. It is not intended to be read from beginning to end. My best advice is to dip in and out, like you would with a newspaper.

Monumental thanks and a rousing 'knockdown' go to Patrick Madden for assembling the main body of the picture sections. And a subeditor's salute goes to photographers Ronan Quinlan, Austin Finn (RIP) and his family, Cyril Byrne, Pat Cashman, Colman Doyle, Brian Barron, Colin O'Riordain, Brenda Fitzsimons, Colm Mahady, Bryan O'Brien, Seán Larkin, Tom Hanahoe, Russell Banks, Bob Hobby, Gary Barton, Tony Gavin, Mick Slevin and Niall McInerney.

Finally, I'm eternally grateful to Justin Corfield, Edwin Higel, Dan Bolger, Shauna Daly, Mariel Deegan and all at New Island for immediately seeing the merits of this unique project. I am proud to note that this is the first book of its kind printed in any language, anywhere.

Another 'scoop' for the *Press* gang.

David Kenny
September 2015

Country Edition

The Early Days

The reverend mother told me the fire wasn't worth a fuck

Sean Purcell
(Chief Subeditor, *Irish Press*, 1995)

Even by the standard of the bizarre vagaries of life at the *Irish Press*, the editor's complaint that evening was a bit unusual. One of our subeditors had poked his penis through the letterbox and pissed all over the floor of his office.

There was nothing salacious about how he had identified the culprit from inside the room; he had simply guessed his identity having encountered him showing signs of volatility earlier. About the affront itself he was uncharacteristically sanguine, leaving it to me to contain the fallout. It set me wondering how I had ended up in a madhouse, appropriately enough a converted music hall on the Dublin quays. The building we occupied had been the old Tivoli Theatre, and before that the Lyric. Only now does it strike me: our destiny had been linked from birth with laughter along the Liffey.

I had started out in Waterford, in a dilapidated building, also on the quays, a sixteen-year-old graduate of the tech in Mooncoin earning seven shillings and sixpence a week as a cub reporter with the *Star*. Within months, and long before the term had been coined, I was headhunted by Smokey Joe Walsh, owner/editor of the *Munster Express*. Shamefully, I deserted the *Star* for an extra half crown. Two years later I went to Roscommon, to the *Champion*, and in another two years I was with the *Sunday Independent* in Dublin. Communications colleges and media studies belonged to the future. The route I took was a common way of qualifying as a journalist in the fifties and sixties: one learned the rudiments of local government in the council chamber and the workings of the justice system in the courtroom. It was an apprenticeship that left one short on theory but sound in practice.

I must have been ludicrously cocksure back then because when McLuhan drew attention to the speed at which communications were shrinking the world, I thought he was a bit tardy with the news. Hadn't the *Skibbereen Eagle* been keeping an eye on Russia the year before my father was born? The global village genius was on to something, however, because in the course of my career print journalism dashed, in a decade, from hot metal through new technology to the dubious delights of social media. (Try whistling that to the tune of John Adams's *Short Ride in a Fast Machine*.)

I arrived at the *Press* with fifteen years' experience in the newsroom at RTÉ, a career move I had made for personal reasons, as the saying goes.

The *Press* in the sixties and seventies had been through a mini golden age of women's lib, but that was well and truly over by the time I got there. The campaign for condoms had been shouldered aside by a campaign for cordite. That, certainly, was what Conor Cruise O'Brien suspected as he kept a daily tally of our pro-Provo letters in his ministerial office. Undeniably, our political hue had intensified from grass green to effulgent emerald.

No woman found employment on the subs' desk for quite a bit of my time there, and it was late in the seventies before we even considered it odd that we worked in a woman-free zone. There was a vague feeling – lame excuse, more accurately – that their tender souls would not survive the deadly mix of ungodly hours, blue air, coarse cynicism and a whole deskload of testosterone. Vincent Doyle of the *Irish Independent* was the last morning paper editor in Dublin to concede defeat on the exclusion of women subs, and he did so with considerable reluctance and an indelicate proviso: 'So long as you treat her like the rest of them and work her bollocks off,' he instructed his chief sub.

In those days a warlike rivalry existed among the three Dublin papers, and was fiercest between the *Press* and the *Independent*. *The Irish Times*, then as now, maintained a prissy distance between itself and its noisy neighbours. Amazingly, the Cold War ended every night at midnight when a so-called night-town reporter took over on the newsdesks. Those fellows collaborated freely on stories breaking in the small hours, and if things grew hectic they shared the workload between them.

Maurice Liston, a *Press* man who went on to become a chief reporter and the terror of the newsroom, was collaborating one night with the *Independent*'s night-town man when news broke of two serious-sounding accidents: a fatal car crash and a fire in a convent. The *Indo*'s man was the first to deliver. He phoned across a substantial accident report to Burgh Quay and then enquired if there was any news from the nuns. Liston's response has become part of newspaper folklore. 'I got the reverend mother out of bed,' he said, 'and she told me that fire wasn't worth a fuck.'

Print workers practised an ancient rite called a knockdown to mark occasions such as staff retirements or sudden windfalls of good fortune. It involved a caseroom assembly creating the loudest noise possible by banging metal tools on their metal benches. The din reverberated throughout the house and was kept up for several minutes. Major Vivion de Valera, the managing director and founder's son, was once accorded a knockdown after the staff had received an unexpected bonus. Unfortunately, he misdiagnosed goodwill for hostility and was terrorised by the clangour. Given his military credentials – he had four years' service on the side of Republican neutrality during the wartime 'emergency' – he might have been expected to face the danger with resolve. Dispatches, however, record that discretion trumped valour. The major ran away. He found shelter in an editorial office, complaining that the staff upstairs had gone completely mad. The celebratory significance of the knockdown had to be spelled out.

In an earlier incident involving the major in the caseroom, he went to sympathise with a man whose shoe was coming asunder, the sole slapping noisily on the floor as he walked. 'Ah sure,' said the wretch, 'I can barely keep body and soul together with the money you are paying us.'

'I may be able to help you there,' said the major, and the man watched with eager anticipation as he went deep into one of his pockets and came up with a stout rubber band.

Breandán Ó hEithir swore to the truth of that when he told it to me during our time in RTÉ. Ó hEithir had played a leading role in another incident involving the major. De Valera had returned from lunch one day to find a large human turd sitting on a windowsill inside his office. Who could the perpetrator be, and what was his motive? A discreet inquiry was launched by the major and his inner circle, but after a fortnight of delicate probing they were no nearer to the truth. Enter Ó hEithir in an imaginary deerstalker. Had the window been open or closed? Frequently open in daytime, he was told. The boy from Aran had the answer in a flash. 'Go back,' he advised, 'and tell the major the matter was carried up from the Liffey by a gull, and the gobshite was interrupted before he had time to have lunch.'

Mulligan's of Poolbeg Street was our pub of choice. There were those who fancied Kennedy's at Butt Bridge, but the atmosphere was so sedate there I usually avoided it, fearing I might hear a decade of the rosary from behind the counter. The printers, taking a break on official 'cutline' or unofficial 'slippiers', favoured the White Horse, a hostelry to which Benedict Kiely had given a wide and shady reputation with his story 'A Ball of Malt and Madame Butterfly'. Its renown was strictly local, though, no match for the notoriety of its New York namesake, the place that literary drunks will always associate with Dylan Thomas's last, fatal binge.

Some nights got stretched, like ourselves, and we moved with the hard chaws from Mulligan's to the Irish Times Club. That was a dingy drinking den three floors above a bookie's shop in Fleet Street. The drill for entry was a secret of its doyens. One pressed a bell-push in a nondescript door and a window was opened on the top floor. A head poked through and you moved out of the shadows and presented yourself in the light from a street lamp to be identified and assessed for fitness for admittance. If you passed muster, the door-key came down in a matchbox. Sober, you caught it in mid-air. Half cut, you went looking for it in the gutter. Either way, this was open sesame, and you ascended half a dozen flights to nirvana in the clouds. In truth, the place resembled an upstairs cellar.

The barman I knew only as Charlie. He was a veteran curmudgeon whose moods veered between glum and grumpy. One was advised to indulge him because he enjoyed supreme authority in deciding whether you were served or barred. I recall two merry punters giving him an order for two pints of Guinness and two gin and tonics. He took the order without demur and returned five minutes later with the pints. 'And now, gentlemen, you have two minutes to get the floozies off the premises,' he told them. He had surmised, correctly, that the gins were intended for two women they had hiding on the landing.

At the club one rubbed shoulders mainly with other journalists and printers, and occasionally a guard or two coming off duty in the nearby Pearse Street Station. Now and again the place provided more exalted company. I woke up one night and discovered that the sonorous monologue I'd been half hearing while I dozed was being delivered, to a fawning audience of machine hall dungarees, by Peter Ustinov, sometime actor and unceasing raconteur. It was Thursday night/Friday morning, and the overlarded old windbag was rehearsing a *Late Late Show* appearance. Or maybe it was Friday night/Saturday morning and he was basking in the afterglow. It turned out he had been touring the louche side of Dublin life, and his chaperone, some personage from *The Irish Times*, had condescended to take him to the club, a place in which he himself would not normally be seen, alive or dead.

Around midnight our newsroom could go weirdly quiet as shifts ended and staff drifted away. The last copy had been sent for setting and the final page proofs were being passed down to us to be checked. The rasp of our deputy editor, John Garvey, was suddenly silent; he had retired to his room with a couple of page proofs and a fine moral comb. Garvey, an earnest and quaintly strait-laced journalist, harboured a hidden fear that some smart alec would one day slip a sexual innuendo past him in copy. I used to think he'd find a double entendre in the Lord's Prayer. John Banville, the chief subeditor, and at the time engaged in real life with his early experimental novels, assumed the stillness of a Buddha and sank, luxuriously one imagined, into the labyrinthine sentences of a Henry James hardback. Jack Jones, the night editor, had entered a spell of intensive combat with *The Financial Times*'s cryptic crossword.

A musical soundtrack for this tableau was provided by John Brophy, a subeditor and occasional music critic who worked late shifts by choice. Sometimes it was a lively tin-whistle jig, more often a plaintive nocturne on his flute. Brophy has a head crammed with the kind of esoteric information useful to no one but a sub. The word on the desk was that to ask him for the time was to risk getting a history of the cuckoo clock. Offered a read of someone else's *Irish Times*, he turned it down with the observation that life was too short. We fancied ourselves for our rigorous way with verbose reporters, and that oblique comment can be seen as Brophy's two fingers to prolixity at *The Times*.

Down in the reporters' area, close to the big window that overlooked the Liffey, Frank Duignan, a former Galway footballer and like myself a refugee from RTÉ – the Irish-language *Nuacht* desk in his case – helped himself to generous tipples from a bottle of whiskey he kept locked in his drawer. Frank, or Proinsias, must not be knocked; there was a night in 1981 when he, working alone and against the clock in the early hours of St Valentine's Day, turned in an exemplary first account of the Stardust disaster.

In that quiet hiatus around midnight I once noticed a boozy fellow wake up in panic on the sports desk. He had just realised that he was not going to make the lavatory in time. He swayed out of the room, dropping here and there the sort of solid samples of which his doctor would have been proud. (Me too. Boxer shorts or nothing, one supposes.) A sports desk copyboy, working well beyond the line of duty, scurried in his wake and, with a pooper-scooper hastily fashioned from an old *Evening Press*, removed every vestige of offending matter. Passing through our area, he gave me a complicitous wink, and implicated me in a conspiracy of silence that has endured for almost forty years.

Younger readers should know of the indignities that attended our demise. The major had gone to a final knockdown in the sky, and de Valera mark III, a.k.a Major Minor, had assumed control with the title of editor-in-chief. In a fit of financial desperation, and with Vincent Jennings, editor of the Sunday paper, as his best man, he had climbed into bed with an American carpetbagger in what he described as a marriage made in heaven. It turned out to be a disaster made in hell. In preparation for the Irish–American nuptials, de Valera and Jennings had started to shrink the kids. The *Irish Press*, the firstborn and the flagship, was reduced to a tabloid. And then, after a fractious cohabitation and the goriest of divorce proceedings, plus a couple of years of unrelieved gloom, all three papers were gone. There would be no more laughter on Burgh Quay.

21

The final meltdown. Just seeing the words reminds me that in our hot-metal heyday we had a man upstairs called Gary, and he lived in a permanent lather of sweat. He worked in the foundry, melting down used metal for recycling and fetching on a bogey the pages of type the compositors had locked together in chases and which in his domain would be converted into flongs for the presses. (Notice how quickly even the words of our era are falling through the sieve of history.) We knew Gary as the bogeyman. The caseroom fellows, who revelled in creative christenings, called him the Incredible Melting Man.

Rumours used to reach us in those days of strange goings-on among our colleagues on the evening paper. They occupied the same desks as us, but during daylight. There was an old man there who always took his bicycle to work, by which I mean all the way upstairs to his desk. In quiet moments between subbing stints he liked to work on this machine, and in the year of his retirement he became fixated on fitting it with a sail. When eventually he achieved a satisfactory marriage of cloth and iron he brought his strange contraption to ground level, where, following adjustments in Poolbeg Street for wind conditions, he was last seen passing east under the Loop Bridge. With a fresh sou'wester behind him, and a few startled motorists in his wake, he was scudding, like a clipper, towards the harbour.

The past, as the man said, is another country.

From tea with Prince Charles, Bill and Hillary to hatch nineteen on Dole Street

Michael Keane
(Copyboy/Reporter/Northern Ireland News Editor/
Editor, *Sunday Press*, 1965–1995)

Maurice Liston was a big man in stature and in reputation. He was the doyen of the national media agriculture correspondents, a very important role as agriculture was the only real driver of the Irish economy in the sixties and early seventies.

Once, attending the Thurles Agricultural Show, a major event in the world of agriculture, Maurice was sitting in the press tent waiting for the show committee to deliver to him the day's results, champion heifer, prize bull etc. A young reporter from the *Tipperary Star* sat alongside Maurice and, awestruck at being in the presence of the great man, enquired politely: 'Mr Liston, what's it like working in the *Irish Press*?'

Maurice put down his generous glass of Jameson (without which no self-respecting agriculture correspondent could operate) and replied: 'Son, the *Irish Press* is like a three-ring circus. And I would be like a trapeze artist in that circus, going swing, swong, swing, swong. And there is always some bastard there to grease the bar.'

Despite Maurice's jaundiced view of the *Press*, it is extraordinary that some twenty years after its closure, and despite the bitterness that surrounded its last days, the well of fond memories and

23

endearment that is evident amongst those who worked there for their days in Burgh Quay still persists. When ex-*Press* people meet for any convivial occasion, and sadly they are rare enough these days, stories soon tumble from their lips – hilarious stories about the most bizarre happenings in Burgh Quay, but also in the nearby hostelries such as Mulligan's, the Silver Swan, the White Horse, the Scotch House, and on assignments far and wide.

The wonderful characters, the messers, the occasional weirdo, the drunks, the religious fanatics, the rabid Republicans, the anti-Republicans, the right-wingers, the left-wingers, the misers, the geniuses, the superb craftsmen and women, the chancers, the workaholics, the dossers, the brilliant reporters, the superb layout men, the astute subs, the outstanding writers, the reporters who could get a story but who couldn't write English, the wonderful shorthand writers who could take dictation in both English and Irish, the speedy copy-takers, the parties, the drinking, the rows, the romances, the craic – all of these will get an airing when the meetings occur over a few pints or glasses of wine.

One thing that transcended the often chaotic nature of life in Burgh Quay was great journalism. The Press newspapers had, and still have, a reputation for producing some of the outstanding journalists and journalism in Irish media history, with its reporters and photographers rated at the top of their respective fields.

When I joined the Irish Press Group as a copyboy/trainee journalist in 1965, the *Sunday Press* was the biggest selling of the Sunday papers, the *Evening Press* was coming into a golden age when it came close to outselling the *Irish Independent*, and the *Irish Press* was about to experience a renaissance with some brilliant journalism. It was, therefore, a very exciting time to be embarking on a career in journalism. I was allocated to the newsdesk as diary clerk, and my job was to ensure that a record was kept of all forthcoming events such as Dáil and court sittings, inquests, tribunals, festivals, courts martial, official openings, commemorations, press conferences, presidential comings and goings, etc.

It was also my job to ensure that country correspondents were covering events for the papers, so very quickly towns around the country became known by the names of the correspondents that sent stories from them. Thus, it became Maddock Rosslare, Hemmings Crolly, Joseph Mary Mooney Drumshambo, Molloy Ballina, McEntee Cavan, Gillespie Castlebar and so on, because that is how they announced themselves to the copy-takers. Two of the outstanding ones were Áine Hurley and Olive Dunne, who were brilliant at taking down long and long-winded reports from correspondents who were paid by the word.

Our staff man in Waterford in those days, John Scarry, rang through one morning with a story about the city being hit the night before by Hurricane Áine. Mick O'Toole, the *Evening Press* news editor, got the story and enquired: 'John, who christened it "Hurricane Áine"?' to which John confessed: 'I did, I named it after Áine the copy-taker!'

The same John rarely came to Dublin, but on one occasion he was cajoled by the chief news editor, Mick O'Kane, to join him in the city for lunch. The following day the redoubtable Betty Hooks, then the diary clerk, and one of the 'stars' of the newsroom, asked him how his lunch with the boss had gone.

'Ack, it was useless, aetin' raw mate in a cellar,' was his verdict on Dublin's finest medium-rare sirloin steak.

Drink played a huge role in the life of the *Press* in the days before a mid-seventies' house agreement brought much better wages and a higher standard of living for all concerned. Before that, however, the 'free drink' was particularly welcome, and especially welcome to some was an assignment that involved nuns who might be opening a school or a hospital extension. At the inevitable reception after the formalities, the whiskey bottle came out and, as 'Little Ed'

McDonald, a veteran snapper, told me, you got to experience the 'Reverend Mother's pour' because nuns poured whiskey as if it were red lemonade!

So you can imagine that the annual arrival of Good Friday was not something to be relished by the thirsty newsmen. The accommodating O'Connells, who ran the White Horse, did a brisk trade in their upstairs lounge, however. The doors below were locked, of course, so that unwelcome guests would not intrude. On one such Good Friday, as the boys were enjoying their pints and small ones, who should come into the newsroom but the Man in the Mac, Major Vivion de Valera, TD, controlling and managing director AND editor-in-chief.

'Where is everybody, Mr Hennessy?' he enquired of the man holding the fort in the newsroom, Mick Hennessy. 'Oh, they're all out on jobs, major,' lied Hennessy. The major flounced off, not a bit convinced. Mick quickly slid out of a side door, but could get no response from upstairs in the lounge. There was nothing for it but to climb up a drainpipe to knock on the window and warn the lads. Just as he reached the top he heard the dreaded voice of the major from below: 'Is this where the jobs are, Mr Hennessy?'

Meanwhile, back to the newsdesk. Each morning a list of what was on that day was handed to the chief news editor, who allocated jobs to reporters. A lengthy news list had to be prepared for the *Irish Press* editorial secretary, Maureen Craddock, to type up for the evening editorial conference, when the contents of the following day's paper would be discussed and decided upon.

Working as a diary clerk was wonderful training because you got to know how the system worked in detail, but in my case it went on for a year and a half, about a year longer than I thought necessary. I couldn't wait to be made a junior reporter and join the exciting team. Once I became a reporter I was like a bird freed from captivity, and a great adventure began that only ended thirty years later. That adventure took me to every part of Ireland and also to the UK, Germany, Italy, the Soviet Union, the United States, Israel, Lebanon, Norway, Holland, France, and perhaps most importantly to Northern Ireland, where I was Northern news editor for five years.

My role as a reporter meant work five days a week. It could be 'day-town' for the *Evening Press* starting at 7 a.m. to 9 a.m. if you were one of the elite *Evening Press* team, 10 a.m. if you were on duty for both the *Evening Press* and the *Irish Press*. On that shift you could end up in the courts or chasing fire brigades around town on a breaking story. The 3–11 p.m. shift was for *Irish Press* duty solely while 'night-town' was the graveyard shift, usually occupied by one-time Éamon de Valera minder and character Paddy Clare ('I carried Vivion de Valera on my shoulders to hear his daddy speak at a rally in O'Connell Street one time; he's been carrying me ever since!')

Each week one reporter was allocated *Sunday Press* duty. This involved joining a photographer on a three-day trip to some part of the country to suss out what we called the 'two-headed donkey' stories – in other words, unusual, entertaining local stories that would appeal to the wide readership of the paper. It was fun and somewhat pressurised as you had to come back with a few picture stories as the leads handed out by the *Sunday Press* news editor, Gerry Fox, were usually thrown out of the window at Newland's Cross. On one occasion the photographer was ordered to stop the car in a small hamlet in Co. Clare, the reporter hopped out, walked away and was never seen in Burgh Quay again.

The newsroom was a very noisy place, what with the constant clatter of typewriters being thumped at high speed by reporters racing to meet a deadline, news editors screaming instructions or demanding copy, phones ringing … in other words, controlled bedlam.

On one occasion, late, lamented colleague Sean MacConnell was trying to get information from the postmistress of an outpost in deepest Mayo about a local girl who had been knocked down and killed crossing a street in Paris. The line was so bad we all had to stop typing so he could hear. The postmistress gave out the required information: 'She went to the local national school, played camogie for the local club, a Child of Mary, a lovely girl, from a respected farming family; the funeral is on Thursday next.'

Finishing up, Sean shouted down the line: 'So they are bringing her home then?'

Postmistress: 'Oh yeah, sure she had a return ticket!'

The newsroom mayhem could be interrupted by the sight of rampaging caricaturist Bobby Pike, a repentant Mick Barber on his knees before an embarrassed news editor, George Kerr begging forgiveness for being two hours late back from a job, calls from the front office where Brendan Behan was slumped in his special chair demanding money for an article that had not yet been published, or the signal that a major disaster had happened, which sent the whole place into frantic overdrive.

The competitive battle with the *Irish Independent*, in particular, was intense. It was Munster v Leinster in present day intensity. We strove might and main to ensure that we got the big stories and got them first. *The Irish Times* seemed to be happy as long as it appeared, never mind that it was a day late.

The excitement of the big story was matched only by the satisfaction of beating the *Indo* hollow or getting a major scoop on our rivals. Some big stories didn't work out as planned, however, and it had nothing to do with the *Indo*. That was the night we buried Robert Kennedy prematurely in the *Sunday Press*. The phones went mad the next day with readers complaining, and one was somewhat mollified when I chanced my arm by asking him if he had never heard of the time difference. I only got away with that one once.

I had joined the *Evening Press* team in the late 1960s, and was being sent to cover the North on a periodic basis, which was harrowing enough. And then in 1972 Mick O'Kane asked me if I would take up the role of Northern news editor based full-time in Belfast. It was a difficult decision, but I agreed on condition that every second weekend I would leave for a break and would only disrupt my weekend if I decided to do so. It was the only way to manage the stress and maintain some sort of normal life with family and friends.

Going there in November 1972 to take up the position in succession to Vincent Browne, I was joined by a popular Scottish reporter, Laurie Kilday, who had been asked at his interview if he was willing to report from Northern Ireland if appointed. Little did he know that within a few months he would be sent up there full-time.

I will not dwell here on the difficulties and dangers of reporting on some of the worst violence during the awful Troubles. They have been well documented. What is perhaps not appreciated so much is that the people of Northern Ireland, even in their darkest hours, have a black sense of humour.

Laurie was caught one day in the middle of a riot involving Falls Road youngsters and the British Army, and took shelter in a doorway as the battle raged up and down the road in front of him. Only then did he notice a little old lady standing in the doorway beside him, shopping bag in hand.

'The bastards are not fightin' fair – they have shields and helmets and ambulances and everything. Our fellas have nothing,' she observed to Laurie.

Laurie gave a terrified 'Aye' in response.

The old lady realised that the 'Aye' was not from her part of the world, and asked: 'Where are you from, son?' to which Laurie replied: 'The Gorbals in Glasgow.'

The Gorbals was one of the toughest housing slums in Europe at the time. The old lady responded: 'The Gorbals? In Glasgow? God, I'd hate to live there. I believe it's fierce wild,' not a bit bothered by the mayhem around her.

On my return from Belfast in February 1978, I was appointed assistant editor of *The Irish Press* working with Tim Pat Coogan, John Garvey, Michael Wolsey and the chief subeditor, John Banville. It was a totally different type of job, producing the paper, writing editorials, editing letters etc. I badly missed the cut and thrust of the newsroom, the buzz of chasing the great stories of the day. So when a job came up as deputy chief news editor under Mick O'Kane, I went for it, and my life took off once again. It was like having a new career.

The newsdesk is the control centre of the news-gathering operation, and when a big story breaks there is nothing better than the excitement it generates. It was the time of 'Gubu', the era of the three elections, the Haughey heaves, the Pope's visit, President Reagan's visit, and of course the continuing Troubles in Northern Ireland – a wonderful time to be a journalist.

From there I went to the *Sunday Press* as deputy editor and news editor, which was demanding but very interesting, and I worked with some excellent journalists. Just a year and a half later I succeeded Vincent Jennings as editor, and filled that role for eight years until the house of cards came tumbling down.

When that happened I was in Washington DC attending President Clinton's economic summit on Northern Ireland, where we witnessed IRA and UVF men standing at the bar having a singing competition in the early hours, something that would be completely impossible back home. And we were entertained at a fabulous party on the White House lawn where we met Bill and Hillary Clinton. On our return I found an invitation to a party in the British ambassador's residence to meet Prince Charles. I said to my wife, Jenny: 'Let's go, we won't be getting many of these again,' and off we went and met the Prince.

So in the space of two weeks I had the pleasure of meeting Prince Charles, President Clinton, Hillary Clinton – and Miss Kelly at hatch nineteen at the dole office. I can assure you that Miss Kelly was much more beneficial to me in the days that followed than Charles, Bill or Hillary.

There's a man in the front office with a gun

Michael O'Kane
(Reporter/Group Chief News Editor, 1959–1995)

It's hard to believe that it is now two decades since I vacated my seat in the newsroom of the *Irish Press*, that bastion of 'The Truth in the News' from whence the Irish people got their daily dose of news for more than half a century. Looking back, it was a miracle that any newspapers emanated from our head office at Burgh Quay at all – with all the problems we had it took a Herculean effort almost every day to get a publication onto the street. On many occasions we did not produce a paper at all, what with rowing trade unions, imported so-called American press barons and atrocious in-house management – the less said about the latter, the better. Suffice to say that between them they wrecked three great newspapers, the *Irish Press, Evening Press* and *Sunday Press*, media organs that had served their country and democracy well for the greater part of the twentieth century.

When the blinds finally came down on Burgh Quay in 1995, and my umbilical cord was cut in such an ignominious way, it was probably all for the best. Even before that awful event, with more than half a dozen years still to serve I was not looking forward to retirement. The parting in 1995 was premature and traumatic, but if I had had to face normal retirement at sixty-five, I would have found it just as difficult.

There was little sense of the passing of time in that newsroom – everybody was a reporter and it didn't matter what age, or indeed what sex, you were – old and young, male and female – we were all equal. I attended lots of retirement parties over a period of thirty years, and none was a happy occasion. The body transplant from the hectic world of headlines and deadlines to the solitude of unrelenting home life was too much for most of them, and in time they just withered away and passed on.

The late Frank Neilis and I arrived in the *Irish Press* newsroom on the same day in 1959, he from a little paper in Newport in Co. Mayo, and me from the *The People's Press* in Co. Donegal. When I made my appearance that first day, word got around that I had joined the *Press* from a Blueshirt stable in the north-west. Bets were taken by veteran buffs like Arthur Noonan, Maurice O'Brien, Sean Ward, John Healy, Michael Mills, Aidan Hennigan and George Douglas – all except Aidan sadly gone to the great newsroom in the sky – that I would not last a month in the heartland of the Republican press. Ted Nealon, who afterwards became a minister in a Fine Gael government, was giving generous odds that I would not last until Christmas.

But my new-found colleagues did not reckon on this hard-nosed northerner from Co. Tyrone. I needed to show them that they had underestimated me. On just my third day in the newsroom I took the initiative and rang the general manager, Jack Dempsey, told him I had just arrived from the North, and asked if I could meet the boss, Major Vivion de Valera. He was a bit taken aback by the request, but my bold stroke worked: a few days later the news editor, George Kerr, called me to the newsdesk and announced in a loud voice that the major wanted to see me.

As it turned out, he was at that particular time in the Mater Private Nursing Home suffering from a nervous breakdown. I found my way to his room in the hospital, but hesitated when confronted by a large notice hanging on a nail on the closed door. '*No Visitors*', it read, and '*Do Not Disturb*'. I waited until a nun came along, explained that I had an appointment and asked what she thought I should do. She went inside and emerged leaving the door ajar. 'Don't stay too long,' she whispered, then disappeared down the corridor with a swish of her habit.

The man in the bed, whom I was seeing for the first time, looked ill, and lay almost inert during the brief interview. He told me to sit down and asked me a couple of questions about my family and experience as a reporter, and then told me I could go. I was glad to oblige. It was an uncomfortable, awkward first meeting, one of many I had with him during more than twenty years as news editor of the *Evening Press* and later chief news editor of the group. Not all of them were as cordial as that first encounter.

Word soon got around among the reporters that I had had a private audience with the major, and thereafter I was treated with much more respect. George Kerr, who was news editor at the time, aided and abetted me by whispering in a few well-placed ears that he heard there was 'a connection' between the O'Kane and de Valera families. George was one of the three real 'gentlemen of the press' that I befriended very early on. Another was the late Dan O'Connell, a Cork man, and of course Willie Collins, who happily is still with us and keeping well.

I spent the next thirty-six years on Burgh Quay, and loved every day of it. I met and worked with some of the most professional journalists this country ever produced, people who took great pride in the job they were doing, men and women who often put work before their home life because they felt they had a mission to keep the people of Ireland informed, giving them the facts, not trying to bend their minds. It was their job to dig deeper than their colleagues in other newspapers and produce the information that kept our readers better informed than anybody else.

Large newsrooms, such as we had in Burgh Quay – at one stage I directed seventy reporters working full-out to serve three newspapers – were by their very nature places apart, inhabited by a breed of people who had no equal in the world outside. For the most part they were talented people, but that gift was used to compete with colleagues and with journalists in other enterprises rather than to impress our readers. Behind the red-brick facade on Burgh Quay and the drinking establishments such as Mulligan's, the White Horse or the Scotch House, they existed in a rarefied atmosphere, a world apart.

Among journalists, drinking was a form of escapism from the real world. The work they produced for publication was based on hard facts, no matter how vivid or disturbing they were. You got no frills or trimmings or comment. Yet among the staff there was no limit to imagination when it came to tall tales, and the more fantastic the story, the better the reception. But that was not for the readers; by the time a story was written the facts had been distilled, bottled and made ready for delivery to the paying public. The spicy trimmings were for the ears only of colleagues.

One of the best illustrations of this split-personality existence among journalists was the late Sean Lynch, a Dundalk man who spent some years in America, and (he led us to believe) served with the Americans in Vietnam. He was a very knowledgeable fellow with a vivid imagination. In the newsroom one evening he was chatting to Major de Valera and to everybody's surprise demonstrated how to take an (invisible) M16 machine gun to pieces and put it together again in minutes. The major, who had some knowledge of ordinance from his years in the army, was so impressed that he suggested to me afterwards that Sean was good officer material, wasted as a reporter. In fact he was promoted soon afterwards to deputy news editor, and when he later left Burgh Quay for the *Independent* newsroom they recognised his qualities and he was given a news editor's job there. Sean Lynch was a kind of Walter Mitty character, but he never allowed his imagination to interfere with the facts when it came to writing a story. And he was typical of a lot of journalists – and a much-loved character as well.

When he was very ill in St Luke's Hospital, and it was clear he would soon be leaving us forever, I visited him a couple of times expecting him to be in the throes of depression because of his plight, but he was as upbeat as ever. He told me how he had the services of a brilliant blood specialist who came all the way from Scotland to treat him. He directed me to charts hanging at the end of his bed showing steep upward curves, proof that he was making a miraculous recovery. When I mentioned this to another colleague who had been to see him, he shook his head. It appears that Sean had drawn the graphs himself and hung them on the bed when he knew he had visitors coming. He died in 1981 leaving a wife, Gillian, and a young son. His passing was a sad event, not only for his family but for Dublin journalists who had served with him in both the *Irish Press* and the *Independent*.

Burgh Quay was an exciting place; never a dull moment. Every day brought some surprise scandal and gossip. I remember a Sunday afternoon in the mid sixties when Mona in the front office rang to say that there was a man there with a gun demanding to see a reporter. The chief news editor, Bill Redmond, waved his finger in my direction and told me to go down and see what it was all about. Reluctant as I was when I heard about the gun, like a good soldier, I followed orders. I remember that Barney Kavanagh, another northerner, volunteered to go in my place, but was told to sit down and get on with his own work.

Downstairs there was a man leaning against the counter with his arms folded and a gun in front of him. Two terrified girls huddled in a corner of the front office trying to get as far away from the revolver as possible. He looked at me. 'The last time I came here to see a reporter they said they were too busy,' he said sarcastically.

I recognised him immediately and put out my hand. 'Glad to meet you, Mr Breen,' I said. 'I loved your book.'

'Dan Breen to you,' he said, and shook my hand. The situation was immediately defused. He took the gun off the counter and put it in his pocket, and we went into a café beside the *Press* and ordered two teas and two sausage rolls.

It was one of the oddest encounters I ever had. It helped that I had read his book, *My Fight for Irish Freedom*, a couple of years before when I was in Republican mode up north. He complained that he had tried to get admittance to the Dáil and had been thrown out by the usher, and he thought this was a downright scandal perpetrated by a Fianna Fáil government that he had helped put in office. He made it clear that he had no love for the new party leader, and once he got that off his chest he calmed down.

He told me that he was ill and did not have a lot of time left. I think he said he had gangrene and that recently it had begun to spread. We chatted over the tea for about half an hour before he shook hands and I promised to see if I could get something into the *Irish Press* the next morning about the way he was treated in the Dáil. I wrote a couple of paragraphs, but they never saw the light of day. Bill Redmond confided afterwards that he had 'referred it upwards' and was told to spike it.

Not long after that, Dan Breen went into a nursing home and died in 1969, but not before he sent me copies of letters that passed between him and Éamon de Valera years before. I read the letters, which were about events that happened during the Civil War and of which I had no knowledge. I was advised to place the letters in the library with Aengus Ó Dalaigh, and I never heard of them again.

There was never a dull moment. On a lighter note, on another hot summer Sunday afternoon, Bill Redmond asked reporter Brendan Ryan to open the windows to let some air into the stuffy newsroom. Brendan obliged, but when he was stepping down from the second window the pocket of his trousers caught a fire extinguisher knob and set it off, spraying foam around the room. Bill Redmond shouted at him to do something quickly. Brendan did the only thing he could think of – he pointed the nozzle out the open window, not realising there were hundreds of people queuing for the 45 bus to Bray down below. There was panic as the foam poured over them, which threatened to turn into a riot until the *Press* management undertook to honour all receipts for dry cleaning of their clothes. The total cost of the fiasco was in the region of £300, and both Brendan Ryan and Bill Redmond were lucky to hang on to their jobs. To put it in perspective, that year the *Press* made a total profit of £25,000, losing £5,000 of that in a libel action taken against them over a music critique.

This was the same Brendan Ryan who was on duty the night Nelson's Pillar was blown up. After covering the story he dragged Nelson's head all the way to Connolly Station on a piece of wire and persuaded the guard on the night goods train to Dundalk to help him get it onto a wagon and off again when it reached his hometown of Skerries. Brendan buried Nelson unceremoniously in a hole in his garden, and for all I know it is still there.

Like any newsroom, there was a mix of talented people and drones. The former were deployed on the better stories to give them a chance to exercise their talent, while the latter did the humdrum work like covering courts, courts martial, inquests, unfair dismissal tribunals and the Dáil and Seanad. Coverage of the Oireachtas was largely the province of the political correspondents. The actual reporting on debates was for the most part boring, but it did keep your shorthand speed up to scratch, and the food in the Dáil dining room was well subsidised.

During the Troubles in the North and the Dublin bombings, kidnappings and robberies that were a feature of the seventies and eighties, the *Press* newsroom was blessed with a body of young reporters who could use their initiative to get the best angle to a story, often at great risk to their own safety. Many of them later went on to greater things inside and outside journalism. Those were the really exciting years, the most eventful since the Civil War – President Kennedy came in the early 1960s shortly before he was assassinated; the Troubles that were to last for a quarter of a century in the North started at the end of the 1960s; there were terror bombings in Dublin and Monaghan in May 1974; the Pope came to visit Ireland in 1979; and forty-eight young people lost their lives in the tragic Stardust disaster in 1981.

There were people who could get stories and others who had them assigned to them. There were also people who could get information but had trouble putting it together in a story. Two of the latter were women – the late Sheila Walsh in Dublin and Jean Sheridan in Cork. They regularly came up with great stories about political and social life that they could not write themselves lest they blew their contacts. Among the men, the late Tony Gallagher picked up more stories than anybody else. He had worked for English newspapers in Dublin before joining the *Press*, had great technique, and was a constant source of good stories. And he could write a story too, with a bit of embellishment here and there that did not take away from the facts.

Tony Gallagher's expense claims were legendary, never fraudulent, but never understated. He never benefited personally from any monies he procured in this way. Any expenses he managed to get he spent again while working for the papers, whether it was drinking in local hostelries where he picked up his stories, or buying drinks for contacts who fed him a steady stream of information that was otherwise impossible to come by. To him goes the credit for the introduction of 'advance expenses', up to then unheard of in any business. It came about when he persuaded the chief news editor to write a voucher so that he could draw money from the petty cash box before he went on a job.

When he was sent to Wales to cover the story of the Aer Lingus Viscount in 1968 that went missing on a flight from Cork to London, he managed to persuade Jack Millar, the airline press officer, to procure from the airline a substantial cash advance to be repaid later. On his return from Wales his expense sheets were so prolific that when I approved them and sent them to head office to get the money to reimburse Aer Lingus, the then general manager was so shocked that he rang me to ask if the *Irish Press* was 'now a substantial shareholder' in an airline! Yet when Tony came home from Wales, he was stony broke. When he had money in his pocket he spread it around like turf on the bog.

Sometimes pictures told a story far better than any words, but when it came to photographers, journalists were not always happy. Reporters, subeditors and feature writers, members of the elite National Union of Journalists, contended that photographers were craftsmen and should be in a craft union. This caused a lot of rancour, especially in the sixties when RTÉ television was being launched, and the problem was resolved at Montrose by moving the photographers to the ITGWU. Fortunately, the situation in print journalism did not change. The Press Group had more than its share of talent when it came to camera work, whether it was the dramatic picture of a doomed driver frantically clawing at the window of his car as it sank in the Liffey at Butt Bridge, a young man jumping to his death from the parapet on O'Connell bridge as he called out 'Goodbye, cruel world' to astonished passers-by, or a panoramic half-page picture of the Irish Sea on the front page of the *Irish Press* used so effectively by editor Tim Pat Coogan to illustrate the hopelessness of finding any survivors from the unexplained Viscount crash.

In many ways news reporters were the glamour boys and girls of the editorial department, and they looked down on colleagues in other departments who were subediting material and seeing it onto the paper pages. They found it hard to accept that it was the clever headline or the way subeditors presented stories that encouraged people to read them. The *Press* had some excellent subs producing headlines that immediately caught the eye of the reader. When Russian ships were spotted off the west coast of Ireland, the *Evening Press* had 'Red Sails in the Sunset' emblazoned across page one. I once covered a murder trial in Belfast about the killing of a girl called Pearl Gamble. When the paper arrived in Belfast that afternoon the headline read 'Band Played "It's Now or Never" the Night Pearl was Murdered'. The *Evening Press* in particular was well known for its topical, catchy headlines.

Neither could the news reporters come to terms with the fact that the majority of people who purchased our papers were mainly interested in the sports pages. They envied the sports reporters for the relaxed way in which they were able to go about their work, hobnobbing with the great and famous of the racehorse industry, travelling the world covering sporting events such as the Olympics and rugby internationals, always having an entrée to activities of the GAA, and gaining access to the worlds of athletics, boxing and soccer.

As far as the printing department was concerned, apart from the editorial make-up people who worked alongside them, most journalists had little or no regard for them. They were seen to be belligerent, under the thumb of unions who often artificially manufactured disputes that stopped production – stoppages that in the end contributed more than their fair share to the demise of the Press Group.

From the early 1980s things were not going well on Burgh Quay, and with a young family I decided it was time to get another string to my bow in case I had to jump ship. So I became a barrister and practised as such on a part-time basis, spending my mornings in the Four Courts and afternoons and evenings in Burgh Quay. The *Press* had a long tradition of journalists studying law and becoming solicitors and barristers. Many were very successful, rising through the ranks of the courts to the High and Supreme Courts. The late Rory O'Hanlon became a High Court judge; the late Rory O'Connor BL was Head of News in RTÉ; David Andrews BL was a minister in several government departments, and Hugh O'Flaherty SC went all the way to the Supreme Court. When I practised, two colleagues from the newsroom, the late Tom Fallon BL and Damien McHugh BL, were also plying their trade in the Four Courts quite successfully.

I had a modest practice there for a few years after 1995, but could not make up for the earnings lost with the closure of the *Press*. There was also a world of difference between the atmosphere in the law library and what I was used to during thirty-six years before the mast on Burgh Quay. I found the courts very formal and submissive – there were times, believe it or not, when you actually had to grovel before a judge so that your case could get a fair hearing. This was something I never had to do as a journalist, not even as a court reporter.

After the closure, when it became clear that the Group was gone forever, for the first time in my life I felt pangs of depression setting in, and no matter how much golf I played or how much coffee I drank in the law library, I could not shake it off. It was a feeling shared with some of my former colleagues – despair at the thought of all those years of hard work and journalistic idealism gone down the drain. Thirty-six years of my working life and nothing to show for it. Luckily I got through it, and found myself another life working in a family company.

At this juncture I sometimes feel that the closure might have been for the best. The vast majority of journalists who lost their jobs found other things to do in their lives, and I often wonder if the *Press* had not closed how we could ever have adapted to the form of journalism that permeates the media today. Perhaps that's the real reason we were forced to close. Readers do not want the facts any more to help them make up their minds; they are more interested in having journalists do the thinking for them – 'mind benders' we used to call them. Mind benders or not, they are still with us and the *Press* newspapers are long gone.

Enough said.

How to be a rebel
(and still know how to dye a rug)

Mary Kenny
(Reporter/Women's Editor/Newspaper Legend)

The most optimistic moment at which to live – and the moment with the greatest opportunity – is when a conservative society is becoming liberalised, and towards the end of the 1960s I could see signs of optimism that were quite evident in Irish society. I had been working in London as a journalist on the *Evening Standard*, and that period of my life, from 1964 until 1969, was the equivalent of university for me. That's to say, I learned a great deal, made many pals and had enormous fun, as well as some catastrophic failures and broken romances. I was in my twenties, and that's the way it should be.

The 1960s seemed to us – the generation who had been born in the 1940s, at the end of the Second World War – a sparky and revolutionary time, and like every generation before us we thought we had invented sex, drugs and rock 'n' roll. The Americans, or more specifically *Time* magazine, dubbed London 'Swinging London', and we thought we were in the vanguard of everything trendy.

My sister then lived in New York City, and on trips to the States I became excitedly caught up in the Women's Liberation Movement there, which was flowering from the mid 1960s, and was particularly strong in 1967–1968. I reported the Paris students' street rebellions in May 1968, and got similarly involved with events there. In Ireland, the Civil Rights Movement in the

North was stirring up the old contours of society, and it looked as though Northern Ireland was embarking on a promising new future. In the Republic of Ireland itself, the economy was visibly picking up, and the many modernist influences coming into the Catholic Church after Vatican II seemed a harbinger of cheerful winds of change.

So, when Tim Pat Coogan, then editor of the *Irish Press,* asked me to return to Dublin and become the woman's editor of the newspaper, I thought it a fabulous opportunity. I remember sailing into the bay of Dublin – we still quite often took the boat in those days, particularly with heavy luggage – and thinking that a whole new vista of life was beginning for me. And, after all, at the age of twenty-five I knew all the answers to everything, didn't I?

'Women's pages' in newspapers have been abolished in broadsheet newspapers these days, although some of the tabloids still retain the tradition, as with the *Daily Mail's* 'Femail' section. In the 1960s they were a rather cosy section of the paper – some would have called it a 'ghetto' – in which safe subjects such as knitting and cooking and baby care could be discoursed upon. The advantage of having such a ghetto is that the menfolk on the newspaper didn't really take it very seriously, and for that reason there was less close editorial control and more leeway, at least until an awareness developed that these ladies' pages weren't always so safe and so cosy, notably when Rosita Sweetman wrote a trenchant article in which the word 'masturbation' was mentioned in the first line. On the editorial floor I believe there was a fit of the vapours from the chaps, and most especially from Major Vivion de Valera, when that was glimpsed on the page.

I would be called to the major's office to offer an explanation of such disturbing language, and Tim Pat warned me that the major's office, situated in the grander *Irish Press* business annexe in O'Connell Street, was something like Mussolini's: it was on a large scale so that the individual feels small. I duly took myself to the Mussolini-like HQ, and the major, pleasant in the way of a fusspot old aunt, took me out to lunch and spoke of this, that and the other, but never of the actual case in question, except to say in an allusive code that we shouldn't offend the readers. Funnily, I can't now remember whether the readers actually were offended.

Tim Pat had never given me any instructions as to what I should do with the woman's page, save for one piece of advice: that the most successful article that had ever been published within this format was called 'How to Dye a Sheepskin Rug'. Years after it had appeared requests were still being sent to Burgh Quay asking for the correct formula for dyeing a sheepskin rug. I came to see that this was shrewd advice. However hi-falutin' a newspaper thinks it may be, it should never forget the simple and the practical, which will always have a place. To this day, the *Guardian*, while it may have high-flown ideas about gender theory, nevertheless derives a strong following for its cookery items.

Did I set out to shock, stewarding the women's page? Yes, I loved to shock, for I was a bold brat who had been expelled from convent school at the age of sixteen, sent unfinished into the world, and keen to get my revenge on the holy nuns and all the stuffiness they represented, and I was drawn to a kind of faux Marxism, partly because I had been ideologically seduced by the excitement of Paris in 1968, and partly because I believed the holy nuns would never have treated me with such disdain if I had been the daughter of a doctor or a High Court judge (their favourites among their pupils' fathers) rather than of a widow without means. And yet, though I liked to shock, I suppose I had a canny enough eye for survival as well as for opportunism – my husband would later dub me Becky O'Sharp, after Thackeray's minx in *Vanity Fair*, and I also perhaps knew something about what worked in journalism, and that the driving force in any journalistic endeavour is curiosity.

It was certainly a time of change, and we began to reflect it. One day on the stairs of Burgh Quay I encountered Máire Comerford, the veteran *Cumann na mBan* activist from the War of Independence, and she gave me a shy smile of approval. I think I was armed with a poster demanding the abolition of the anti-contraception laws. There's always a bit of a *grá* in Ireland for the Rebel Girl.

We in the women's page had a top floor office in Burgh Quay. Anne Harris wrote a splendid series about going begging with the travelling people, and after it had appeared an envelope containing £100 (maybe equivalent to a thousand today) arrived at Burgh Quay, discreetly bearing the blessing of the Archbishop of Dublin, John Charles McQuaid – money to be distributed 'to the poor travellers' whose lives had been so poignantly described 'by Mrs Harris'. Tim Pat, if I recall correctly, plucked a fiver out of the hundred and told me that Anne and I should spend the fiver at Mulligan's, which we duly did.

Rosita Sweetman did a superb campaigning piece about the abuses that took place at Marlborough House, an institution for young offenders, alerted by whistle-blower Peadar Kelly. But journalism needs to be a mixture of the serious, the revealing and the frothy, and I think we tried to bring that diversity to the pages. I came to appreciate the *Irish Press* readers very much: they represented, to me, the heart of an old Ireland I have always liked, rooted in the traditions of faith and fatherland, but still stimulated by change, appreciative of culture and not lacking a sense of humour. Many were in the west of Ireland, where there has always been an anarchic streak anyway. We brought the pages, too, to various parts of the country having a special focus on parts of Ireland outside of Dublin. I knew there was grass-roots support for Women's Liberation, even if not for every aspect of it, because of the letters we'd receive from rural Ireland.

The office itself was gloriously informal and slightly ramshackle. Was it male-dominated? Most workplaces were more male-dominated in those days, and the heavy-lifting side of industries, such as the hot metal on which a newspaper was printed, was exclusively male. When I mentioned this aspect of life to a younger woman journalist about ten years ago she replied, perhaps surprisingly, 'Weren't you lucky? Having all those guys around?' Yes, when women have scarcity value, sometimes a certain privilege goes with it.

One of the big shifts in journalism today is that the influx of more women (and often very able women indeed) has made it much less of a drinking culture, since women as a group are historically less tolerant of excessive boozing. I don't think the *Irish Press* journalists were particularly boozy – my recollection is that *The Irish Times'* people were seldom out of the Pearl Bar – but one or two were noted topers, and I guess I became one of them. I think I rather shocked the late Terry O'Sullivan by lying across his desk for a few moments' repose after a drinking session, and he was no stranger to the bottle (he was an amiable colleague; his daughter, Nuala O'Faoilain, painted a much darker picture in her memoir *Are You Somebody?*)

In many ways it was a magical time to be a journalist, not just because we were living through periods of interesting and often optimistic social change, but because journalism in the last third of the twentieth century seemed to be thriving. I am far less optimistic about the future of the written word – how often do you see anyone under thirty today actually reading a newspaper? I look back at Burgh Quay days with affection, occasionally embarrassment, and a certain ruefulness that I didn't appreciate better at the time the golden age through which I was living.

Sometimes it does seem as though it were just yesterday

John Kelly
(Reporter, Feature Writer and Father of the Chapel,
Sunday Press, 1966–1995)

We learned a lot in the old Tivoli Theatre. Within ten days of what had been an apparently successful interview for an attractive job in the *Sunday Press*, I learned that you had to be careful about the way in which you conduct affairs with the powers that were in Burgh Quay.

The year was 1966, and I was then one of the youngest acting editors in the Republic of Ireland, sitting in the chair of the highly respected *Nationalist & Leinster Times*, Carlow. I was almost totally wet behind the ears, two years out of UCD, and three years after I had my first experience of working for a newspaper.

There, in the absolutely hectic newsroom of the *New York Daily Mirror* in 1963, I was what they called an 'editorial assistant' (posh for copyboy) in the second biggest newspaper in the five boroughs of the city. Yet, ironically enough, it shut forever that same year, mainly the result of the printing strike that closed down the inky trade in Manhattan. Really, it was primarily because it had just not kept pace with changing technology whilst its main competitor, the *Daily News*, had.

I could tell you stories about some of the world-famous people who still worked in the editorial area when I was there, people like Walter Winchell and William Randolph Hearst Jnr., but that would be name-dropping. This piece demands name-dropping too, but closer to home, names like Bill Redmond.

The late Mr Redmond, who invariably referred to all staff journalists with the prefix 'Mr' and to the few women who worked there as 'Miss', or even more seldom 'Mrs', as indeed they were named on the duty rosters, was one of a trio who interviewed me for the job advertised in the *Sunday Press*. It sounded highly promising: there were good staff rates and plenty of travel. It demanded talent for feature and reporting skills. Best of all was the fact that the national newspaper rate was then almost three times the provincial rate.

Peculiarly, during the interview, the tall and imposing Mr Redmond seemed slightly disparaging about the *Sunday Press*, reminding me that there were plenty of vacancies in the newsroom, the general reporting pool that was the heart of the entire news-gathering operation. The problem was that it would involve shift work, and I didn't want shift work. I had worked long hours in the *Nationalist*, desperately trying to perfect skills that I hardly possessed. I was twenty-three. I needed to live a little, and what could be better than spending lots of time on the road, and on expenses, in the best hotels of Ireland?

The next morning I got a call from Mr Redmond. He cheerily assured me that he was pleased to inform me that I had the job. While he would provide me with a letter of confirmation later, he advised me to submit my resignation to the late Liam D. Bergin, the editor who was constantly absent from the *Nationalist*. He travelled quite a lot, especially to the US, where he lectured on journalism in the University of Illinois.

So I wrote a rather lengthy, slightly acerbic, resignation, and I heard nothing from Burgh Quay – no letter of confirmation, absolutely nothing, not a peep. I rang Bill Redmond. He was very comforting, very conciliatory. Unfortunately, he told me, the job in the *Sunday Press* had been put on the long finger. He assured me, however, that he would write a letter of confirmation immediately, guaranteeing that I had a job as a general reporter in the newsroom. Boy, oh boy, was I wet behind the ears!

Luckily, I was just as stubborn. I stuck to my guns. I had not burned my boats with my resignation notice. No newsroom, just the *Sunday Press,* I insisted, as it was advertised. Two days later I got a call from Bill Redmond. He had discussed my position with Frank Carty, the elderly editor of the *Sunday Press*. They had reconsidered. I had the job. And so it came about.

What was it like way back then in the mid sixties?

The *Sunday Press* was the biggest-selling newspaper in Ireland. It had a tiny staff, cramped together on the third floor of the older part of the Burgh Quay building. On the floor above was a ladies' toilet that occasionally leaked right onto the sports desk, occupied by the late sports editor, the highly innovative Tommy O'Hara.

The news editor was the absolutely unflappable Gerry Fox, a Roscommon native who doled out news leads, mainly clips from provincial newspapers accumulated over weeks and months. He also kept his well-thumbed contact book, containing names and telephone numbers of journalists throughout the thirty-two counties, fully up to date. He was a reporter of the best sort, trained in the old school, with perfect shorthand, proficient typing, and above all a readiness to listen to almost anything. Nothing surprised him.

Also central to the *Sunday Press* operation were Dick Wilkes, deputy editor, Willie Collins and the late Steve Sennett, all intensely occupied in the editing process. Dick Wilkes's son, Alan, became chief subeditor on the staff of the *Evening Press* while Willie Collins's two sons are Stephen, now of *The Irish Times*, and Liam, of the *Sunday Independent*. All are consummate newspapermen. But the *Sunday Press* in those years had its idiosyncrasies – no doubt about that.

Well do I recall one of the first editorial conferences, held every Tuesday morning, shortly after I joined. At that time the paper featured a single column strip that gathered supposedly riveting opinions from people on the streets about changing social mores and controversies of the week. The topic selected after some debate that particular week posed the question as to whether turn-ups on men's pants were a fashion trend of the past.

Yes, we just never knew what was likely to turn up in the weekly vox pop.

I scanned my eyes quickly around the room. Turn-ups – almost everywhere! I was one of two who had none. The fact that it was 1966, long past the end of the 1950s and Teddy Boys, did not quite dispel my fleeting pangs of guilt. Such momentous questions were enough to drive anybody to drink … ah, yes, the drink….

The three most popular watering holes in the immediate environs were Mulligan's (of course), Kennedy's, the Silver Swan, known more familiarly with conscious irony as the 'Mucky Duck', and the White Horse, not to forget the Scotch House either. Press-relations people, showbiz promoters and many of their rising stars, as well as top city models, tended to congregate in the Swan's downstairs bar. Mulligan's was much more proletarian, as might be expected, while the upstairs lounge of the White Horse was something of a quiet retreat unless, of course, the indefatigable, justifiably great writer, Benedict Kiely from Omagh, happened to be there, in which case it would be uproarious.

Irish Press staffers tended to be much more sociable and colourful than their competitors in the *Irish Independent* or *The Irish Times*, which is hardly to mention the Dublin-based staff of the then *Cork Examiner*.

Even now, the more honest journalists on rival publications will be prepared to admit that all three Press Group newspapers were rarely beaten to a story. Astoundingly, those who are even more honest than honest will also readily concede that, for all of the undoubted influence of the de Valera and Fianna Fáil connections, the group played it fair in general.

Staff members kept their political affiliations off their typewriter keyboards. Views or prejudices rarely, if ever, made it into print on the news pages. The journalists of those changing times often held highly vehement opinions, but their generally progressive views were rarely reflected in what they wrote. News was strictly news, views were views, and it was better to be temperate than to be radical – features were always carefully vetted.

Hours and wages were appalling. A scheduled eight-hour shift on paper was often extended by one, two or even three hours, depending on the story. There was never any compensation. If you were on a breaking story you stayed with it. That was the professional attitude, and *Irish Press* journalists were nothing if not professional. Wages, the Dublin rates as they were known throughout the rest of the island, were as minimal as they could be. They were fixed in negotiations between the DNMC (Dublin Newspapers Management Committee) and the NUJ (National Union of Journalists, Dublin Branch), usually on a yearly basis.

Many excellent journalists gave up in despair and took jobs in the much more lucrative public relations field. Others headed off for Fleet Street, never dreaming of the possibility of Canary Wharf, or RTÉ, where they became hugely successful.

The recruitment drive in the mid 1960s provided the *Irish Press* with younger staff than any of its competitors. Older staff, like the veteran Maurice Liston, who was a founder member of the *Irish Press* 'chapel' (as print and journalistic unions were called), along with Bill Redmond, were on their slow paths to retirement. Yet, even though he was long past his best days, and although his legs were bad, Maurice still insisted on walking down to the High Court, which he covered for many years. I met him one morning as he trudged down the stairs from the newsroom and offered my sympathy because he looked particularly weak.

'Maurice,' I suggested, 'why don't you ask one of the lads to give you a black?'

A 'black' referred to a carbon copy provided by a journalist, often employed on a rival publication, and sometimes deliberately not containing the full facts. Maurice smiled knowingly as he replied in his inimitable west-Limerick accent.

'John,' he said, 'the trouble with blacks is that they're very often half caste!'

He was right, of course. You had to be very confident of the honesty of those who offered blacks!

The *Irish Press* was infested with characters. Many of the reporters, indeed most, were the most serious professionals on this earth. They were careful to get their quotes right, keen to ensure that they wrote the best possible lead paragraph in the 'intro' of the story, getting all of the facts right and writing it as closely as possible to the required size. When they finished their shifts they had to let off a lot of steam. They sometimes overstayed their welcomes in the neighbouring hostelries, with hilarious consequences as comical as anything displayed on the stage of the old Theatre Royal at the rear of the Press Building.

One lunchtime in the Mucky Duck, a highly experienced reporter who seemed to return home only rarely was propped up comfortably over the bar when a woman walked in carrying something that for all the world looked like a plate wrapped in a cloth. She walked up to the errant reporter, banged the plate down on the counter in front of him and snarled, 'There's your dinner!' as she turned on her heels and stormed out.

Then, of course, there was the late inimitable Sean Lynch, native of Dundalk, another top-class reporter, although a consummate

Walter Mitty in person and the origin of many hilarious incidents. On one occasion he was called by Mr Redmond, who was carefully inspecting his monthly expenses at the newsdesk. He was informed by the imperious editor-in-chief: 'Mr Lynch, you are spending too much money on taxis,' while he crossed out his entries.

'Mr' Lynch said nothing. He held his fire for his inevitable outburst in the Mucky Duck at the close of his shift, but carefully prepared his revenge in the month that followed. Then, at the end of the period, he cheerfully approached Mr Redmond's desk at the top of the newsroom in full view of all of his colleagues. In his hand he carried a spike festooned with innumerable bus tickets. Plonking it down on his desk, he gestured to Mr Redmond and said, loudly enough to be heard by most, 'There's my travel expenses for the month!'

Representing all of these diverse, unique people, except executives, who were not supposed to remain active members of the National Union of Journalists after promotion, was the *Irish Press* chapel of the same union. The name 'chapel' was borrowed from the print unions and owed its title to the earliest days of craftsmen responsible for the production of copies of the Bible. All chapels had to have a leader, the elected 'father' or 'mother' as he or she was called, a clerk and a treasurer. Usually, a 'deputy father' was also elected.

When the violence in Northern Ireland had passed the simmering point, reporters and photographers were deployed in teams. I was frequently there myself, always liaising with the then Northern Ireland editor, Paddy Reynolds or 'Paddy the Hat', and his assistant, the late Paddy Topping, a.k.a. 'Paddy the Top'. Paddy Reynolds, incidentally, is the author of a hilarious memoir, *The Late Paddy Murphy* – an account of his invention of his alter ego, a fictitious young Belfast columnist.

Without realising that 'Paddy Murphy' was in fact Paddy Reynolds, the powers that were in Burgh Quay hired him as a commentator. Paddy the Hat gave him a fictitious address and collected the weekly pay cheque. It all went well until Mr Redmond signalled his intention to meet Paddy Murphy and offer him a staff job. The panic-stricken Paddy Reynolds rang Burgh Quay immediately to tell the editor-in-chief that the unfortunate 'Mr Murphy' had died suddenly – while also enquiring if he could take time off for the funeral service.

After watching the incredibly bigoted antics of Ian Paisley and his supporters on the streets of Belfast while the fires of hatred were stoked, talking to the likes of the late Paddy Devlin and Seamus Mallon and meeting the people of Ballymurphy and Andersonstown, I realised that this latest outburst of northern sectarianism was not just going to be a spark in the grate; this was for the long term. Yet, the chapel at that time, approaching the turn of the decade, was debating whether it should continue to allow dangerous coverage without an increased allowance, the equivalent of danger money. The committee recommended that action should be taken. Coverage of Northern Ireland should be put off limits until extra money was paid to photographers and reporters.

I opposed the committee, arguing that northern coverage was too important to be suspended. I felt that it was all important to keep the people of the island fully informed of the truth of whatever was to happen there. In the event, coverage was not banned. Instead, realistic claims were submitted, and about two weeks later, after a conversation with the FOC, the late Michael Cronin, and his deputy, also, alas, the late Niall Connolly, I was appointed as clerk of the chapel. Little did I know at that time where it was all going to lead me, and that increasing union involvement would steer me further away from the mainline journalism I loved. But that's the way it went....

On foot of developments in the UK, newspaper managements and unions set out to rationalise newspaper production in formal agreements, containing job specifications, holidays, wage rates, dispute procedures and job descriptions. The *Irish Press* followed in the wake of the *Irish Independent*, which was the first group to finalise an overall editorial agreement between the NUJ and management. Later, all other sectors followed in their footsteps.

Weekly wages were trebled in many cases. Rates in the Press Group became the highest in Ireland. Generally, house agreements were subject to annual review between the union and management. It entailed secondment from work duties for elected chapel officers.

In the early years we were the envy of journalists in other publications, and, for the first time since its foundation, in RTÉ as well.

The greater NUJ, representing journalists all over the island, soon began to initiate house agreements in every sector of the journalistic profession. Achievement followed achievement so that working conditions, and of course wages, were greatly improved everywhere. There were hitches of course, especially in the case of the *Irish Press*. Management insisted that in the first agreement a clause deploring the journalistic predilection for strong drink, while also recognising that it was a serious professional problem, should be included. The ruling body of the NUJ, the NEC, based in London, was firmly opposed to allowing the *Irish Press* chapel to come to any such agreement. Finally, after many hectic exchanges and a mass threat from the majority of journalists in Burgh Quay to resign from the NUJ, a mutually agreeable solution was achieved.

Times could be tough in those years. And what do I think now that it's all over? The problem with beginning to remember is remembering much too much. Let me say simply that the *Irish Press* was crowded with life, often uproarious, sometimes misguided, but always eventful, and in the end full of serious purpose.

And let me finish with a short final word from a photographer I travelled with on numerous occasions, the late Douglas E. Duggan. He was a religious, considerate man, something of a philosopher. We discussed many eternal questions over miles of country roads. One sun-struck day I decided to goad him on foot of a discussion on the possibility of a life hereafter. I had argued that life had no predestined purpose other than its own temporary existence.

'Look at that windscreen, Duggie,' I said, pointing out at the blood-smeared glass. 'What was the purpose of those insects?'

Duggie took his pipe from his mouth, throwing me a mischievous glance, 'Maybe their purpose is to make us ask what our purpose is,' he said.

And maybe he was right.

Adrian's new book

Dick O'Riordan
(Copyboy/Subeditor/Assistant Editor/ Travel Writer/
Deputy Editor, *Irish Press*, 1987–1991/ Editor, *Evening Press*,
1991–1995)

On a summer afternoon in 1988, we all gathered at the top desk in the *Evening Press* for a long-awaited event – the arrival of a new book written by Adrian MacLoughlin, one of our subeditors. The beaming new author was sitting with a few copies of his *Historic Guide to Dublin*, which had just been delivered by Gill and Macmillan. He was trying hard not to look ecstatic, but he was.

Staff swarmed from all around the newsroom to deluge him in congratulations and of course to voice their opinions. Some thought the orange-brown a bit too 'loud' for what was essentially a serious work; others thought the book stinted on decent pictures; and there was split opinion on the humorous cartoons that were spread throughout its pages.

None of this really mattered, because everyone realised that the book had required a superhuman effort by a splendidly stylish writer whose talent and personality had been shattered by drink problems for nearly two decades. Adrian had only recently succeeded in pulling himself out of a spiral of destruction and self-loathing that had brought nothing but humiliation and some notoriety. The book may have had its faults in literary terms, but in real human terms it proved a life-saver. Adrian's new book was simply a miracle.

The author's love of his native city and his knowledge of its highways and byways was well known. Down the years, since his arrival from *The Irish Times* in the early 1960s, he had written many fine articles about it. His explosive temperament was an ever-present danger on a subs' desk not short of eccentrics. But he kept his most vitriolic eruptions for those who got their facts about Dublin wrong. These included eminences such as John O'Donovan, who wrote a popular weekly 'Time Was' column in the *Evening Press*, radio broadcaster Éamonn Mac Thomáis, and even James Joyce himself did not escape a lash. His attack on Joyce was particularly interesting. Some years previously he had contributed an article to a book compiled by features editor Sean McCann. At the time there was a growing fallacy that Joyce had written purely from memory about Dublin while in exile. It was a nice romantic notion, but Adrian didn't believe it, and by poring over *Thom's Directories* of the period he made a credible case for his contention. Bursting Bloom's bubble did not go down well with an emerging new wave of Joyceans.

My own awakening to Adrian's fierce passion for Dublin, warts and all, came on a dreary Saturday evening some years previously when we were both working a *Sunday Press* shift and decided to cross the Liffey to Di Mascio's facing the Abbey Theatre. At that time it was the oldest chipper in Dublin and a byword for the best fish and chips, particularly its 'long' ray. Even the paper's social diarist, Terry O'Sullivan of Dubliner's Diary, was not averse to dining there after a hectic night on the trail.

As we walked over O'Connell Bridge, an old codger peering up the docks through a black drizzle spoke to us without turning around.

'It's a grand oul' city all the same,' he uttered.

'Sure is,' I replied, quickening up to get past him.

'It is and my arse!' he roared after us. I cracked up, but Adrian became apoplectic.

'Dublin is full of those old geezers who know fuck all about this city and care less.' He then launched into a rant about those who were destroying Dublin – everyone, it seemed, from 'those ignorant culchie clowns in the Corpo' to architects, builders, John Charles McQuaid, and now, apparently, me. The tirade lasted right through our 'one-and-ones' and only ended when I made some casual remark about the nearby Abbey Theatre and uttered the awful words 'Ernie Blythe'. That, I later learned, was below the belt as far as Adrian was concerned, and maybe that was the reason why he dried up and was almost silent all the way back to Burgh Quay.

Adrian's drinking sprees were legendary in an office not lacking hard cases. His odd fellowship with the much younger Aidan Madden, a truly gifted writer, became a source of much speculation. Both had been appointed critics, Aidan for theatre and Adrian for films, so they had ready-made social scenes that were amply serviced with watering holes. The friendship, however, was a toxic cocktail that was comical, corrosive, and often mutually destructive.

Adrian's humour and bitchiness often became intolerable for those around him. In one famous incident a veteran subeditor actually tried to throttle him at his desk because of personal abuse. One night I picked Adrian up (literally) outside Mulligan's pub in Poolbeg Street, just a few steps from the *Irish Press* office. My car was nearby so I bundled him into the back and drove him home to Fitzroy Avenue, beside Croke Park. The hall door was ajar, and when I pushed it open, his mother, whom I had met many times, was standing inside with rosary beads wrapped tightly around the knuckles of both hands. She was praying for his safe return, as she probably did most nights. She thanked me profusely, but in her confusion and anxiety did not recognise me, because when I got back to the office I realised there was a £5 note sticking out of my breast pocket. Taxi men of the Good Samaritan kind were frequent visitors to Adrian's hall door.

The real turnabout in his life came about through the concern and decency of husband and wife journalists, Maureen Browne and the late Michael O'Toole. When all seemed hopeless, and everybody else acquiesced in the inevitable, they took action. Formerly of the *Irish Press*, Maureen was then news editor of the *Irish Medical Times*, and she and Michael convinced Adrian to see Dr John O'Connell, its owner/editor and leading Labour politician, who became Minister for Health. O'Connell set out a strict alcohol-free regime that was adhered to only spasmodically until, obviously near the end of his tether, he issued a death warning with a timeframe of weeks, not months.

That shook Adrian's jittery foundation. Over the following months he became increasingly quiet, remarkably calm, and intensely busy. A different person began to emerge with a new agenda for living. The writing of his *Historical Guide to Dublin* was an immediate focus, but, once that was completed, other interests and ambitions opened up. His addictive and obsessive nature, which had previously shackled him almost exclusively to alcohol, had somehow been suppressed, and its energy focused in other directions.

The Dublin guidebook was followed a couple of years later by a second book, the immensely impressive *Streets of Ireland*, a guide to the history and architecture of twenty-five of the biggest towns and cities in the Republic. His style, though always scholarly and informative, never failed to dip into the quirks and oddities of regions and communities. This required a huge physical and mental effort in terms of travel and research as he was still working full-time as an assistant editor, having been promoted by editor Sean Ward.

A guide to Belfast was soon completed, having been accomplished during some of the worst days of the Troubles there. Both of these books were published by Tara Publishing under the title Swift Publications, a noble gesture by managing director Fergus Farrell, a hard-nosed businessman in terms of his magazine empire. However, he allowed his admiration of Adrian's work to supersede any ambition of a profitable return. Adrian wanted to complete the job by continuing through the main towns of Northern Ireland, but these were dangerous times and the RUC advised against it.

Through the travelling involved spanned the length and breadth of Ireland, the books opened up a love of travel again, something that had been snuffed out almost totally in his wild days. True to character, travel was also embraced with characteristic eccentricity. He began going regularly to weekend soccer matches in Glasgow and Liverpool, supporting Celtic and Everton and rarely failing to return in the jersey of visiting clubs, which he wore to work, without comment, on Monday mornings. Everybody pretended not to notice, but it was difficult enough to remain calm, particularly when some of the more flamboyant team kits were involved.

He also became obsessed with Abba – especially the blonde. Though he had never seemed much interested in music of any kind, he bought every record the band had produced – he particularly valued the Swedish products – and even sought out the pre-Abba albums of Agnetha. There was a general consensus among the staff that if he began wearing Abba gear on Monday mornings we would all have to vacate the building.

We were spared that, but much later on he told me he had once gone to Stockholm for a few days in the hope that he would spot the blonde walking down the main street. He had read somewhere that the group did that sort of thing to try and keep themselves grounded in normality after the fans' frenzy of their tours. They didn't turn up, so Adrian compensated himself with some atrocious new gear from a boutique, none of it capable of stretching over a pot belly. He wore it nevertheless, a furry belt remindful of an attack of shingles being particularly memorable.

Then there was Adrian's weird method of choosing a holiday. In fact, he didn't really bother about holidays per se, but just liked to remain on terra firma. Nor did he have any interest in, or appreciation of, scenery, however glorious. He was totally urban in his choice of destinations: he liked streets and roads, cathedrals and buildings, parks and public places.

On an occasion when I was in his kitchen while helping him edit his *Streets of Ireland*, I happened to mention that I was taking off soon for a holiday with the family in France.

'Have you organised anything yourself?' I asked.

'No,' he said, 'but I'll do that right now.'

He went to his bookshelf and took out a large hardback atlas and opened it on a double-page spread of Europe. He then picked up a large pin, circled it around above the book and then plunged it down aimlessly beside the city of Worms in Germany. Being short-sighted, he could not read the name easily, so he asked me. 'That's Worms,' I said, 'where the Diet comes from.'

'That's where I'm going then,' he declared. 'Worms, where the Diet comes from. Do you know anything else about it?'

'Not a thing,' I replied.

Sometime after, he did the trip, by boat, train, bus and taxi across Britain and Europe. And all the way back.

When his Abba fascination subsided, he took to model railways with a passion, buying a couple of engines or carriages or rail stations every week in a shop behind McBirney's on Arran Quay. His mother had died some years earlier and he had taken a flat near the top of Home Farm Road, to which he invited me to see his 'set-up'. I didn't realise it was a railway system he was referring to and not his new accommodation of two fine, big rooms that were linked. There were trains running all over the place, all making a terrific racket as they passed under chairs and tables and even over the end of his bed. He became totally immersed in timetables and schedules and spoke of the trains in 'he' and 'she' terms as if they were human.

It struck me that the elderly landlady on the ground floor beneath must have been at her wits' end as Adrian's locomotives and diesels sent their echoes through the ceiling overhead. I could hear them as I entered the house. 'Be quick, the 3.30 to Euston Station is about to depart,' the landlady advised me sardonically. I think it had become a mantra for Adrian's visitors.

This was the scenario that Aiden Madden – who for some reason had changed his name to Aodhan – used as a theme in his script for the 1998 film *Night Train*. The film debut by director John Lynch, it followed the romantic pursuit of an ex-prisoner (John Hurt) with a passion for electric trains and his landlady's daughter (Brenda Blethyn). Madden said that constant rewriting of his film script had diluted considerably his original intention in regard to the 'Adrian' role. Intriguingly, Hurt's character in the film was named Poole, and the irony of Madden's little in-joke was not lost on his *Evening Press* colleagues. Another subeditor, Harry Poole, was Adrian's nemesis in the 1960s and 1970s. Harry presided Buddha-like over a large wooden drawer in which he stashed an enormous haul of stationery – pins, clips, rulers, elastic bands, etc. Every so often he would open the locked drawer, inch by inch, so as to check that everything was in place.

On the other hand, nobody else seemed to have enough of anything, particularly pins and clips, so one day Adrian reluctantly had to ask Harry for 'a loan of a pin' until the stationery lady came around. Tut, tut, said Harry, producing a single pin and handing it over with a ceremonial flourish. Adrian was incandescent, but said nothing. The following morning at about 6.30 a.m. he came into the office – probably from an early house on the quays – with a hammer and an eight-inch nail and drove it straight up through the drawer and into the thick wooden table. Harry pulled and puffed for over a day before he eventually cottoned on to the fact that he had been 'nailed'.

Adrian faced yet another interesting challenge that he quickly turned into an obsession. He discovered a letter indicating family links with long-lost relations in Hawaii and the Azores. A paternal forebear had apparently worked on a whaling ship. He pursued the information relentlessly until he discovered distant cousins on both islands and decided to visit them. This meant facing up to a lifelong fear of flying, which he did. These contacts brought him much joy, a lot of correspondence, and he kept in frequent contact with both islands. He was particularly proud to pass pictures of his long-lost cousins around among colleagues at the desk.

During all this he made one of the most important decisions of his life by buying a house in Marino and settling there very happily with Marilyn, his extra-bandy Jack Russell terrier. To celebrate his trip to Hawaii, he named his house OAHU after the main island there. It was an enormous crude sign (he painted it himself) that could be read from a hundred yards away. Marilyn was always at the gate when he returned from work in the evenings and began barking even before he came into sight. He loved that, and taking her for walks in Fairview Park and on the prom at Clontarf, where he chatted happily about doggie matters, now a big part of his daily routine.

Adrian's health began to decline, and following an operation for cancer he died in the late 1990s.

Nowadays, I pass his house in Marino quite frequently and never fail to recall the satisfaction and stability it brought a troubled soul who succeeded in replacing crushing insecurity with contented eccentricity. Gone is the great sign OAHU – a name that still resonates more like a shout of jubilation than the name of an island in Hawaii.

OAHU – it rings through the years like Adrian's last hurrah.

Curtseys, spy stories, and the hack who mistook a teapot for a telephone

Maureen Browne
(News Reporter, 1967–1969)

The circulation of the Press newspapers trebled in Bruff, Co. Limerick, the day the news broke that I had got a job at 'the base'. Drinks were put in front of me in the local pub, and my father was congratulated on having given me an education. It was hinted darkly that the family's Fianna Fáil credentials had done me no harm, and I was advised to mind myself from the traffic in Dublin. It was confidently expected that within weeks I would be the political correspondent for one of the three papers and be able to give them all the inside track on the latest stories.

I'd be up at the Áras every week getting a briefing from 'himself,' one guy suggested – my native Bruff after all was only a few miles from President de Valera's ancestral home in Bruree.

'Not at all,' he was contradicted. 'Sure the major is the head man in Burgh Quay, and he has all the information from the horse's mouth.'

Hardened from two years in the *Limerick Leader*, where I had picked up the rudiments of journalism along with a healthy scepticism of mankind in general (including those who bought me free drinks in pubs), and of interfering politicians and my fellow hacks in particular, my main objective was not to make a fool of myself in the sophisticated world of the national media.

In my first week in the *Leader* I had been told by the editor that my job depended on my being able to borrow 'a bucket of hair spaces' from some of the other papers in the city. I was also instructed by my fellow scribe – and later my husband – Michael O'Toole, that I should curtsey to the judge when I left the court (where O'Toole was instructing me in the art of legal reporting). I didn't feel too badly about the hair spaces as I reckoned I couldn't be expected to know that, in those days of hot metal, a hair space was the narrowest space between two letters. However, I would long remember the goggling solicitors and the judge blushing scarlet as I swept him a low curtsey – an invaluable skill taught to me by Mother Columba in the confident belief that all her pupils, despite our peasant origins, would hopefully be presented at court, or at the very least marry colonial governors.

I arrived at the *Press* determined to enjoy the fun and fashion of the capital and to give a wide berth to O'Toole (who, by then, was a senior reporter there), with his passion for 'ball-hops', newspapers, literature, theatre and aviation, and his beguiling talk about endless sunlit walks by crystal seas on Howth Head and Portmarnock Beach.

I got the job because the Sligo-born journalist Paddy Clancy had taken himself off to pursue his career in Brighton, en route to Fleet Street, and there were dire murmurings in the newsroom about what a loss he would be. They admitted, however, that he had one failing: he didn't like getting up in the morning and was frequently half an hour late for work. His Rathgar Road flatmates, who were also colleagues, got tired of this and decided to put the clock forward half an hour one night. As Clancy was passing through Rathmines he noticed the time on the Rathmines Town Hall Clock. Muttering imprecations, he got off the bus and went back home for another half hour's sleep.

Halfway up the broad Burgh Quay staircase that first morning I was brought to a dramatic halt when two hands clasped my ankle, while an upper-class voice declaimed: 'A half crown for the love of God – your mother won't have sent you to the big city without money in your pocket.' The great cartoonist Bobby Pyke was sitting on the stairs, intent on supplementing the day job by extracting baksheesh from newly arrived young reporters. Torn between the honour of being asked to contribute to such a famous man and my reluctance to be separated from the small store that my mother had indeed given me, I dithered until a booming voice instructed 'Mr Pyke' to 'unhand Miss Browne,' and to let the two of us go about our work. To my deep embarrassment I was swept into the newsroom by Mr William J. Redmond, the managing editor. 'WJR,' as he was known to his peers, or 'Big Daddy' to his disrespectful staff, told me to take off my coat and sit down.

The *Evening Press* news editor, Michael O'Kane, promptly told me to put on my coat and take myself off to the National Gallery, where one of the more famous paintings had just been stolen. It could make the lead for the evening paper, so he asked me to ring in a piece as soon as I got there. He sounded harassed and was obviously very short-staffed and a tad unhappy to have to send a rookie out on this job. I was surreptitiously looking at my map of Dublin to see where the National Gallery was when the photographer who was going on the job bore down on me, festooned with cameras.

'I'm Douglas Duggan,' he said. 'Are you just up from the country?' Meekly, I agreed that I was. Half an hour later we had spoken to Dr James White, the formidable director of the National Gallery, I had taken copious shorthand notes and Dougie suggested we should get a cup of tea.

'Oh no,' I protested frantically, the weight of the city edition on my shoulders, intros swimming around in my head. 'I have to ring in the story.'

'We'll just have a cup of tea first,' Dougie insisted placidly. 'You'll have to find a phone and there'll be one in the café.' Protesting every step of the way, I was ushered into a nearby café. By the time the tea arrived Dougie had written out five paragraphs and handed them to me with 4d. 'Ring them and read that out to the copy-takers and they'll all say you're great.' I did, and they did, although I felt slightly ashamed when the legendary *Evening Press* editor, Conor O'Brien, himself told me that it was a good piece.

Basking in the glory of a page-one piece on my first day (even if I hadn't actually written it), I thought the *Press* was a great place. I was overawed by the senior men – and they were all men, women reporters being very scarce. There was Tony Gallagher, ex-Fleet Street, who wrote the memorable intro 'Two Guinness boats got locked on the Liffey last night' when two of the Guinness barges crashed on the river. The burly 'Cryan the Crime,' the Group's crime reporter, dressed in long navy coat and broad hat, who would arrive at a crime scene and nod at the nearest young garda on duty – who nine times out of ten saluted and let him through, thinking he was at least a superintendent. The agriculture correspondent and founder of the NUJ in Ireland, Maurice Liston, from Knockaderry in west Limerick, took me under his wing because I was from the other side of the county. Michael Mills was the fiercely independent political correspondent whom the pub drinkers in Bruff presumably expected me to supplant. There was also the ebullient Sean Lynch; the learned and courteous Niall Carroll, who was also an Abbey playwright; 'Dubliner's diarist' Terry O'Sullivan, who on hearing my husband was going to Chicago on a marking one cold winter, and knowing he had no coat suitable to combat the freezing lake winds, gave him his own sheepskin coat; the urbane motoring correspondent

Alan Wilkes, who marshalled three colleagues to act as a human jack when I had a puncture outside the office in a car that did not boast a jack; the court reporter, Paul Muldowney; the young Tim Pat Coogan; Mick Finlan, newly returned from Canada; and the older men, Willie Collins and Dick Wilkes, who kept up the tone of the newsroom.

Then there was Mick Hennessy, who claimed the doubtful skill of being able to tell which women were virgins by looking into their eyes (this expertise did not extend to men). There was a journalist who, overly fond of alcoholic refreshment, laboured under the delusion that if he had a bath after a skinful of drink it would completely sober him, with the result that he was frequently to be found stark naked trying to bathe in the gents' hand basin. The 'night-town man,' and veteran of the war against Franco, Paddy Clare, memorably fell asleep one night at his desk, which had a phone and a full teapot. When the phone rang at about 2 a.m., Clare reached for the phone shouting 'What? What is it? Is it an accident? Is there much blood?' as he emptied the teapot over his head. There was also a journalist who hadn't bothered to go beyond Paris when sent to cover the opening of a new basilica in Lourdes, and wrote eloquently about the flags fluttering in the sky, never realising it was an underground basilica.

Some people were driven to taking a hand in the stories. When the famous film star Jayne Mansfield visited Ireland it was proving to be an unfortunately tame event. At his wits' end, as he was following her down a country road, our reporter suggested to her that she might like to slip into a church and say a little prayer for her family. As she fell to her knees (photographer at the ready) he was knocking on the parish priest's door, urging him to turn this 'scarlet woman' (she was one of the earlier *Playboy* 'playmates' and had posed partially nude at least once) out of his church.

In the newsroom, they were still telling the stories of the retired Máire Comerford, who in her pre-journalistic days was a member of *Cumann na mBan*. The Black and Tans had captured Máire and decided that to soften her up they would lock her up for the night in a room with a corpse. Arriving next morning they opened the door expecting to find Máire pale and shivering. She was peacefully asleep on the bed having tipped the corpse onto the floor. If the news editor asked her to do a job she didn't fancy in her *Press* days, she had been known to dial the direct line to Áras an Uachtaráin to complain to 'Ned.' (The locals in Bruff would have loved her – and she them.)

I was also learning how to deal with Dublin. The unfortunate garda who told me he couldn't let me into the docks area, where there had been a murder, as women were forbidden there after midnight, wasn't long out of Templemore and blushed as red as my old friend the judge in Limerick when I asked if I looked like a prostitute.

In those days you frequently had to fight for a chair and a typewriter in the newsroom, as a first-come first-served policy applied. The industrial correspondent, George Douglas, had solved the typewriter problem for himself by removing all the letters from one keyboard. As the only touch-typist in the place, this ensured that he had a personal typewriter – until I arrived. 'Use this one,' the lads told me, having learned of my accomplishment, then sat back to enjoy his wrath when he arrived in to find the newest recruit having appropriated 'his' typewriter.

It wasn't so easy to explain to the *Evening Press* editor, Sean Ward, how I had managed to 'miss' a miracle in Lourdes involving an Irish pilgrim – Lourdes always seemed to lead to trouble. I didn't think it prudent to tell him I had written my daily reports before I went, and on the day in question had been on an amazing trip in the Pyrenees. O'Toole, who by then was a news editor in the paper, was unsupportive, guessing correctly that I hadn't been on my own in the mountains.

We all suffered Ward's wrath when Limerick man Sean Bourke helped to spring the British spy George Blake from prison. Seeing a few colleagues from other media in the Silver Swan pub inspired a great ball-hop. We whispered excitedly how the *Evening Press* had an exclusive on Bourke escaping to join Blake in Moscow, and our best reporter was travelling with him. It became an international story – in every media except our own. The story took legs with confirmations that Bourke had been seen passing through Paris, having coffee in East Berlin and boarding a flight for Moscow.

'But there's no truth in it,' we told a furious Ward.

'There mightn't be, but they've all got a great story and we've been stuck on it,' he snarled.

No quarter was given either when the reporter sent to the US to cover the funeral of the late Robert Kennedy described for the *Sunday Press* the harrowing scenes as the former attorney general's coffin was lowered into the ground. As he had to file the copy early because of the time difference, our man could not have known that the funeral would be delayed because of the crowds who had held up the train bearing Kennedy's casket from New York to Arlington, and the tragic accident when the funeral train hit and killed two spectators.

I had been hired at a weekly salary of £15, and inflated by a year's experience, a couple of bylines and my success in prising the cost of a hot-water bottle from a reluctant Big Daddy when I had been consigned to a damp B & B rather than the hotel I had wanted on a country marking, I proposed to him that I should get a modest increase. He was courteous and affable – he would love to give it to me, but he just didn't have the money. I cut to the chase – I had an offer of doubling my salary from a PR company…. I was a journalist. I wouldn't go over to the dark side, he said. I might have to, in the interest of feeding and clothing myself, my mother's store long expended. I didn't have to give notice for a week, so maybe he would have another try at getting me an extra few bob? A week later I arrived into his office in my highest heels, outwardly confident, inwardly in fear and trembling, an envelope bearing my resignation in my hand, already sorry I had invented this non-existent PR job. He could do nothing, he said. Wordlessly, I proffered the envelope. Wordlessly, he took it, looked at it and then handed it back to me. At great personal cost, he had managed to get me the increase. I would stay, wouldn't I? I would – even though the PR company would be disappointed.

The days of youth, craic and ball-hops were all too short. A little over two years after arriving at the *Press*, I left – seduced by my beautiful blonde, blue-eyed baby daughter, Orla, whom I could not see fitting into the mad, turbulent world of the *Press*, which might suddenly demand I pursue midnight murders in the docks, drive to Cork, get a train to Belfast or a flight to the Arctic Circle. She and her two brothers, Feargal and Justin, propelled me into a new world, new happiness, new people and new friendships.

I kept in touch with those who came after me, many of whom became dear friends: David Davin Power, who went on to become RTÉ's political correspondent; Denis McClean, award-winning journalist and the man who became all our consciences in the third world; the beautiful Muriel Reddy, who broke the men's hearts while scooping them and whom we lost too soon to Australia; Alan Byrne, who became editor of the *Racing Post*; Stephen O'Byrnes, who went on to be secretary general of the Progressive Democrats; Frances

O'Rourke, who went to *The Irish Times*; and Con Houlihan, who memorably bought a new *geansaí* for my son Justin's christening, something he assured me he would never do again, so I could stop having babies. Then there was Austin Finn, Donal McCann, Noeleen Dowling, Tom McPhail, Aindreas McEntee, Sean Lynch, Kevin Marron, bestselling author Claire Boylan, the much-loved honorary *Press* man John Hooks (Hooxi), and so many others who were snatched from us all far too soon.

The country, and the world of journalism, were changing too. We had begun to discover corruption in high places – when Michael O'Toole revealed that Taoiseach Charles Haughey had personally kept a jewelled dagger, and his wife, Maureen, a jewelled necklace, which had been presented by the Saudi royal family and which should have been handed over to the state, it rocked the country and was one of the earlier stories to shake our belief in politicians. There were other scandals such as passports for sale, brown paper envelopes stuffed with cash, the fate of 'illegitimate' babies and their 'illegitimate' mothers.... Clerical sexual abuse would follow, ending the innocence of our youth and our generation.

Then guns and bombs, hunger strikes, intimidation and threats to ourselves and our families and to the state itself, made the work of the Fourth Estate a much more serious and hazardous affair for those whose job it was to pursue free speech and ultimately hold the line on democracy.

The Press Group, for so long teetering on the verge of closure, would not survive the turbulent changes as the old millennium died. It left a gap in the world of journalism that has not been filled, particularly in the areas of hard news and social issues.

By then the locals in Bruff had long ceased to buy me drinks. I had failed miserably to become the confidante of the political movers and shakers, and they had little faith that in my new career as a medical journalist I would be able to get them free treatment or even faster treatment.

For me, the *Press* was a time of youth and fun that would pass too quickly, of hard work, long days and nights, sunlit walks on Howth Head and Portmarnock's Velvet Strand (Michael snatched time for this in between plane crashes, chasing foreign spies and Irish politicians), of long, discursive evenings in the Silver Swan, of great friendships and a love that would last forever.

Big Daddy, and how I tried to save Johnny Rotten from jail

Paddy Clancy
(Reporter, 1965–1967)

He was called Big Daddy – not to his face – and it is so far back in the history of my time in newspapers I cannot really remember why.

He was a blustery sort of man who ruled the newsroom at the *Irish Press*. It was my first national newspaper, and I was fresh up from a weekly in Donegal at the age of twenty-two. I was convinced that I got the job not through merit but because the *Press* had about half a newsroom to fill after a strike in 1965 and was desperately seeking staff.

I think it was a strike – it was some sort of stoppage anyway – and it led to a mini-invasion of rural hacks stepping onto the newsroom floor for the first time of a daily national. We were wound up big-time to produce the greatest stories and whip the asses off our rivals in the fast-selling *Indo* group in Middle Abbey Street and the posh scribblers in the Old Lady of D'Olier Street. Younger newspaper employees nowadays never take their eyes from their laptops and iPads to bother talking to their colleagues. They don't even bother going to the boozer for a chat. They may need reminding that the paper I just mentioned is *The Irish Times* of Tara Street. The staff there seriously lacks the conviviality and sheer professionalism of those who worked at the paper when it was known as the Old Lady of D'Olier Street.

There I was one day in early 1966 about to change the face of Irish journalism when I got a call from a booming voice.

'Mr Clancy!' it said. Note the 'Mr'. Oh boy, I was finally in the big-time where even the bosses tipped their forelock as they were about to send you on a major scoop. It was Big Daddy, otherwise known as Mr Redmond, the managing editor or maybe it was chief news editor, and he scared me stiff. He had a commanding presence, and when he slipped out of the office for a drink it was usually with the two guys I thought had the scariest jobs in the business. They were crime reporters Sean Cryan and Tony Gallagher. Was I about to be raised even a small step towards their status?

Like hell I was. Big Daddy wanted to know why I had, in recent weeks, been missing my Monday morning sessions at a journalism course in Rathmines College. Let me tell you about that course, or what little I remember of it.

So far as I recall it was the first journalism course agreed between the NUJ and the nationals, and if you were under twenty-four you were required to attend on Monday mornings. As far as I could see it was designed for young Dublin-based journalists starting their work in newspapers. I had already done four years in the provinces, eighteen months as a sole staffer covering all of south Donegal. I couldn't see the point in studying what I reckoned I had already learned in the previous four years, so I took Monday mornings off to catch up on lost weekend sleep.

Strangely, despite my stupid big-headedness, Big Daddy, after ticking me off, indicated that he understood that I would be more useful in the newsroom, but he was obliged to send me to the course.

After that, he wasn't so frightening, and a few weeks later I dared to avail of a kind of freebie older reporters had told me was easy to organise. In those days the papers distributed free rail passes to reporters without cars 'going down the country' on a job. I was told that not too many questions were asked, if any at all, about some of the stories that were likely to fizzle out.

Putting it another way: it was an excuse to get a free train ride home to the west of Ireland. So I put in for a free rail pass to Sligo. I hadn't even thought of a tale, I was so confident no questions would be asked. But Bill Redmond – by now I could think his Christian name, although I daren't utter it – was still in Big Daddy mode. He wanted to know what the story was. I was so flummoxed I blurted out that there was no story; that I was on a couple of days off but I hadn't got money to go home. He offered me a loan of a fiver of his own cash. I protested that I would have to pay it back and I didn't think I could afford to for several weeks.

I won't swear to the outcome of the situation, for memory forty-nine years later serves me poorly, but I think it was resolved when Big Daddy found a story in Sligo and gave me my rail pass. By the way, some years later when I returned on holiday from England to *Irish Press* pubs, Bill Redmond was one of the first to buy me a pint.

My eighteen months on the *Press* was a ball, a very hazy ball admittedly, taking into account the numbers of hours spent in the Mucky Duck/Silver Swan on Burgh Quay, or in the White Horse or – when finishing on 'night-town' at 4 a.m. – in the Waldorf Hotel on Eden Quay.

I think the Waldorf is now called the Clifton Court. Way back in 1966 it was the nearest out-of-hours bar for a newspaper night worker ending his shift. I'm talking about the days before Leeson Street clubs were even a dream. It was when I first got to know, and appreciate, subeditors, for at that time of the morning they were the only drinking companions around for the lone late-night-duty reporter. One I remember with great affection – but unfortunately not his surname – was a man called Des. His title was something like 'late-night chief sub'.

The Waldorf played a role again when, after a number of years on the *Brighton Evening Argus,* the *Daily Telegraph* and the *Daily Express*, I returned to Dublin to start earning a living as a freelance. Johnny Rotten, formerly of the Sex Pistols, got arrested in a pub on Eden Quay in October 1980, and later that night I was tipped off that he was released from custody and was in the Waldorf. Between stops at phone kiosks – no mobiles in those days – to ring Fleet Street papers in London for orders for the story, I eventually arrived around midnight at the Waldorf. I found Johnny – real name John Lydon – in the bar, and to my amazement he turned out to be a very nice guy and not at all the punk of his public image.

He was quite worried about appearing in court on the next day, and he didn't know any solicitor in Dublin. Being just a year back in Dublin, my list of legal contacts was very short, so short that in fact I had only the home number of one in my contacts book because he was the one I most dealt with on stories over previous months. He was the solicitor most IRA suspects hired when they were due to appear in the Special Criminal Court, where I spent much time producing stories. I am 99 per cent certain I remember the name of the solicitor, but that 1 per cent doubt means I can't say for fear I will commit libel. Suffice to say the legal eagle was alerted, which was why spikey-haired Rotten was represented, to the bemusement of other reporters who were unaware of how the contact was made, by an IRA solicitor on his first appearance in Dublin District Court.

Rotten ended up being returned to custody and spent a weekend in Mountjoy Prison before he was sentenced to three months, which was suspended pending an appeal, and he was given bail.

Shortly after I joined the *Irish Press* a young man called Michael Keane started work there as a newsroom messenger. When I returned to work freelance shifts at the *Sunday Press* many years later, the same Mr Keane was then the editor. Presumably, he had the good sense not to touch up his managing editor for a free rail pass or to embarrass him into offering a fiver loan.

The *Press*, of course, carries many personal stories despite my short time in it. A young civil servant I first met in Donegal and then introduced to one of my Dublin flatmates, John Hooks, was Betty O'Driscoll. Her marriage to Hooxi, a non-journalist, should have got him away from the evil scribes he met through me and our other flatmates, Pat Chatten and Michael O'Toole. But Betty switched from the civil service to the *Irish Press* newsroom, where she became known through the good offices of Mr O'Toole as 'Miss Betty'. So Hooxi's life became more deeply involved in journalistic friends until his sad death some years ago.

When I left the *Press* as a staffer in 1967, O'Toole was joined in the newsroom by Maureen Browne, like him a product of Limerick journalism. Clancy's departure was definitely the *Press*'s gain, for Ms Browne was one of their greatest recruits. Her marriage to O'Toole meant that another of my friends had found a great woman. Sadly, Michael also passed away too soon.

There have been many more deaths in my fifty-two years in journalism, including ex-IP reporters Brendan Burke and Tom McPhail, who moved to work with me for a while as freelances.

One of the most recent deaths was of former *Evening Press* editor Sean Ward, whom I first met in my digs in a pub in Donegal when he was travelling around Ireland to have a chat with stringers.

Many years later he reminded me that he was puzzled how he kept buying the drinks in my digs when I didn't return the favour. I had to admit I was flat broke when he arrived, and I owed the landlord too much rent to risk asking him for a further favour when he might refuse in front of a man I hoped to work for one day.

My pub digs was directly opposite Donegal town courthouse, so a couple of months ago I thought I might finally return the favour for one member of his family when I was covering a case involving the arrest of the world's largest trawler, which is longer than Croke Park. One of the main witnesses in the Donegal courthouse was the Irish Navy's LÉ *Roisin*'s former skipper, retired Lieutenant Commander Terry Ward, Sean's son.

Unfortunately, by the time I slipped out of the *Press* box, Terry had disappeared – so I still owe a drink to the first news editor I ever worked for in the Irish Press Group.

New York cops in a time warp and IRA Armalites in coffins

Frank McDonald
(Correspondent/Subeditor/Reporter, *Irish Press*, 1973–1978)

Hard to believe, but it's true: I started my journalistic career at the age of twenty-two as freelance New York correspondent for the *Irish Press*. It only happened because I had been involved in student politics at UCD and had good contacts in the national papers. So, having fled to New York City after getting my degree (in history and politics), I wrote to them asking if there'd be any chance of freelancing from there.

Michael Kirke, then education correspondent of the *Irish Press* and a member of Opus Dei, passed me on to foreign editor Joe Carroll, and he gave me the break. So I bought a Remington portable typewriter (I still have it, in case everything else breaks down) and set about becoming a proper journalist; I even managed to get an 'I' visa (for foreign press) to legitimise my stay in the United States.

Seán Cronin, a former chief of staff of the IRA (going way back), was writing for *The Irish Times* from New York then, and Owen Dudley Edwards was also contributing a 'letter from America' for the *Times* while on an extended academic sabbatical in the US. He was the son of Robin Dudley Edwards, one of my old history professors at UCD, whose wild white hair made him look as if he had just been electrocuted.

I had a wonderful time, writing about Watergate, Irish Noraid (what dinosaurs!), how the IRA was using coffins to smuggle Armalites to Ireland, Broadway and off-Broadway shows and offbeat stuff about New York City. I met Pete Hamill and Shirley MacLaine, interviewed the great Siobhán McKenna in the Grammercy Park Hotel, and watched Senator Sam Erwin and the Watergate hearings on daytime TV. The 1972 US presidential election was on while I was there, and it was pretty devastating. Richard Nixon won forty-nine of the fifty states, with the single exception of Massachusetts, which voted for George McGovern. After the Watergate scandal broke, eventually forcing Nixon out of office in 1974, car drivers with Boston registrations put up bumper stickers saying: 'Don't blame me – I'm from Massachusetts'.

It was Noraid that unnerved me most. I'll never forget interviewing its chief, Michael Flannery, in the bleak Irish ghetto of Astoria in Queens. He had left Ireland in 1926, deeply disillusioned by Éamon de Valera's decision to establish Fianna Fáil and participate in Free State politics, and his mind was frozen in that era of betrayal and 'empty' oath-taking; he knew almost nothing about contemporary Ireland. This was when members of the New York City Police Department, and other officially approved contingents in the annual St Patrick's Day parade, carried green banners fringed with gold tassels bearing the message (in gold lettering): 'ENGLAND GET OUT OF IRELAND' – a whole generation living on the bitter folk memory of the '800 Years of Oppression'.

Flannery believed that the 'armed struggle' would bring about a united Ireland, and he worked tirelessly to raise funds, ostensibly for Sinn Féin, but in reality for the Provisional IRA. Good sources told me how they would pack coffins with Armalites and other weapons for dispatch on Aer Lingus flights to Ireland – banking on these not being discovered due to the traditional Irish respect for the dead.

The Irish deputy consul general in New York at the time was Paddy McKernan, an astute, brilliant and personally engaging diplomat whose job included keeping an eye on the Noraid crowd. He was nothing if not unconventional, with poster-size portraits of Marx and Lenin on the walls of his Upper East Side apartment. But that early left-wing dalliance didn't stand in the way of McKernan's stellar career.

I didn't even know what a subeditor was when Tim Pat Coogan offered me a job as one in the autumn of 1973. Although I had been freelance New York correspondent for eighteen months, I hadn't a clue about how the stuff I wrote was processed for publication. All I knew was that my copy was turned into a ticker tape at the Reuters office, not far from the Flatiron building, and then sent on to Dublin by Telex. Now, suddenly, with no training whatever, I found myself on the subs' desk in Burgh Quay one Sunday evening, having been escorted there by deputy editor Fintan Faulkner, an absolute gentleman. (His younger brother, Pádraig, had been a Fianna Fáil minister and went on to become Ceann Comhairle of Dáil Éireann. But then, even the dogs in the street knew that the *Irish Press* was a Fianna Fáil paper).

Fintan introduced me to chief sub John Garvey, who promptly gave me a 'two-of-eighteen' to do. Maurice Sweeney, whom I had known from UCD, was one of my new colleagues, and he helpfully explained that what was needed was a two-paragraph 'short', topped by a two-line heading in eighteen-point type, using a brief news story some reporter had done as my raw material. I soon got the hang of it.

My starting salary was £28 per week, topped up by £11 in lieu of a productivity deal then being finalised between management and the NUJ chapel, headed by militant Niall Connolly, who later went over to the other side. I'll never forget him pledging at a mandatory meeting in Liberty Hall that they weren't going to settle for anything less than a basic of £80 per week. £80 per week?! It was unimaginable to me.

As a subeditor I had to get to know the *Irish Press* 'house style', which had its own peculiarities. In obituaries of Old IRA veterans (Fianna Fáil ones), it was the practice to say that they had fought somewhere-or-other in 1916, took part in the War of Independence and 'remained on the Republican side' during the Civil War – clearly implying that those who joined the National Army were traitors. No wonder the paper was nicknamed *Pravda* by then Minister for Posts & Telegraphs Conor Cruise O'Brien, who announced, menacingly, that he was keeping a file on its editorials and letter writers about the situation in 'the North', 'the Six Counties' or Northern Ireland, as we would eventually come to call it. For a time it looked as if he would nobble press freedom, à la Section 31 of the Broadcasting Act, but the *Irish Press* was not propagandist in the way that *Pravda* was. Its political correspondent, Michael Mills, was a man of the utmost integrity, and he reported the news from Leinster House in a non-partisan way. Only when it came to elections was the paper pro-Fianna Fáil: its managing director, Vivion de Valera, son of the party's founder, was also Fianna Fáil TD for Dublin North-West.

The *Irish Press* subs' desk in the 1970s was legendary. It was populated by so many interesting characters, fellows who knew Latin or Greek, alcoholics, historians, literary types, poets and novelists. One of the assistant chief subs, John Banville, gave us all signed copies of *Long Lankin* – his first book, a collection of short stories – after it was remaindered by London publishers Secker & Warburg.

Joycean scholar Terence Killeen was also on the subs' desk then, along with mild-mannered poet Hugh McFadden, Dermot Keogh, who went on to become professor of history at UCC, and diminutive Derry man Séamus McGonagle, a great raconteur when he was sober, artful cartoonist and author of a slim volume called *The Bicycle in Life, Love, War, and Literature*. It was an enjoyable place to work.

John Garvey, from Co. Down, was the most decent man I ever met, as well as being a great journalist with an instinct for a good story. He was ably assisted by deputy chief sub Liam Moher, an edgy Cork man and former army officer who brought a sense of order to the chaos. Other fine colleagues included John Spain, who became literary editor of the *Irish Independent*, and gentle Galwegian Seán Conway. We amused ourselves by thinking up joke headlines, and the rule was that they had to fit in a single column, using the *Irish Press* typefaces and font sizes. One I remember, a 'two-of-eighteen', was 'Cat devours Pro-Cathedral', but the winning headline by a mile – coined by John Brophy – was 'Rabbit carnage as train hits magician'. It fitted perfectly in three lines of thirty-point Tempo heavy condensed.

Our half-hour break – 'cutline' at 10 p.m., was spent in local hostelries with the hard chaws going to Mulligan's, whereas we moderate drinkers went to Kennedy's on George's Quay. Mind you, the only food available there was a bowl of soup or a toasted ham-and-cheese sandwich, served up in a piping hot cellophane bag; that was pretty well the range of 'bar food' in Dublin in the 1970s.

Another option was the Scotch House, a great old pub on the corner of Burgh Quay and Hawkins Street. It was pulled down for a nondescript office block, leased (inevitably) by the state. There was also the old White Horse at the corner of George's Quay, which has since been transformed beyond recognition. It was a favourite haunt of our colleagues, the printers who claimed direct descent from Gutenberg.

As a subeditor you had to be conscious of the strong demarcation line between compositors and journalists. This was most visible on 'the stone', where we stood facing each other over the frame of a page as columns were filled with cooling hot metal and headlines formed from a matrix of steel letters. Before the page proof was produced you got used to 'reading' the headlines upside down AND back to front. If you touched any of the metal, you were dead. That was exclusively the preserve of compositors, those princes of the printing trade. They took precedence over the Linotype machinists who, by some magic, turned molten lead into columns of material to fill the pages, reading from the often heavily subbed stories sent down for printing by chief sub John Garvey after he had gone through them all.

Behind Garvey sat the night editor, Jack Jones, whose main job was to lay out pages. A gentleman and good Protestant, he'd say things like 'Would you mind awfully, old chap?' before asking you to do something or other – perhaps even taking a badly written report and rewriting it from top to bottom on one of the typewriters in the newsroom. I once did that in front of the offending reporter.

Not long after I joined the *Irish Press* subs' desk, the Burgh Quay building was redeveloped around us with the exception of a Georgian house adjoining the Corn Exchange. This was where Tim Pat had his office. At 8.30 p.m. one night I popped in with an urgent query to find him sitting back in his wooden swivel chair, legs crossed on the desk, dictating his latest book to his long-suffering secretary, Eileen Davis.

Incredibly, the extensive construction work was not financed by a bank loan or anything like that, but rather from day-to-day receipts from the sale of newspapers – the *Irish Press*, *Evening Press* and the *Sunday Press*. The latter was the biggest seller, allowing its editor Vincent Jennings – nicknamed 'Jenocide' long before he presided over the Irish Press Group's demise – to preen himself like a peacock.

On my way to work one evening in May 1974, I heard at least one of the three car bomb explosions in Parnell Street, Talbot Street and South Leinster Street – the Dublin Bombings. The city's emergency plan was activated and ambulances with sirens blaring were soon rushing the victims to hospital. Twenty-seven people were killed and a further seven perished when a car bomb went off in Monaghan. The atmosphere in Burgh Quay that night was sombre; after all, nobody knew whether relatives or friends were among the casualties, and it took a while before the names of those killed were released. Although a car bomb had exploded outside Liberty Hall in 1972, the widespread carnage in Dublin and Monaghan that day – caused by the UVF, it was suspected – brought 'the Troubles' to our doorsteps.

It was also while working as a sub that I realised Dublin was dying. Cycling home after finishing work at either 1 a.m. or 4 a.m., when the city centre is virtually taken over by squawking seagulls, I began to notice derelict sites all over the place and reckoned that there was a story behind every hoarding. So I started writing about what was happening, and some would say that I made a career out of it.

In 1976, after three years as a subeditor, I had finally made a switch to the newsroom, working under Mick O'Kane and Dermot MacIntyre. O'Kane, who was from Northern Ireland, was the quiet man, while MacIntyre, his deputy, was always barking orders at us like a chef in some busy restaurant. I can still see him standing at the newsdesk at lunchtime, wolfing an apple. No doubt he thought lunch was for wimps.

I was rostered for everything in the news area – the Children's Court, the Dáil, day-to-day stories and the Special Criminal Court, where I covered the Sallins mail train robbery case. I saw there that one of the judges was falling asleep and mentioned this to defence counsel Séamus Sorahan SC. He told me that he had seen it too, and he and Paddy MacEntee SC would be making an application for a mistrial. This was rejected by the three-judge court, so Sorahan and MacEntee appealed to the Supreme Court. To the incredulity of those of us who had seen Judge John O'Connor asleep, the highest court in the land held as a matter of fact that he had been alert all the time. Not long afterwards the sleeping judge died from heart failure, and Nicky Kelly, Osgur Breatnach et al had to be put on trial all over again.

One of my biggest assignments as a fledgling reporter was to cover the St Patrick's Day parade in New York City and interview Judge James J. Comerford, long-serving chairman of the parade committee. It was regarded as so important that Tim Pat even took me to see Major de Valera in advance, and he gave me a little lecture about the political independence of the *Irish Press*. I didn't believe a word of it. I only discovered afterwards that Comerford, who had emigrated from Co. Kilkenny in the mid 1920s, had been the *Irish Press* bagman in the US for many years. And it was through the Delaware-registered Irish Press Corporation, which held in trust the shares of thousands of Irish-American investors in his newspaper venture, that Éamon de Valera and his family were able to control the company for decades. In this, the de Valeras were no different to Major T. B. McDowell, chairman and long-serving chief executive of *The Irish Times*. When its ownership was transferred to a trust in 1974, the Articles of Association specified that the major would be the sole 'A' shareholder, and in the event of any attempt to remove him, the 'A' shareholder's vote would be equivalent to all of the others, plus one vote.

I went to work for *The Irish Times* in January 1979. The first big story I covered was the aftermath of a deadly explosion on board the *Betelgeuse*, a French oil tanker, at Whiddy Island in Bantry Bay. I can vividly remember phoning it over to a copy-taker in Dublin from a wind-up telephone in a kiosk on the main street in Bantry. That was not yet forty years ago – before fax machines, internet, email and iPhones.

From Fleet Street, we watched the *Irish Press* going down the drain until it finally ceased publication in 1995. For at least twenty years it had been obvious that the company was not investing in its flagship paper, preferring to put money into promoting the Evening and Sunday titles. But it's to the *Irish Press* that I, and so many others, owe our early training in journalism. For that, it was the best in the business.

Hot metal, Poison Pricks, smoked haddock and the 'lead' story

John Brophy
(News Subeditor/Stone man)

The first things you had to learn were the nicknames. There was one person called Rasher, the traditional Dublin name for a thin person, but he was also known as Lazarus, from the pallor of his complexion. But Laz/Rasher was not to be confused with the Wicked Chicken, or Bonaski, or Little Waxy, or Freddie the Fearless, or Clumper, or The Crake, or The Howler, or Liver. And there was the Dickensian name for one comrade: The Horrible Boy.

The only rule was that no considerations of charity or delicacy of feeling, much less of propriety, were ever allowed to obfuscate the accuracy of these appellations. Once bestowed, they stuck. And they could be inherited. For instance, one person was dubbed The Greyhound, and when the son followed him into the trade, not an unusual happening, he was duly named The Whippet. Only once have I encountered a soubriquet to better what was available in Burgh Quay. This was in the case of a man who had been married three times, and all three ladies had predeceased him. That's how he graduated to being called Poison Prick, and knew better than to object.

Now before those of another generation become suffocated in an orgy of political correctness and condemnation, let me explain that to have a nickname conferred status and acceptance. As the saying was, 'You mightn't like him, or spend your night off with him' (precious indeed was that, only one in every fortnight), 'but if he's in any trouble, we'll go to war for him.' The manuals of what is now, sickeningly, called Human Resources' Management will identify this bonded corporate identity as something very precious – except when there's a wage claim in process.

The printing process I knew hadn't changed much since stereotyping arrived in around the 1820s, and the Linotype at the end of that century. The hot metal referred to nostalgically was mostly made of lead, with tin added for hardness and antimony. The fumes, when inhaled through a cigarette, did very nasty things to the human frame, which is why, when there is a memorial service as there is each September in Haddington Road Church, followed by a reception in the National Print Museum, we look with quiet trepidation to see who isn't there. Most of those named at the start of this piece – all very real people – are gone from us.

Consider, too, that there were stereotypers working with three tons of this molten metal, and it's no wonder they drank enormous quantities and sweated it out in similar amounts. By law they were entitled to free milk to help counteract lead poisoning from the fumes. There was a time when the editorial desk was perched on top of this cauldron of lead, with only a flimsy floor in between. That's why we called it Short Kesh: it took a threat of industrial action to change things. Also, the lads downstairs had a playful custom of wrapping their lunch of smoked haddock in aluminium foil and reheating it on top of the metal pot, which left us above trying to compose a headline and salivating like Pavlov's dogs.

Speaking of 'dogs' ... apprentice printers studied at the Technical College in Bolton Street. It was a formal setting where decorum was inspected. The first class involved reviewing the letters of the alphabet, the numerals and the other characters, the 'sorts'.

'So we have the interrogation mark, also called the question mark, and we have the exclamation mark. What other name do we have for that?' Teacher was expecting a respectful reply.

'Please, sir, we sometimes call it a drumstick.'

Polite chortles were then permitted. But from the back of the room they heard: 'Jaze, we always call that a dog's mickey!' and everyone knew at once that the speaker was from the *Irish Press*.

Looked at from a modern standpoint, all of the above sounds primitive, indeed savage. But there was a pride in the job, in beating the opposition, in getting the story and getting it right. There were tales coming from across the river that hacks would form a queue in the Oval, waiting for the privilege of being allowed to buy the editor a drink. In Mulligan's it was more likely that the editor would buy you a drink and take the sting out of any dispute that had blown up in the heat of racing against deadlines. It was the triple Republican policy of Liberty, Equality and Fraternity.

Mulligan's wasn't our only watering hole. Much late-night drinking took place in the Irish Times Club. It was located, for most of its existence, in the top storey of a building opposite the back door of *The Times*. I once spoke to a family member of the Kilmartin clan who ran a bookie's shop on the ground floor. He confirmed that they had often been afraid the whole place might collapse under the weight of the traffic. It was a well-run establishment, though the walls and ceilings were a shade of dark gold from the cigarette smoke.

In earlier times access was achieved by ringing the doorbell and waiting until someone, four floors up, threw down a latch key. One room featured the dartboard, another the pool table (formerly the bar billiards/bagatelle board). The third was the bar room and the fourth too small for much except talk. The seating was hard chairs: some old dining chairs with the backs cut off. The bar shut at 4 a.m.

The only other rule was that people on shift, who came in for their break, had precedence in calling drinks and getting seats.

It happened one night that Peter Ustinov was in town, and after a TV appearance he was taken out and ended up in the club. He was in the middle of a spate of anecdote and repartee, regaling the company, when the men came in on their break, also known as the 'cut-line'. And the cry went up: 'Chairs for the cut-line men.'

The steward who was on the rounds collecting empty glasses noticed that Ustinov was supporting his ample frame on not one but two stools. So, with an adroit flick of the ankle, he dislodged a seat from under the distinguished visitor with the remark: 'I suppose you think that your arse is twice as good as anyone else's!'

It was a remark that Ustinov greatly enjoyed and told against himself thereafter.

So what went wrong with the *Press*? I remember reporting for work on Sunday evenings when they would still be clearing up after the Saturday night run. The *Sunday Press* sold over 420,000 copies, a figure that's not likely to be equalled again. But the technology meant that it was limited to thirty-two pages. Even allowing for pre-printed colour and supplements, it was not enough. By the time of the Pope's visit in 1979, the opposition had colour, and we couldn't match them. Contrast this with the famed 1947 All-Ireland Final, played in New York. The *Press* was the first to have a wire picture machine. There was dynamism in management with names like Lemass and Dempsey (later Aer Lingus chief executive). These had followed iconic names like Pierce of Wexford and O'Meara's Bacon.

The Fianna Fáil party lost interest in the papers: they had a tame RTÉ with Section 31 and the rest of the Broadcasting Act. Indeed, management was perceived to favour the Progressive Democrats rather than their own roots. There was the unedifying spectacle of Vincent Jennings attending the monthly soirées of Maureen Cairnduff in Waterloo Road (reported to include British intelligence personnel). The expertise and initiative had vanished, and so had the dream.

I remember the night of the Brighton bombing. I was finishing off some work on a classical music column when the news broke just before 4 a.m. We tore open the front page and two others, and within twenty minutes had banner headlines. We were the only Dublin paper to have the story. In the days that followed I waited for an acknowledgement or even a reproof for having wasted resources. None came, and it was a sure sign that it was time to get out. But we couldn't: we loved the place too much.

In the last twenty years, many people who have got jobs elsewhere have dreamed of getting back to a place where there was good, principled journalism, and where colleagues supported and cared for colleagues. Once you had known Burgh Quay, you couldn't go elsewhere and settle for less.

The day I nearly killed Dev

Liam Flynn
(Reporter/Feature Writer/Deputy News Editor/Group
Art Editor, 1956–1995)

The *Irish Press* hit the streets and hamlets of Ireland in September 1931 when Miss Margaret Pearse, sister of the 1916 patriot Patrick Henry Pierce, pressed a button of the old Hoe printing press with Dev by her side.

That was the year I was born. Twenty-five years later I joined the staff, and remained for forty years, during which time I was reporter, feature writer, deputy news editor, and for thirty years the group art editor. The closure in 1995 was a devastating blow to 600 staff and their families, an episode in Irish journalism that for years would be debated as to what and who caused the demise. Burgh Quay was a great news centre and was sorely missed by staff and readers throughout the country. Despite the tragedy of its closure, though, memories are filled with stories, anecdotes and occurrences that happened on the fringes of the avaricious demands of the printing presses. One such affecting me was The Day I Nearly Killed Dev.

When it happened my entire lifespan flashed across my mind, as they say happens when death is nigh. Cold sweat on the back of one's neck is an abiding experience. And so it came to pass that one of my early markings was to cover Dev in his favourite native tongue when opening An Óige Hostel in Glenmalure, Co. Wicklow. I travelled on a gorgeous sunny Sunday morning with Arthur Noonan, who was delegated to cover the English language version (Arthur later became political correspondent for RTÉ). It was a common joke amongst journalists that Dev would often open his speech with a few lines in Irish and then announce 'as I have just said in Irish,' and speak for another hour in English, though I must record that that was not the case on this occasion.

Dev was then in the unusual position of being the leader of the opposition in the Dáil. But he was also our boss, the founder of the paper, and had proprietary entitlements to appropriate coverage. When you were 'on' Dev you had to be on your mettle. That certainly meant being on time. Eddie McDonnell (deceased) was the driver of the VW Beetle as the photographer always had the use of the car and since in emergencies he would have to leave a marking early. Most times wiring facilities were unavailable. Eddie always boasted that he was called Eddie after The Chief, de Valera himself. On this occasion he was concerned to be on time when Dev opened the hostel.

So he sped on with Fangio-like enthusiasm until we tailed Dev's car. Steady Eddie, nothing to worry about.

Rising up the Wicklow Hills presented its own driving problems. Where did Dev's car turn off to go down into the valley? Obviously, Christy Cruise, Dev's driver and bodyguard, was a little unsure too, and passed the narrow laneway leading to his destination. He stopped suddenly, so suddenly that Fangio Eddie ran into the back of the much larger car, a Packard given to Dev, it was said, by John A. Costello (a Taoiseach not now remembered too well) as a gift. The language in the VW was not in Dev's favourite tongue.

The cars were locked together, bumper to bumper. The three of us jumped out of the VW as fast as you could say with Sean O'Casey 'we're all Shanghaied now.' So too did Christy, with the face of a man doomed for the gallows. The four of us heaved and swore as we tried to undo the bumpers. I think I heard Eddie say under his breath: 'Jaysus, we're all fired now'.

Meanwhile, seated in the back seat of the Packard was the world-renowned statesman Dev, himself engaged in conversation with Dorothy McArdle, the author of the definitive work *The Irish Republic*. Sitting in pensive or in vacant mood in the passenger seat was Dev's secretary, Pádraig Ó hAnnracháin – a lot of history in the one car. To this day the tiny curling hairs stand up on my neck when thinking about it. Once the bumpers had been unlocked, the quartet breathed a sigh of relief. Christy especially. He had an immaculate record, but was still looking forward to his impending retirement. His visage I remember well – it was as white and as cold as a slab of Carrara marble. He dabbed his brow with the back of his garda hand and turned with satisfaction to return to his car.

Horror of horrors, the lovely Christy had forgotten to put on the brake, and as the bumpers had been unlocked it started to move across the narrow roadway towards a ravine on the other side. Disaster loomed. It looked as if Dev, Dorothy and Pádraig were heading for the Golden Gates sooner than was planned.

It is amazing what unplumbed energies can surface when needs must. Christy, well into his sixties (then regarded as old), leaped like a ferret chased by a hound and slammed on his brake to save both Tom O'Neill and Lord Packenham from rewriting the history of Dev. I ask you just to imagine what role Eddie, Arthur and I nearly played in history. In a thrice, all was forgotten. No one was bothered.

In due course Dev stood on a grassy knoll and said his usual piece in Irish, which I took down fully in my Gregg shorthand; Arthur got his vernacular piece and Eddie took his pics. All was forgotten until one Sunday when I wrote the story for 'Sunday Miscellany'. I had no sooner finished hearing the story on radio when my home phone rang. It was the famous and great writer Benedict Kiely. He yelled down the phone: 'And why didn't you kill the so-and-so?!' Ben had once worked for the *Irish Press*.

I joined the *Press* following an interview on a sunny afternoon in May 1956. I never had any regrets. It was a terrific newspaper, nearly always first with the latest news, and especially hard news stories. It was generally accepted that the newsroom was the best in the land. So it was.

While the staff were held in high esteem, the conditions within the building itself were almost Dickensian. This impression started with my interview. It took place in what seemed like the attic of the ancient building on Burgh Quay, once Conciliation Hall, the meeting place of Daniel O'Connell, the Liberator, and later the Tivoli Music Hall, (some say the Tivoli never closed). The two interviewers (Joe Walsh, who was later to become editor of the *Irish Press*, and the chief news editor, Bill Redmond) sat on a rostrum some four or five feet above me, making me 'look up' to my future superiors. I got the job, but not before I had convinced them that I could take a good note, that I could review theatre, that I could take a good note in proper grammatical Irish (especially from Dev), and that I was available for all shifts.

Bill was my first boss, and despite any contrary opinions that were nurtured he was an excellent if somewhat gruff deskman. (Remember your *Macbeth*. Was it King Duncan who said: 'There is no art to find the mind's construction in the face'?) Shifts were worked from 7 a.m. for the first eight hours, and the latest from 4 p.m., with a special shift known as 'night-town'. When the entire staff had gone home, 'night-town' kept contact with the guards.

The area in which the staff worked was a total shambles. For the squad of reporters, the phones were in short supply, and the kitchen chairs seemed as scarce as scoops on a Good Friday. Indeed, so rare were they that one industrial correspondent when leaving the office on a story would tie the chair he was using to the legs of the table with a roll of hairy twine to ensure that it would be available for him when he returned.

Apparently, typing was not essential, and reporters were not generally supplied with typewriters. A number of upright Remington machines were provided, so if one was available one could choose to use it or otherwise write the story longhand on the copy paper provided. This paper was cut in sheets from the newsprint that was left over after the rolls had been put through the printing presses. Notebooks were not provided either, so reporters going out on stories would bring a pocketful of copy sheets to use while making notes. There was no such thing as a phone recorder or a computer back then.

The industrial correspondent I refer to was a first-class typist and note-taker, and actually played the Remington like a machine gunner on an Isis raid. He played the piano too, which he also played like a typewriter – the same space between each note. All the notes were there, but not the melody.

I recall one morning when he was rushing a story for the *Evening Press* when he slammed the phone down with the retort: 'And I never killed the Parish Priest!' Sometime later I discovered that the 'killer' was the PRO for Aer Lingus who in earlier days had been the local correspondent for the national papers. A report on the death of a parish priest was always worth some money. The 'PP' had been very ill, and a daily call to the Presbytery was made to find out if he had passed away. The sympathetic housekeeper told the correspondent that the PP was in bed in the front bedroom, and to save him the trouble she would pull the blind down when his final moment came. One morning, of course, the sun was blinding, and the poor man had asked that the blind be pulled down, so the correspondent thought that he had left us. He immediately phoned the three dailies to inform them of the death. Hence, 'I never killed the Parish Priest.'

The newsroom then was littered with would-be writers, poets, playwrights and enthusiasts of all types.

There was Niall Carroll, brother of the internationally renowned Paul Vincent Carroll, who wrote West End and Broadway hits. Niall didn't achieve the same fame. Since his days covering the Louth County Council meetings he aimed to write a play about the shallow tide that drivelled into Blackrock beach. He eventually wrote it, and titled it *The Wanton Tide*. The Abbey Theatre accepted it, but it wasn't a hit. In fact it lasted only for a very brief spell. It was a great disappointment to him and he never wrote another. If he had got it out of his system he may have had later success.

There was John Healy from Charlestown, Co. Mayo, who wrote *No-one Shouted Stop*. It was a significant hit. He later edited the *Evening Mail* when it was purchased by *The Irish Times*. Douglas Gageby was a great admirer of John's energy, and surely gave him the same advice he gave to all aspiring journalists: write as much as you can on any story. John took him at his word and wrote by the yardage. 'How much copy do you want – that much, or that much?'

There was Ted Nealon from Co. Sligo. Ted was more pragmatic than most and liked to spend ample time backing winners and buying property. He became editor of the *Sunday Review* and was later a renowned political commentator on RTÉ. He stood for Fine Gael in the general election and was appointed Minister for the Arts.

I'm writing mainly about the pre-RTÉ days when the public depended, almost exclusively, on the newspapers for their information. Hence, journalists were held in the highest esteem.

The demands on journalists were great, especially in terms of time. When you were marked on a story you generally stayed with it. There was no overtime payment back then.

Covering Dev brought its own degree of anxiety, not only because he owned the paper but because he delivered many of his speeches in Irish. Consequently, I was marked on many of Dev's sojourns down the country. One example will suffice. Joe Shakespeare (the photographer and my driver) and I left Dublin at 7 a.m. to travel to Donegal, where Dev, that Sunday afternoon, was unveiling a monument to Neil Blayney's father. Niall was the Fianna Fáil TD and his father was an Old IRA man. Having covered that I went on to Jackson's hotel in Ballybofey, where Dev was still speaking coming up to midnight. To get the story back to Dublin I had to hurry to a neighbouring village, Stranorlar, where the only phone available was a public phone.

With no computers or laptops to help us, all copy on stories outside the city had to be phoned in to the newsroom, where a team of patient copy-takers crammed into tiny cubicles to type out the copy. Frequently, one would hear the desperate cries of: 'How do you spell that? S for what?' On that night, poor Arthur Noonan, who later became political correspondent for RTÉ, spent over an hour taking copy (the copy-takers had long since gone home). Oh for a laptop or a mobile! No extra pay, no overtime. Yes, things were different back then.

That night I stayed in the same hotel in Bundoran just as tired as Dev must have been after a long, long day. But I thought the trip and effort were well worth it when Dev asked to meet me over breakfast the following morning. I had heard that he did not like boiled eggs, but there he was eating one. We spoke in Irish, of course, and as a result he invited me to travel with him to Sligo where he was to deliver his valedictory before quitting his seat in the Dáil.

I was thrilled to join him in the back seat, and the main topic of conversation in the first language was W. B. Yeats. It was a mere coincidence that Yeats's son was a subeditor in the *Irish Press*. By the way, how do you put Irish on: 'I will arise and go now' or 'Lake water lapping with low sounds by the shore'?

In all my years I never had a complaint that Dev was misquoted, but then I had devised a method to take a shorthand note of the man in Irish. I'm sure Walsh and Redmond made a perfect choice when they took me on, especially when Dev himself would phone the office with a statement in Irish. The cry always was 'Where is Flynn?'

It is inevitable that journalists have a myriad of stories, and most journalists have cultivated the art of survival. I like to mention a story regarding the greatest survivor of all, a man who was always in control despite the extraordinary manner in which he lived: Con Houlihan.

He was the most admired journalist in town, and I like to feel that I played some part in his coming to the *Evening Press*. A simple recollection of reading his wonderful contributions in the *Kerryman* when I casually met him in the Silver Swan started a lifelong friendship. I introduced him to Sean Ward, editor of the *Evening Press*, soon after, and from there his back-page column developed. Thankfully, when we first met he wasn't on the brandy/milk libation that was his favourite tipple. Sean and I always got honourable mention in Con's recollections for his introduction to the back page.

When the *Press* decided to go tabloid, however, management took over Mulligan's pub for one day when all could go and have free drinks to celebrate. After many hours, and late in the afternoon, I spotted Con sitting disconsolately on his stool. I asked him what he thought of the changeover to tabloid. He replied in his usual muffled Kerry tongue, fingers over nose: 'Oh it's bloody awful. It's dreadful. I'll never write for Burgh Quay again. It's a disgrace.'

Just then, the door into the side bar opened and Dr Éamon de Valera (who was editor-in-chief and controlling director) popped his head in, saw Con and asked: 'Well, Con, what do you think?'

With the survivor's flash, Con answered: 'Oh magic, magic'.

He was the greatest.

Memories from the other side of the Stone

Harry Havelin
(Compositor/Con Houlihan's
Personal Typesetter, 1964–1991)

On Monday 6 July 1964, I started work in the *Irish Press* offices on Burgh Quay. I was sixteen-and-a-half years old, just out of school, and commencing my six-year apprenticeship as a compositor. In those days the Press Group was a highly successful company – its three papers enjoyed huge circulations, and many of the country's top journalists were on the payroll. Though the offices and works on Burgh Quay were dilapidated and badly in need of refurbishing, the Hoe-Crabtree and K & B rotary presses churned out over two million newspapers each week.

The caseroom, where the pages were made up, was an incredibly busy place. Not only did it produce three newspapers, but also all of the company's stationery (business cards, invoices, labels, forms, letterheads, envelopes, posters, etc.), plus the Fianna Fáil party newspaper, *Gléas*, and the annual Palm Sunday charity paper, *The Advocate*.

It was a twenty-four-hours-a-day, seven-days-a-week operation: when the day staff were going home the night crew were coming in, and vice versa. Twelve and even fifteen-hour shifts were not uncommon. Overtime was guaranteed – indeed, it was absolutely essential to ensure that the papers went out on time. The caseroom, in its chaotic pre-1970 layout, contained twenty-eight Intertype typesetting machines; three Ludlow headline-setting machines,

106

plus the area known as the stone, where the pages were put together. There were also a couple of electric circular saws for cutting the metal type; mitre wheels, which were used for trimming rules so they joined together neatly; and 'randoms', where type was collated on 'galleys' (long, narrow metal trays) prior to being handed over to the 'stone men' for assembly into the pages.

The supervisor's 'box' stood at the top of the caseroom, leaving plenty of 'hiding places' in between the machines where cups of tea were regularly drunk outside official break times. Mind you, tea wasn't the only beverage consumed in those dark passages!

In decades long past, an apprenticeship in the printing trade was much sought after and highly regarded. The Print Union controlled entry into the trade. At one time it was a requirement that an aspiring apprentice had to have a close male relative in the trade in order to gain admission, though this had changed by the late 1960s when the government-appointed body *An Comhairle Oiliúna* (ANCO) took over control of training for all trades. Apprentices in the printing trade worked hard for very small reward, particularly in their first couple of years. My starting pay was £3. 10*s*. 8*d*. per week.

During my first four years in the *Press*, I had to attend classes in the School of Printing at Bolton Street College of Technology. The format for year one was: morning in the 'Tech', afternoon in the *Press*. Year two was: morning in work, afternoon in Bolton Street. In my third and fourth years, it was a full five-day working week, with attendance in 'Tech' on Monday, Wednesday and Friday nights (7.30 to 10).

In the 1950s, printing trade apprentices 'served' seven years before they were fully qualified tradesmen. By the time I started, the apprenticeship period had been reduced to six years. By 1970, however, it had been reduced to five years by ANCO. As things turned out, I actually served five-and-a-half years.

Alongside the areas in the caseroom, which I've already mentioned, there was also the reading room, fitters' workshop, monocasting room and upper stereo. The fitters' shop was where the mechanics, whose job it was to service and maintain the Intertype and Ludlow machines, were based. The monocasting room was where all hot metal spacing and rules (six-point and twelve-point) for the newspaper pages were cast on two rather antiquated machines. The upper stereo was where the newspaper pages were pressed into 'flong' moulds prior to being cast in semicircular metal plates in the lower stereo for the printing presses.

The reading room in the 1960s was like a home for retired soldiers. Most of the readers were older men, several of whom had seen action in the War of Independence and the Civil War. Some had fingers missing, bad limps, and other physical legacies of conflicts past. A few of these men had been on opposite sides in the Civil War and, even more than forty years on, the deep bitterness between them was still very evident. I recall one of them, a big man from Co. Tipperary, who was on the Free State side in the Civil War, who wouldn't look at, let alone talk to, a work colleague who sat a few feet away from him and who had been on the 'Irregular' (IRA) anti-treaty side. Wasn't it the great playwright Brendan Behan who said that anytime he went into the *Press* offices on Burgh Quay he had to be careful to dodge the flying bullets? He wasn't far wrong!

Each reader had a copyholder with him. The copyholder read the original hard copy while the reader, who had to be a fully qualified compositor, checked the typeset galley proofs. It was not uncommon for apprentice compositors to be sent into the reading room to 'hold copy' for a reader. This was very useful experience, and I did it on many occasions in my first two years there. On the day I started in the caseroom I was put in the hands of a man named Billy O'Neill, who was affectionately known to one and all as 'Naylor'. He would have been well over seventy years old in 1964. 'Naylor' wore a distinctive well-worn brown shop-coat, which stretched down to his ankles, and as the oldest compositor in the caseroom one of his jobs was to take the junior apprentices under his wing and 'break them in'. To the best of my recollection there were about twelve apprentices in the *Press* in the mid 1960s. I spent a short period of my first year with 'Naylor' before moving on to another man named Billy Geoghegan, who also trained new apprentices.

As well as learning my trade, I also had to make tea for the caseroom staff and go for the 'messages' in the morning and afternoon. The afternoon messages were for members of the day staff working a few hours' overtime that night. As far as I was concerned, doing the morning messages was an absolute nightmare. It involved going to everyone in the caseroom to ask if they wanted anything from the shop in Townsend Street. The list was always huge, and no matter how careful I was with the money it never seemed to balance. I was very glad when I reached my third year and became a 'senior apprentice', and therefore no longer had to perform this daily chore!

One of the things that always amazed me through my years in the *Press* was the absence of a fully-serviced canteen where you could get a proper meal. While both *The Irish Times* and the *Irish Independent* had cafeterias open all hours on their premises, the *Press* had nothing more than a room with tables, chairs and a machine that dispensed the vilest-tasting coffee, tea and soup known to man. This machine was almost always faulty. It was not unusual to put in your money and get a cup of cold water in return.

Throughout those happy and prosperous years of the 1960s and 1970s there was a vibrant social scene in the *Press*. There were several very active clubs in Burgh Quay – fishing, tennis, golf, soccer, swimming and hiking/mountaineering. The annual 'Gathering' was the occasion eagerly looked forward to in mid December when all the staff came together for a bit of pre-Christmas craic. For many years there was a black-tie dinner dance for staff from all departments held in the month of January, but this had ceased by the early 1970s.

Also in the 1970s, an *Irish Press* team participated several times in the then hugely popular John Player Tops of the Town variety show. I took part in the show in 1978 and 1979. In the latter year the team finished fourth in the Dublin region, which was a great achievement. Shortly after our successful run in the 1979 competition, the *Press* team put on a show for charity in the old Stardust Ballroom in Artane, which was the scene of the terrible fire on 14 February 1981, which claimed forty-eight lives.

The old *Press* offices on Burgh Quay were completely rebuilt over a period of years in the late 1960s. It may surprise many to hear that not a single edition was missed during the rebuilding, when, on occasions, concrete was being poured and iron girders bolted into place as compositors made up pages just feet away. Conditions for the caseroom staff during the rebuilding were uncomfortable to say the least. For a couple of years the entire caseroom area was covered by a protective ceiling of transparent plastic sheeting to prevent dust and grit falling onto the made-up pages and, of course, the long-suffering workers. This plastic created a sweltering glasshouse effect in high summer, while in winter there were freezing draughts blowing from all directions. Eventually the move to our new caseroom, one floor up, came in June 1970. We now had a clean, airy, bright environment in which to work. For some strange unexplained reason the draughts we had suffered in the old caseroom followed us up onto the new floor, and most of the following two decades were

Rolling off the Pearses: Éamon de Valera and assorted luminaries watch Margaret Pearse kickstart the presses on a rainy September day, 1931. Note Mrs Pearse's muddy hemline and the cleric's umbrella

The vanguard: Drivers and their chariots await the arrival of the papers on Burgh Quay

Snack happy: *Press* photographers, from left, John Rowley, Dick Rowley, Sean Larkin, Paddy Whelan, Brian Barron, Sean Bourke, Eddie McDonnell, Mick Loftus and Fred Ludlow

Horsing about: Subeditors Hugh McFadden and Shay McGonigle enjoy a tipple upstairs in the White Horse, 1976 (photograph courtesy of Niall McInerney)

Flip off: Michael O'Toole gets a lesson in pancake tossing from Sheila Walshe

By George: Bestie is feted by, from left, Dave Guiney, Sean Diffley, Vincent Mathers, Cyril Byrne (senior) and Brendan McKenna

Kelly Hero: John Kelly and John O'Reilly enjoy a scoop in Mulligan's while the Cusack brothers man the pumps

Bums in the pane: Dublin kids make a pitstop to buy sweets
(photograph by Austin Finn)

I am a camera: Austin Finn, who was one of the best-loved snappers of his day
(photograph courtesy of the Finn family)

On the shoulders of giants: The late, great Austin Finn snaps JFK (circled) on his
historic visit to Ireland in 1963 (photograph by Brian Barron)

Farewell to Johnny: John Giles leaves the field after his last game for the Republic of Ireland in 1979 (photograph by Austin Finn)

Lady and Gentlemen of the *Press*: Mary Moloney takes a breather with newsroom colleagues Michael O'Toole, Oliver Weldon, Steve Sinnott, Liam Flynn, Adrian MacLoughlin, Pat Chatten and John J. Dunne (seated)

Simpler Times: Jim Kerr of Simple Minds is 'doorstepped' before a gig in Dublin by Presser Joyce Buggy and Alan O'Keeffe of the *Herald*

Metal heads: Bearded *Sunday Press* editor Michael Keane watches Willie Collins (second from the right) put the final touches to the last hot metal page one

spent trying to locate their source. Experts were brought in countless times to try to trace where they were coming from, but to the best of my knowledge the problem was never solved. Wooden screens were provided to protect the Intertype operators from the scourge. A few of the men who were paranoid about draughts often sat working at their machines wearing overcoats, scarves and caps!

On countless occasions over the years I typeset Con Houlihan's columns on Intertype machines or on computer keyboards. His thrice-weekly sports column appeared without fail on the back page of the *Evening Press* every Monday, Wednesday and Friday for many years. He also wrote a weekly arts-type 'Tributaries' column, as well as theatre reviews. Con's handwritten copy came to the caseroom for typesetting on quarto (10" x 8") newsprint paper. He usually wrote a paragraph to a single page, which meant that it was not unusual for one of his articles to take from fifty to eighty sheets of paper. Con's skill with words was legendary; the same, however, could not be said of his handwriting.

At times it was very difficult to decipher words or phrases, but having said that it was my experience that if one got his copy to typeset on a regular basis one's eyes and brain became attuned to his writing. Con always got a proof of his articles before they appeared in the paper. He abhorred errors, and was particularly fastidious about correct punctuation.

Despite the pressures of maintaining such a prodigious output, I never saw him lose his temper. Con was a true and generous gentleman.

On the first Sunday of February 1975, a new productivity agreement came into operation, and a four-day/four-night week, with improved pay, made life much better for the caseroom staff. Every line of type we set was given a specific value, every galley of type was measured, and each individual's weekly output was calculated in the work study office. The top performance was 'band 11', and a fairly concentrated effort was required to maintain this, day-in, day-out. The arrival of the productivity scheme had the effect of reducing the amount of overtime worked, which it was, in fact, designed to do. In due course the overtime crept back, however, to the dismay of the management.

I was not a huge fan of overtime myself. In the sixteen years between the introduction of the productivity scheme and my leaving the *Press* in February 1991, I worked just one hour's overtime, and that was as the result of a request from an overseer late one night in 1981 when a hunger-striker died in The Maze Prison in Northern Ireland and there was widespread rioting in Belfast, which had to be covered in the *Irish Press*. The productivity scheme continued up to mid 1985, when new technology arrived. Retraining for new technology had commenced in the autumn of 1984, when members of the caseroom staff were sent to learn the qwerty keyboard in the Keytrainer company's office, which was located on the top floor of a building in Fleet Street, just around the corner from Westmoreland Street.

This was followed by an intensive two weeks of training on the Harris typesetting system. Younger members of the staff coped reasonably well with all of this, but, understandably, for the older men it was much more difficult. Most newspaper companies (both at home and abroad, and including *The Times* and the *Independent*) introduced new technology on a phased basis. But the *Irish Press* went for a complete changeover after a six-week shutdown when all three papers were off the streets. This proved to be a critical mistake. Inadequate training left staff struggling to come to terms with the qwerty keyboards, not to mention the complexities of the Harris Composition System. A few days after the new technology commenced I recall being given the *Evening Press* television programmes to set for the next day's paper: it took me the whole day to do what previously I would have done in less than two hours.

The result of all this was that the newspapers suffered – deadlines collapsed, distribution connections were missed. The *Evening Press*, which normally left the caseroom at around 11 a.m., was not going until 2 or 3 p.m., and the same was true of the other two papers, the *Irish Press* and *Sunday Press*. The three papers had been suffering some circulation decreases prior to the introduction of new technology, but the decline in their fortunes accelerated from 1985.

Though it is now thirty years ago, I still remember very clearly the depressing atmosphere in the caseroom at that time. There was great pressure on the men, particularly those with young families, and we all could see that our once-proud trade, which had been around for hundreds of years, was dying, if not already dead. Several 'corporate plans' had been produced by management in the period 1985–1991, all of which envisaged drastic staff reductions. As far as I, and indeed many others, could see, there was no future for us in Burgh Quay.

American newspaper magnate Ralph Ingersoll came to the *Irish Press* with great fanfare in the summer of 1989 and looked like he would be saviour of the company, promising to introduce state-of-the-art production technology, the latest marketing techniques and, of course, significant rationalisation. I left the *Press* in February 1991 under the Ingersoll rationalisation plan. I was sorry to depart from a company I loved and respected and was very proud to work for, but there was no future in it for me after twenty-six-and-a-half mostly happy years.

The *Irish Press* played a huge part in my life. The building that was once the *Press* office on Burgh Quay was demolished and rebuilt and is now the headquarters of the Garda National Immigration

Bureau. Though it is greatly changed, every time I pass that building on the corner of Corn Exchange Place and Burgh Quay I recall the many characters, the laughs, the hard work, the rows, the three great newspapers and, of course, the draughts, which were part of parcel of our days and nights there.

Who left that turd on the MD's windowsill?

Seán Ó hÉalaí
(Group Irish Editor/Assistant Editor, *Irish Press*)

I can never pass Burgh Quay without looking at the glass building that housed the *Press* and remembering the moments of drama, hilarity and sadness that I witnessed there. It is no architectural beauty, but was probably seen as really modern and 'hip' when it was built. According to one *Press* veteran, the construction had taken a long time and was paid for piecemeal as it was done – no question of debt, apparently. I don't know if that was the reason, but I did hear from enough of the older staff of the inconvenience of going about their work inside while it was happening.

According to one account, when Éamon de Valera himself came to inspect the almost finished building, his entourage was amused by the innocence of one unexpected question: 'And where will the staff bar or canteen be?' One can imagine the knowing looks that passed around behind hands cupped over mouths at the very suggestion of a bar.

Coming from Derry, I had been aware of the *Irish Press* and, of course, the *Sunday Press* from an early age. Both had particularly good coverage of Donegal and the north-west, and unlike the other big Dublin papers they appeared to care about Northern Ireland. In a strange way, that was important and reassuring. Between news, outlook, features and sport, they merited a regular appearance in our house.

When I moved to Dublin as a student I met the brash and louder sister, the *Evening Press*, and saw it in action for the first time one day after attending a court case in the Four Courts. I had run into some Galway friends and decided to have a pint with them in one of the bars on the quays. I'm quite certain I was only there an hour, it being early in the day, but when I bought an *Evening Press* on my way home, there, to my astonishment, was a full account of the court case. I know in this age of Twitter that an hour may be regarded as intolerably long, but to me, at the time, the *Evening Press* performance was almost magical.

One had to marvel at the operational strategy of all three papers. The Daily and the Sunday had gained a fiercely strong loyalty throughout the country, and the Evening, with its various editions, had the capital nailed down. At their high point one could easily believe the stories of buckets of advertising in metal having to be dumped to accommodate stories. This was a newspaper group to be reckoned with, and one that was deeply embedded in the history of the state and in the national fabric. The old circulation manager, Pádraig Ó Críogáin, used to tell the story proudly of how, when the *Press* started, the isolation of Kerry was cracked by hiring a train of donkeys to take the newborn daily over the mountains. Interasal in action!

Of course, the paper's origins and associations were recognised and the regular charge of being Fianna Fáil's *Pravda* would be made, especially by Fine Gael and competitors. But essentially its news operation and editorial judgement were regarded as trustworthy and dependable. The appointment of someone like Michael Mills, long-serving political correspondent of the *Press*, as Ireland's first ombudsman shows that even in political coverage there was a recognition that, while the paper would endorse Fianna Fáil at election time, the individual journalists were not just party hacks.

Working in RTÉ, I realised very quickly the remarkable respect in which the *Irish Press* journalists were held. A lot of broadcast media programs then, as now, are based on filleting the papers and, slim as it was, the *Irish Press* would often provide the most reliable source of items.

Most of the older generation in RTÉ admired the spadework of the *Press* papers in breaking stories and following up on them. As one elder journalist said to me one day: 'It's like a high-powered intelligence organisation. They have contacts and sources in every village, maybe even in every street, in Ireland … the fuckin' Stasi aren't in it.'

Of course, a lot of the RTÉ journalists had actually been trained in the *Press*, as had many reporters in the other newspapers. You only had to look at the big bylines in the *Independent* and *The Times* to see that Burgh Quay had become the cradle for a whole generation of journalists who looked back on their days there with nostalgia. Breandán Ó hEithir spent his early years as a young journalist in the *Press* at a time when 'austerity' meant that most journos didn't know where the next drink was coming from.

He used to paint a vivid picture of the anarchic life in the features office, which was dominated at the time by Benedict Kiely and finance editor Joe McCauley. Late-night sessions led to security being ordered to close down the area throughout the night and not allow anyone, no matter what title they held in the firm, to enter. This applied especially to those 'who might want to sleep there.'

Ó hEithir also recounted how a rain-drenched Brendan Behan would often arrive in the front office and sit on a radiator with clouds of steam rising from his coat while he loudly demanded payment for a piece that had not yet been published.

Dick Walshe, who ended up as political editor of *The Irish Times*, also told a story about Benedict Kiely that has done the rounds since. Walshe was a copyboy in the *Press*, and one day the deputy editor asked him to find 'Mr Kiely'. Try as he might, Walshe couldn't locate him in the building and he duly reported that back. The irate deputy editor brought him into the features office, which overlooked the bar of the White Horse, and pointed at the window. 'Do you see the man sitting on the third stool from the left, young Walshe? That is Mr Kiely, and I want you to go over there and tell him that if the copy for his column isn't in my hands within the hour he needn't come back.'

In trepidation, Walshe went over, approached Kiely, who was telling a story in his deep, cello-toned voice, and delivered the message. Kiely took the threat very calmly and told the young copyboy to go back to his desk where he would find a copy of an American literary magazine to which he had contributed recently. He was to bring that back with a page of copy paper and a pin.

When Walshe came back with the required items, Kiely ripped three pages out of the magazine and on the top corners he wrote 'Kiely 1, Kiely 2, Kiely 3.' He then wrote on the copy sheet: 'Here are some observations on the development of the short story which I made recently in a widely read American literary magazine,' pinned it to the magazine pages and bade Walshe deliver them to his tormentor. Calm and serenity returned to the Quay.

Good raconteurs like Ó hEithir and Walshe may have embellished some of the tales from the annals of Burgh Quay, including one involving an investigation into how a human turd appeared on the second-storey windowsill of the managing director's office. Interpreted by the management as the extreme protest of an aggrieved employee, it took the islander Ó hEithir only a minute to provide, Poirot-like, the culprit: a curious seagull.

Even allowing for exaggeration, however, it was clear to anyone listening that the *Press* was not just a cradle of nascent journalism;

it also had a fatal attraction for eccentric characters, some of them brilliant, whose exploits helped to relieve the necessary tension of a place ruled by deadlines.

That element had not changed by the time I arrived in the front office of Burgh Quay. The news teams and photographers who were servicing the three papers were second to none, and some of the best features writers in the country were blazing a trail to greater things.

Mary Kenny, who had reputedly enlivened the place by strutting around in hot pants and smoking a pipe, had already moved on, but the 'sisters' had poured in through the breach and were much in evidence in what had been a man's world.

Ironically, I found myself working in the very features office that had once been the fiefdom of Kiely and company. There I found that, while Kiely had long since physically decamped to literary pastures new, part of his epicurean spirit still presided in the person of the dapper Belgian foreign editor Julian de Cassells. Julian's favourite trick was to arrive back after a long lunch with some ambassador or other and loudly itemise the treats he had enjoyed from a gourmet menu.

The office buzzed from morning to night with activity, housing as it did features editor Michael Wolsey, finance editor Brian O'Connor, and features secretary Beatrice Mullen. In a little side office, the editor's secretary, Eileen Davis, and deputy editor John Garvey worked away feverishly on their typewriters.

The door never stopped opening as a procession of writers and messengers, looking for one or the other, made their way through. You did not know what to expect next, an irate news editor trying to track down a recalcitrant reporter, a stone overseer needing a features sub to cut an article or Bobby Pyke, cartoonist, who would offer you immortality in a cartoon that would hang in the Palace Bar for £5.

Among the occasional visitors, usually seeking the editor, was Major Vivion de Valera himself. He would usually stop and discuss financial stories with the finance editor, but on seeing the new addition to the staff he came over and proceeded to chat to me for half an hour in fluent Irish. This was to happen a few times over the next few years and, though I suspect he only welcomed the opportunity to speak Irish, I found him to be a very engaging and vivacious conversationalist. His knowledge was as wide-ranging as his interests were varied. He reminisced a lot about his childhood, and recalled many events with surprising clarity. On one occasion he recounted how Michael Collins had come to visit his mother, Sinéad, with housekeeping money when Éamon was 'away'. It happened to be Vivion's birthday, and he was sitting on the floor playing with a toy gun. To his surprise and delight, Collins suddenly reached into his coat and sent a real gun skimming across the floor to him, saying: 'Here, try a real one.' When Sinéad saw the gun she started up, seized it and upbraided Collins while he protested that it wasn't loaded and he was only letting the child have a look at it.

Life in the Quay was anything but boring. All that wonderful noise: the clacking chaos of the newsroom, the humming and grinding of the wireroom, the clanking and metallic chatter of the printers, the jet scream of the presses and, in that era, the smoke that hung over it all. There was hardly a typewriter without a packet of cigarettes beside it. Above all there were the people themselves, the writers, the subs, the copygirls, the printers and transport workers, all forming a very large family. This was a warm, close-knit community that worked against the clock every day and wouldn't stint if an emergency suddenly hit like the Stardust or the Dublin bombings. No one was looking at their time sheets when the *Press* was up against a big story – and from the 1970s on, there was no shortage.

Even in its last years, the ailing newspaper group was sending forth another generation of young journalists whose names you can see prominently now in other publications and in television and radio credits today. Open any paper. It was still nurturing that talent.

The more I reflect on those days, the more I confront the surreal ambience of the old *Press*. From outside it looked like a formidable, highly successful, history-laden institution. But once inside the building you realised that it sometimes had a lot more in common with the music hall it had replaced, the old Tivoli. 'Theatre of Varieties' is apt.

No one who was there can ever think about it without smiling.

Meeting Michael Hand – and how it changed my life

Éanna Brophy
(Reporter/Subeditor/Columnist, 1973–1995)

There was a large man in a mohair suit standing at the reception desk of the hotel in Luxembourg when I arrived to check in. I had been sent by the *RTÉ Guide* to cover the Eurovision Song Contest. The large man was loudly addressing the much smaller and younger man behind the desk. I recognised him immediately. Correction, I immediately recognised that he could only be one of two people.

'Ciarán,'[1] he said, his distinctive Drogheda accent carrying right across the lobby, startling people of several nationalities. The receptionist looked even more startled, and distinctly nervous. 'Ciarán,' the large man said again, brandishing a jacket, 'the Tans are gone! Where are they?'

I was as puzzled by this as was the receptionist. Michael Hand (for it was he) elucidated: 'The Tannhausers! The trousers! I have the jacket, Ciarán, but the Tans are gone.' Understanding dawned gradually. Michael, who was staying in the hotel, had left a dress suit to be dry-cleaned, but the hotel had lost his trousers. They were found later, in good time for Mickser (as we all knew him) to wear to the song contest and its many attendant press receptions (things were more formal back in 1973).

It was at one of those receptions that I asked Michael Hand a question that was to change my life. The *Sunday World* had been launched some months earlier, and Kevin Marron (whose output I

122

avidly read) had been one of those who left the *Press* for those pastures new. I had not seen any announcement of a successor. I was not even thinking of applying, but I did ask Michael, over a loud babble of Euronoise, whether anyone had been chosen to take Kevin's place. 'No,' he said, 'do you want the job?' I jokingly replied, 'Of course I do!' He thrust out his hand and declared: 'You have 'er!'

Knowing that drink had been taken (though I was on Coca Cola myself) I laughed outright and said, 'But you can't go around giving out jobs to people you hardly know!' Michael (whom I knew only slightly then, and could still confuse him with his identical twin brother, the equally ebullient Jim), leaned forward and said, 'I know your stuff in the *RTÉ Guide*, and listen – the editor of the *Sunday Press* thinks the sun, moon and stars shine outa my arse. If I tell him that you're the right man for the job, you have 'er!'

I thought the whole conversation would be forgotten when sobriety took hold, but Michael rang me as promised the following Friday and told me to come in and see the editor, Vincent Jennings. 'Hold out for £50,' he urged me. 'Tell him you'll throw in a TV column as a nixer.'

This was unimaginable riches, and made me very nervous: I was earning about £35 a week at the time, and wages in the *Press* were £45 or so. I didn't want to be turned down. But I took a deep breath and did as he told me. And it worked.

A few weeks later, in early June, I started work in the *Sunday Press* (Frances O'Rourke started the same day). I felt somehow that I had come home, and never looked back until the place closed in May 1995.

Looking back today, twenty years further on, when I was asked to write something about the *Press* it occurred to me to say thanks to Michael Hand. To say he was a colourful character is a rather pale use of words – and anyone who ever saw him in spontaneous performance, or jointly with Jim at the height of their powers, still treasures the memory. But behind the public persona was an extremely good writer with an unerring nose for a good story, an esoteric range of contacts and the rapport to get people at every level to talk to him. His 'country' page for the *Sunday Press* was a large part of its success, covering stories from the trivially eccentric to the deepest human interest. They often made the front page as well. He was probably proudest of the pieces he wrote following Bloody Sunday in Derry: he visited the home of every family of those who had been shot dead, and was made welcome in every one.

Several months after I joined the *Sunday Press*, Michael suddenly jumped ship, having been headhunted to join the *Sunday Independent* (of all papers). Like the rest of us, I was dumbfounded. I was even more so when Vincent Jennings and news editor Gerry Fox called me into the editor's office and asked (told) me that I was immediately to take over the 'country run' as we called it. It was an offer – an order more like – that I couldn't turn down. So in no time I was setting out every week with a different photographer, following in Michael Hand's tyre tracks. It was fun; it was daunting; it was frustrating – especially when, having tracked down some intriguing local yarn, and interviewing some great character, to hear him say something like: 'And sure I said them very same words to Michael Hand when he was here five year ago.'

The memory of 'Mickser' was everywhere. And stories sometimes found him. I heard a great example one cold autumn afternoon in Ballyvaughan, Co. Clare. Along with snapper Cyril Byrne (or it may have been Ray Cullen) we had stopped for a late lunch sandwich in the local pub, having had three stories evaporate on us that morning. We were chatting with the pub owner about this when he said: 'Ye remind me of two other fellas who were here a few years back. They were in the same fix. Michael Hand and Brian Barron it was. Well ye'll never believe what happened next.

That door behind ye opened suddenly and in walked Gene Kelly. Gene Kelly, the dancer, the Hollywood star!' He was staying up the road incognito and very hush-hush in the new traditional Irish cottages.

'He didn't want any publicity, and didn't want anyone to know he was in the country at all. He was flying home on the Friday. Well, you should have seen the way that fella Hand went to work on him. In about ten minutes they had Gene Kelly out there in the street, buck-leppin' and twirling, and the photographer, Brian Barron, lying full stretch on ground, snappin' away good-oh!'

Sure you couldn't compete with that. Shortly after that the country run was abandoned (phones had been discovered in the meantime). I came 'home' to the office – and soon afterwards I began to write the occasional added humorous comment....

So thanks again, Michael.

---

1 The receptionist's name was not really Ciarán.

President Kennedy's copyboy (who missed the cut)

John Redmond
(Copyboy, Sports Reporter, Group Sports News Editor, 1963–1995)

It was a remarkable experience that was to sustain me for over thirty years. A lowly copyboy had been seconded to take on a special assignment on the morning of Thursday 27 June 1963 – the day that John F. Kennedy visited his ancestral home in Dunganstown, Co. Wexford. The team covering Kennedy's visit to Wexford for the *Irish Press* and *Evening Press* included writers Ben Kiely, Mick O'Kane, Barney Kavanagh, Frank Nealis and Jim Dunne; photographers Colman Doyle, Eddie McDonald and Brian Barron; and photographic printer Paddy Whelan.

For those not familiar with the quirks of the Fourth Estate, the position of copyboy is journalistic vernacular for gofer/messenger. Becoming a copyboy was like being apprenticed, and most aspiring journalists of the time started in that modest fashion.

The copyboy's role on that historic day was as 'gofer' to Colman Doyle, the legendary, award-winning and much-celebrated *Press* photographer. The brief was to shadow him as he photographed the US president's arrival for an al fresco late-morning tea party in the farmyard of the Kennedy homestead, take his roll of film and run like hell. When the cacophony of clicking cameras heralded Kennedy's arrival, and Doyle had got his quick-fire shots of the president meeting his cousins, he handed me the roll of film. I took off through the crowded forecourt with naïve recklessness, for the full force of the gardaí and US secret service agents was peppering my route. I then nabbed a bicycle parked against a hedge at the top of a nearby boreen, pedalled furiously down the narrow lane, hopped over a ditch into a field that bounded the River Barrow, and jumped into an awaiting speedboat, which took me at great haste four miles upriver into New Ross.

There, I delivered my precious cargo, gingerly I might add, as I had to find the right balance in the bobbing boat to place the treasured roll of film into a rusty Batchelors beans can, which dangled on a piece of hairy twine that was being lowered with equal dexterity from above by the valiant Paddy Whelan, our photographic printer.

A temporary darkroom had been set up by the quayside courtesy of a local cable company, Driver Harris. Taking account of the limited facilities of the day, Doyle's prize-winning pics were quickly developed and transmitted over the telephone wires to head office in Burgh Quay. There they were processed at great speed onto the front page of the *Evening Press* early edition, and dispatched by our speedster scooter delivery riders around Dublin city and its suburbs. It was still only early afternoon as the paperboys on O'Connell Bridge cried out: 'President Kennedy meets his cousins in Dunganstown – get your *Evening Press* picture special!'

The breakneck logistical operation was heralded as the communications accomplishment of its time. It was my whimsical introduction to a career in the *Irish Press*, and the experience left an indelible mark. The sense of camaraderie, team spirit, professionalism and commitment displayed by the team of news reporters, photographers, printers and 'wireroom' operators was inspiring. And, as I was to experience over a period of thirty years, as copy-boy, then sports reporter, and finally group sports news editor, it epitomised a spirit of comradeship that, in the face of turbulent relations with management, set the staff in Burgh Quay apart. Without them, I believe the *Press* would have closed down long before May 1995.

I 'graduated' from copyboy to the world of sport in June 1964. Over fifty years later I am still haunted by one heartbreaking experience I endured in April 1989. I was in Augusta to cover the US Masters, and my name was pulled out of the hat for the privilege of playing the famous course on the day after Nick Faldo won the first of three Green Jackets. My bittersweet experience and follow-up description in the *Evening Press* of what then ensued elicited the biggest response to anything I wrote during my thirty years in the *Press*. The hearts of most reached out in shared sympathy – but how impending glory changed to utter grief also evoked its own sense of dry, but well-meaning, humour. I bear the scars of it still.

To be drawn to play Augusta, I wrote, from an expectant media entry of hundreds, was the golfing equivalent of winning the lottery. The anticipation was heart-stopping. During a restless night I fretted over what I would do if I hit the ball into those magnificent magnolias, azaleas and dogwoods. To thrash about would be to commit sacrilege. Reverently, I would just take a penalty drop. After all, you are playing Augusta, revered as the Cathedral of Golf, the game's Sistine Chapel. But would I have enough balls to get around? I agonised. Should I buy more to be on the safe side? After all, how the hell could I get through Amen Corner where Rae's Creek provides a watery grave for the world's best players? What club would I select at the notorious short twelfth? Best take not one but two extra clubs, just to be sure of clearing the water. Would I dare try for the carry over the creek at the infamous thirteenth and fifteenth and live to boast of the feat for ever more?

The appointed tee time was 7.30 a.m. sharp on Monday morning. Alarm clock call for 6 a.m. – no, make it 5.30 to be safe. Call a cab for 7 a.m. – no, make that 6.30 just to be sure. Order an early breakfast – no, probably wouldn't be able to eat because of nerves. Lay out my clothing before going to bed. I must respectfully wear my Sunday best. Hop back out of bed and put my slacks in the trouser press, not once, but twice. After all, I'm playing Augusta tomorrow.

Razor gash under chin shows the emotions. Cup rattles off saucer during effort to force-feed breakfast. Knife and fork beat a nervous rhythm. No, it's no good – abandon breakfast. Cab driver, can you go any faster? Cab driver, do you know a better way to beat the traffic? Understand I'm in a hurry – I'm going to play Augusta. Finally, we arrive on Magnolia Lane – the venerated driveway to the most exclusive golf club in the world. A security guard steps from the sentry box and flags us down.

'What's your business, mister?' he snaps in a stern tone of unwelcome.

'My man's in a hurry. He's coming to play golf,' drawled the cab driver, mocking my impatience.

'Well, sir, he ain't playin' no golf here today. The course is closed 'cos of the rain. Now if you'd back up your cab and get your ass out of here, I'd be mighty pleased. Y'all have a nice day!'

And I never got the chance to come out of the hat again!

Hot metal and cold porter

Michael Morris
(Compositor/Stone man/Subeditor, *Evening Press*,
1968–1995)

Mulligan's is almost set in aspic – smoke-stained ceilings, overpainted with decades of yellow varnish, creaky floors soaked in drunken spillages, cranky, oh yes, cranky barmen, but best of all, the perfect pint and the greatest place to have a conversation, even if you have to shout over the crowds.

There are no crowds the day we meet, two of us still living in Dublin with the wreckage of the *Irish Press* closure now buried, and two visiting from Toronto, who left before the paper took a bad turn and spewed its human contents onto the city streets. We have come back almost twenty years later to the familiar haunt, almost the branch office of the paper itself, taking in the unchanged scene and mingling with the ghosts of drinkers past.

Accosted by the stationmaster on entering, I am transported back in time. Peter, for it was he, now retired from the railway and happily married to Cora, another former frequenter of Mulligan's, says: 'Michael, you've just missed Paddy Madden – and his brother, Aodhán. They've been here all day and they're scuttered.' The Maddens had not been there, it turns out. Peter is delusional about the Maddens. He is sitting there, throwing back the pints and selecting his losers from the racing pages. He hasn't changed: immaculately dressed, ensconced in the same corner as the bentwood chair he sits on, his Guinness resting on a card table by the window. He could be mistaken for a well-heeled businessman – but perhaps he is a well-heeled punter?

This encounter gives Martin and Dermot a jolt. Before they took flight to Canada twenty-five years ago, Peter was cheerfully sitting in the same spot, spouting the same fairytales and telling people that they had just missed out on meeting their friends. We settle down into the hard seats, order three Guinnesses and one coffee (Harry doesn't drink) and begin our own personal trip to the past and the *Press* days. We leave Peter in his corner with his paper, his opinions, and his pint.

The lies are trotted out, we laugh, and the slagging goes on. Just like the old days. Martin, the one with the lean and hungry look, butters me up on my youthful demeanour.

'Jaysus, Mick, how do you do it?'

'Easy,' I say. 'Choose your mother and father very carefully.'

'You didn't pick them for their looks.'

Laughter all round, and more slagging. The pints are lowered and more are ordered.

Ghosts emerge from the shadows and corners. It is difficult to reconcile the near-empty premises now with the thronged pub in the past. The great and mighty sports writer Con Houlihan would lean quietly against the mahogany bar counter near where his picture hangs now and sip his pint, or his brandy with milk, and occasionally converse with his friends and enemies, hand cupped over his mouth as if afraid of being overheard. There was little fear of him being heard, such was his low whisper, but what he whispered, if heard, were nuggets of Kerry gold. On many days he would write his column on sheets of quarto newsprint on the very bar top that he leaned on. In between editions the other sports writers would huddle and muddle themselves beside Con – Tom O'Shea, Meagan the Señor, the aforesaid Paddy Madden, and a few junior reporters and subs trying to capture the essence of what a newspaper should be.

Mick Cronin, of the *Evening Press* newsdesk, could be found nearby, briefcase on his lap, expounding on Fianna Fáil and politicians he loved to hate and God knows what else with the way he could mumble a sentence, with his deputy John O'Reilly ordering the drink and hanging on to his every word. The briefcase was always the subject of much speculation as he was never seen to open it until the day he slapped it onto Mulligan's bar, reached inside and produced a fresh trout. The trout was consumed raw while Mick ranted on, with flesh and bones hanging out of his mouth. We never found out how or why the trout was there or when Mick had developed a taste for raw fish. Mick also had a taste for ten-shilling notes. An argument developed one day over who owned the ten-shilling note on the table. It was the change from a round of drinks, and nobody could remember who had bought the round. After much arguing, and not a small amount of rancour, Mick grabbed the note, stuffed it into his mouth and washed it down with a draught of Guinness. The argument was over.

The bar door swung open at that time to a regular beat of *Press* workers coming in for their liquid lunches or others slipping back out after a quick break and a quicker pint. Nailer, our resident socialist and stonehand supreme, could be seen holding court at the corner of the bar, expounding on how to solve the problems of Ireland, the *Press* and the workers while the Guinness dripped off his moustache, with his pal Devereaux beside him shouting vulgarisms at anyone who would listen, and not caring a jot about politics, but about having a bit of fun and taking a rise out of youngsters new to the place.

Coming up to lunchtime – or its equivalent on nightwork (usually 10.30) – the bar would be lined with freshly pulled pints of Guinness, like sentries in a row, in all their blond-headed glory, ready to be dished out to men in a hurry. The women in those days had just begun their breaching of male bastions – Mary Kenny and Nell McCafferty had only just begun to barrack the barmen to serve them pints and not glasses of beer.

Coming up to the holy hour, owner Tommy Cusack would begin banging his sweeping brush on the floor and asking us if we had no work to go to before locking the door and pulling more pints. But before he'd do that he had a ritual every day. There was a man we had christened Buttercrust who was always safely tucked into a corner under a light. The nickname came from an advertisement then running with a cartoon character who used to say 'The world is in a state of chassis.' Buttercrust annoyed the clientele of the branch office by reading out stories from *The Times* at the top of his voice and informing everyone within earshot about what he thought of the story and the journalist who wrote it. While doing this, to the delight of the *Press* journalists, he managed to mangle and mispronounce most of the words. Tommy had to put up with this every day of his life, and had decided in his Cavan-like mind that Buttercrust was put into his bar to be a foil to Tommy's sense of humour. He would switch off the light above Buttercrust's head until he heard that he couldn't read the paper any more, then he would switch on the light and then begin banging his sweeping brush on the floor beside Buttercrust, creating enough noise to drown out the malapropisms. The drama that ensued without fail at lunchtime had everyone in thrall, despite having only one act and one joke.

Many a story was cobbled together in Mulligan's, long regarded as the branch office of the *Irish Press*, over pints and cigarettes. Journalists, compositors and printers would ebb and flow in there throughout the day, exchanging friendly insults, mixing their metaphors and their muckraking with each other and the general public. There would be a continuous stream of *Press* workers slipping in and out for 'tea' breaks, to use the phone, to meet a 'friend', to have the craic – the excuses were varied, but they all had one purpose: drink. Drink was the oil that lubricated many of the workers of the *Press*. For many, lunch was two or three pints and a tea break was a quick pint, thrown down in five minutes flat.

Sitting there, the four of us, the memories bounce off each other and the stories flow. We order another round and sit back, recalling the tales told and characters that passed through the *Press* portals, remembering those long departed and those still with us.

One classic story was of a certain printer, 'S', who was a great supporter of Mulligan's, but also one of the better workers. Many journalists, most of whom were his friends, maintained that he worked far better with drink than without. One particular time, the caseroom manager, Victor Smith, a blunt-speaking man, was having a lot of trouble with men drinking to the detriment of getting the paper out, and threatened to take action against the next one found slipping out for a pint. He let his overseers know of his displeasure and what steps they were to take. A couple of days after he had made this proclamation Victor was striding back from a meeting in the O'Connell Street head office and spotted S lying against the quay wall, almost falling into the Liffey, oblivious to Victor passing by and incapable of walking, never mind finding his way back to the *Press* offices.

Victor tore up to the overseer's box. The overseer was Jem Walton, a gentleman who got the job done quietly and without fuss, the polar extreme in temperament to his boss. Victor told him what he had just seen, practically foaming at the mouth.

'I don't give a shit,' he said. 'He's definitely going this time. I don't care if he's the finest worker we have, get rid of him.'

Jem calmly waited until he had finished. He picked up the roster sheet and looked carefully down it, as if to figure out how he was going to replace S. Victor fumed on, Jem's patient moves clearly infuriating him.

'He's got to go,' he said. 'His presence in that condition is a bad example to everyone else. They'll all think they can get away with it.' Jem continued riffling through the papers, pausing to ask Victor again the name of the man he was talking about.

'For the third time, it's S. Are you deaf?' Jem put the roster down.

'He's on his day off,' he said. 'What do you want me to do?'

Dermot leans back and finishes his pint, relishing the Guinness that he says is unique to Dublin. He sets his empty glass down on the table. The time has come to go our separate ways – to Toronto for our two friends and to the northside for me and Harry. We slipped out of Mulligan's, leaving the empty glasses behind, but taking our memories.

Peter the stationmaster was still there on the bentwood chair, picking his horses, noting the winners and pontificating to anyone who cared to listen.

Boogie on Burgh Quay

Hugh McFadden
(News Subeditor)

It was twenty years ago today that 'Major Minor' stopped the band from playing on Burgh Quay and pulled down the shutters on the Irish Press Building, which once housed the Tivoli Theatre, formerly called the Lyric Theatre of Varieties. My late and great *Press* buddy Shay McGonagle, the foreign pages editor and sometime *Irish Press* cartoonist, often chanted his mantra on the news subeditors' desk: 'It's all showbiz, folks, all showbiz.' And, indeed, very often it seemed to be just that, showbiz: de Valera's Lonely Hearts Club Band.

> *I don't really want to stop the show*
> *but I thought that you might like to know*
> *that the singer's going to sing a song*
> *and he wants you all to sing along*
> *so let me introduce to you*
> *the one and only Eamon Shears*
> *And de Valera's Lonely Hearts Club Band.*

Cut the line, folks, cut the line: he took the money (offshore) and ran … being for the benefit of Mr Dev. (Contrary to the popular misconception, the Press Group newspapers were de Valera papers, not Fianna Fáil papers). Now, sit back and let the future go.

My first encounter with the *Irish Press* Theatre of Varieties dates back to the late summer or early autumn of 1966, after my graduation from University College Dublin with an honours degree in history and political science. The UCD History Department asked me to consider doing a post-grad degree in history and offered me some tutorials in the department to assist me financially while researching a thesis on George Russell (AE) and the Co-operative Movement (this was in the days long before state grants of any kind). The chance to earn some decent pocket money by giving tutorials was very welcome, but I needed to earn more than the tutorials yielded, so I applied to the *Irish Press* for a job as a trainee journalist (a 'copy' youth). A gruff block of a man, Bill Redmond, interviewed me and gave me the job on the news subs' desk fetching editorial 'copy' and taking it out to the compositors, collecting pics from the photographers and the wireroom and taking them to the Klischograph department, then collecting the photographic blocks and taking them down to the stone. My only editorial duties involving the marking of 'copy' was the preparation of the weather forecast and the tides' charts (ironically, on one occasion a much older sub asked me to check a story on Joyce's *Finnegans Wake* that he was editing).

Eight or nine months of this familiarisation course with the various departments and their functions was more than enough for me, so I resigned at the end of the following summer in order to concentrate on research for my two-year M.A. thesis, on which I was not making enough progress due to the late-night work on Burgh Quay and my reconnaissance sorties to 'moral' establishments such as Mulligan's and McDaid's. A then senior editorial person, Hugh Hartnett, tried to persuade me to stay with the *Press*, but it wasn't possible to combine working until 1 a.m. with getting up early enough the next day to do much meaningful research in the National Library.

On graduating from UCD with an M.A. in modern history I was offered work on the editing of *The Correspondence of Daniel*

O'Connell (eight volumes) by the editor Professor Maurice R. O'Connell, a direct descendant of the Liberator. This detailed and mammoth task, along with tutoring in UCD, occupied the next few years until the beginning of 1972, when I decided to leave the country after the trauma of 'Bloody Sunday'. Ironically, it was back to the lair of the imperial beast and the old stamping ground of London, where I had spent a good deal of time in the 1960s expanding my consciousness and enjoying the counter-cultural 'vibe'.

But London in the early 1970s was a very different city from the laid-back place I had known in the 1960s in the days of Harold Wilson's Labour government, the Beatles and Stones and all that flower power Carnaby Street swinging. Not long after my arrival, Ted ('Teeth') Heath's Tory government engaged in a full-on confrontation with the unions, and the lights and power went out at regular intervals as the city was plunged into the cold and dark of a bitter winter of discontent.

Between then and the summer of 1973 I taught at a grammar school in Enfield in the outer northern suburbs of London. The local council had traditionally been a Tory stronghold, but was then almost evenly split between the Conservatives and Labour, who with the narrowest of majorities was trying to convert the hallowed grammar school into a comprehensive school. Fun and games.

In the late summer of 1973 I wrote a piece on the growing anti-Irish sentiment in Britain due to the worsening of the euphemistically named 'Troubles' in Northern Ireland, which were then spilling over into serious incidents of bombings in Britain. For some time I had sent various communications to the periodical *Hibernia* on issues regarding the North. One Sunday an ad appeared in *The Sunday Press* seeking subeditor journalists. I applied, and was called for interview in Dublin, where I duly turned up at the *Press* head office in O'Connell Street at the junction with Middle Abbey Street.

I was ushered into the boardroom on an upper floor and met the *Irish Press* editor, Tim Pat Coogan, and a dapper little man called (Captain) Fitzgerald, who was wearing an RAF fighter pilot's handlebar moustache. I got off to a good start with Tim Pat by quoting Brendan Behan's adage about New York, applying it to the streets of Dublin city below, where workers with pneumatic drills were digging up the pavements and making a ferocious din: 'It will be a great city when they finish building it,' quoth he. Tim Pat scanned a small selection of cuttings that I had shown him, noted my interest in the North, looked over my qualifications, and asked me when I could start. Fitzgerald, who theoretically was the Personnel Officer (HR), spluttered, 'But I haven't had a chance to ask him any questions,' to which Tim Pat replied, 'Oh, of course, what did you want to ask him?' I assured Tim Pat that I could report for duty in a week's time as I had to return to London to tidy up some affairs.

Tim Pat told me to call in first to floor eleven in Liberty Hall and get an NUJ union card and then report to the newsroom in Burgh Quay. The only other issue to be sorted out was my starting point on the NUJ house agreement pay scale: I wanted to be put on the senior journalists' rate, and we argued the pros and cons of my position. Tim Pat agreed to start me at the beginning of the senior rate, acknowledging my qualifications and other career experience. When I seemed to baulk at not being placed further up the scale, he assured me that the rates were about to be substantially increased under a new house agreement in the *Press* that was in the final stage of negotiations, so the old senior starting rate of almost £40 per week would shoot up substantially within months.

For the next twenty-two years, most of my evenings and nights were spent in the Theatre of Varieties on Burgh Quay with its extraordinary *dramatis personæ* – characters whose works were nearly always dramatic, sometimes comic, and sometimes tragic (there was even the *de riguer* house ghost, whose chains, it was claimed, could be heard rattling late at night on the back stairs). Since my first engagement with the *Press* there had been a shift in the type of journalist being employed, with more university graduates being brought in by Tim Pat to beef up the intellectual quotient on the various desks. Many of the veteran old-timers were now retiring.

For a couple of years, though, we had the pleasure of working on the news subs' desk with several true veterans of old: the last editor of the defunct Dublin evening paper, the *Evening Mail*, Louis Walsh, a dapper, thin man, and the even older George Crilly, a rotund individual who had the distinction of having reported the first sitting of the Stormont Parliament in Northern Ireland, and also of covering the first sitting of Dáil Éireann.

Both men were, to put it mildly, no longer young: if memory serves, both of them were over eighty years old when they finally retired. In the winter, George would arrive into work carrying a Foxford rug, which he would place carefully over his knees when he sat at the desk. He would instruct the copyboy to close all windows that were open, whereupon, within a few minutes, the more wiry and hardy Louis Walsh would call over the copyboy and instruct him to 'open the windows, for heaven's sake.' Those were the days when most of the journalists smoked either cigarettes, cigars or pipes, and a cloud of tobacco smoke would hang over the desks like the Sword of Damocles. Between the smoking and the regular imbibing of libations in nearby hostelries such as Mulligan's, the Scotch House and the White Horse, it is a marvel that any of the old hacks ever lived to draw their pensions.

We had a farewell bash in the Pot-Pourri restaurant on Parliament Street in the mid 1970s for these two and several other veterans, including Alec Newman, a one-time editor of *The Irish Times* who had taken to writing editorials for the *Press*. Another memorable farewell bash, though more liquid and less gastronomic, was held upstairs in the White Horse Lounge a few years later for the Kerry-born short-story writer, Seamus de Faoite, who in his youth had been an assistant editor at *The Bell* magazine, to which he contributed a number of stories. The Aran-sweater-clad Seamus was a passionate supporter of the Kingdom's football team, and often clashed with the one-time chief sub from Cork, Liam Moher, especially during the All-Ireland campaigns.

The 1970s were the most enjoyable years at the *Press* in Burgh Quay, before the battles began over the introduction of new technology. Hot-metal production still ruled, with all its ancient and sometimes arcane skills. It was a noisy shop, from the newsroom, where the typewriters clattered and the TV chattered when turned on for news bulletins, and the copy-taker ladies talked incessantly on the phones while taking down copy from reporters in the field and 'stringers' from around the country, to the compositor's room, where the Linotype machines clattered, while in the caseroom the clatter of metal could be heard as chases were deposited on the stone, or taken off and conveyed on metal trolleys to the foundry, from which quarter smoke emanated. When the machine room in the bowels of the building went into action and started the print run, the whole house would shake.

As I was interested in books and writing, the literary/books editor of the *Press*, David Marcus, often gave me volumes of history to review (perhaps on the suggestion of the editor). But I was equally interested in poetry, and covered poetry readings and book launches on my nights off. Another extra-curricular activity was attendance at music gigs of various genres, mainly blues, jazz and rock, at a number of venues around town, particularly at the National Stadium on the South Circular Road. Among the memorable gigs there were concerts given by Chuck Berry, 'Fats' Domino and Canned Heat, the American R 'n' B and blues outfit.

This sometime reporter managed to get into the dressing rooms to meet these music stars after the gigs. One unforgettable night was the occasion when I attended a concert by the legendary bluesmen Sonny Terry and Brownie McGhee, along with my *Press* buddy Shay McGonagle. Shay had started his 'preparations' for the evening earlier, before I met up with him in a nearby bar. By the time the gig was over, perhaps due to the cloud of incense smoke from 'funny' cigarettes that hung over proceedings all night, Shay was a tad *distrait*, even slightly confused. When I asked him how he had enjoyed the concert, he agreed that it had been a great gig, but then added: 'It's a pity, though, that Brownie didn't make it.' To which I replied: 'How do you mean, Shay? Brownie was there; that was Brownie singing and playing the guitar.' Shay shook his head and said: 'No, man, that wasn't Brownie. It was some other dude who is much older than Brownie. I saw Brownie in Liverpool some years ago.' It turned out that he had been to one of his concerts about twenty-five years earlier. Brownie, naturally, had aged a bit in looks since then.

Shay was a great fan of jazz and the blues. He covered the visit of the Duke Ellington band to Dublin and reviewed that gig, headlining it: 'The Duke is King'. One of the most hilarious occasions that I shared with Shay took place one summer's evening in Mulligan's. Both of us were off duty and relaxing, or as they say nowadays, 'socialising', in that licensed premises when a group of American tourists came in and positioned themselves beside us at the bar. After a while, and some desultory conversation, I suggested to Shay that we could liven things up with a few blues numbers. Thereupon Shay launched into a rendition of the classic number 'Peg Leg Blues', banging out the rhythm on the wooden floor with his foot. It was so authentic that one of the Americans asked Shay: 'What part of the States are you from, buddy?' To which Shay replied that he was from Derry City. Puzzled, the American then asked: 'What state is Derry City in?' To which Shay gave the unforgettable riposte: 'It's in a state of chassis.' Still puzzled, the tourist asked: 'But are you an American? You seem to have a stateside accent.' To which Shay replied: 'I'm not an American, but I've seen a lot of John Wayne movies.'

In the early 1980s I covered some other gigs for the *Press*, including two concerts at Slane Castle by Bob Dylan and the Rolling Stones, as well as a Van Morrison concert in the Gaiety Theatre.

The *Press* seemed to be viable enough as a newspaper group at the turn of the decade into the 1980s, but already there were indications of the industrial trouble that lay ahead. Negotiations by the management with the print unions about the introduction of computerisation and new technology were stonewalled and making little progress. Many of the printers' crafts were now outdated, and their very high salaries and substantial numbers were becoming a drain on the company's finances in an increasingly competitive newspaper world, with aggressive marketing campaigns by British papers trying to increase their share of the Irish market. Some of the printers who worked overtime were earning well over £400 per week even as early as the late 1970s.

By the middle of the 1980s, the financial situation of the *Press* companies had become increasingly problematic, leading to a shutdown of the premises for a number of weeks one summer, a shutdown engineered by the management in order to remove the old hot-metal machines and install computers. This writer vividly remembers when, on a Sunday afternoon at about 4.30 p.m., the news reached Mulligan's that a deal had been worked out to allow the reopening of the premises and a return to work. A group of journalists, including the famous sports (and arts) commentator Con Houlihan, entered the newsroom just before Éamon ('Major Minor') de Valera, the grandson of Dev, crossed the newsroom floor heading for the editor's office. Con, all six-foot-something of Kerry brawn, cut him off at the pass, grabbed him in a bear hug and lifted him off his feet, calling out in a loud voice: 'Me boy, ya, I knew you'd never shut it down.'

Alas, that's exactly what the de Valera family did in May 1995 after a decade of disastrous management decisions had led to a serious decline in circulation sales and advertising, following the long drawn-out legal battle with the Ingersoll half of the company and the accumulation of debts totalling about £20m.

To end on a happier note, *The Irish Press* employed many of the country's greatest journalists and photographers who staffed the best newsroom in Ireland. Before my time there had been such luminaries as the first editor, Frank Gallagher, Bill Sweetman, Jim McGuinness and Douglas Gageby. Seán Lemass was an early managing director. Cearbhall Ó Dálaigh, later a chief justice and a president of Ireland, was the first Irish-language editor, and his brother, Aenghus, was the company's librarian. The writer Maeve Brennan's father, Robert, who took part as a youth in the 1916 Rising and the War of Independence, was a business manager and a director of the *Irish Press*, as was Robert Barton, a Sinn Féin TD. Other Republicans included Máire Comerford and the historian and feminist Dorothy Macardle, author of *The Irish Republic*.

Among the well-known authors who wrote or worked for the *Press* were Patrick Kavanagh, Brendan Behan, Peadar O'Donnell, Liam O'Flaherty, Ben Kiely, Seán White and John Jordan. Breandán Ó hEithir, nephew of Liam O'Flaherty, was an Irish-language editor. David Marcus developed the 'New Irish Writing' page, which first published the stories and poems of writers who later achieved distinction and fame.

On the news subs' desk in my time the novelist John Banville was chief subeditor for some years. The desk also included the

Joycean critic Terence Killeen, the historian Dermot Keogh, the theologian Donal Flanagan, the novelist and short-story author Mary Morrissey, the short-story writer Lucille Redmond, the writer on conservation and a campaigner on urban planning, Frank McDonald, and Seán Purcell, who succeeded John Banville as chief sub. The ace layout man and page designer Maurice Sweeney also worked on this desk, as did the Irish-language columnist Seán Ó hÉalaí after the post of Irish editor was discontinued. John Brophy, noted music critic and flute and tin-whistle player, provided musical accomplishment during the increasingly rare quiet moments in the evening's work.

In later years, when the then deputy editor John Garvey would enter the subs' area and ask, 'Who's on duty tonight?', he often got the reply: 'The A-Team'. And indeed it was the 'A-Team'.

Ní Bheidh a Leithéid Ann Arís.

When we were the talk of the town

Patrick Madden
(Deputy Features Editor, *Evening Press*, 1968–1995)

Recently, while walking down Poolbeg Street to meet some friends for a bevvy or two in Mulligan's, I spotted a youngish-looking man sleeping rough on the steps outside the back door of the old Irish Press Building.

He was curled up in a blanket that had obviously seen better days, and by his side rested a bottle – cider, by the look of it. For a millisecond or so I was back in happier times when the world was right and our horizons looked secure. Instead of seeing a down-and-out seeking refuge from the breeze that always blows in from the Liffey and inevitably turns Poolbeg Street into an iceberg, the man in the shadows, for just one fleeting second, was an *Irish Press* nubian, slurping down the last dregs of his night's fun before reporting for the late shift.

The old grey building that brought the world to our doorsteps for so many years may be forgotten, but it is certainly not gone.

Walking past it is like traipsing through a sea of dead flowers in Glasnevin Cemetery. Withered perhaps, but always a reminder of what lies beneath – in the case of the *Press* it's a matter of what used to go on behind those walls that stretched around the corner from Burgh Quay to Poolbeg Street.

More than two decades have passed since the lights went out and over 600 dreams died in the darkness. It's hard to write objectively when the subject matter is close to the marrow of your soul.

For the best part of thirty years, my heart belonged to Dev's shabby old emporium that brought the news of Ireland to the masses with unerring accuracy. I grew up in the place. In 1968 I went in as a callow teenager, all spotty, with ideology in my head and a naïve determination that I was going to change the world of journalism. The smell of printer's ink and the hope of an eventual byline was the opium of those innocent days. I learned how to edit. I learned the skill of writing – short sentences, with one verb – barked by my sports editor, a tyrant with a heart of twenty-four-carat gold from Ballymahon in Co. Longford.

Those youthful aspirations, even the bad days when everything went wrong, still have free lodgings in the deepest recesses of my soul, no matter how long I live. That's why I still find it difficult to find objective or reasonable reasons why the management of Irish Press Newspapers showed us the door in May 1995. In the opinion of 600 workers, who packed their bags for the final time on that sad day, the decision by management was senseless, nasty, malicious, and carried out without a whim of humanity.

Over the following days we did what all ejected workers do: we occupied the building. That ultimately failed. We protested outside Dáil Éireann. That failed too. We marched through the streets of Dublin. That produced much sympathy and a lot of tears, but that ultimately failed too.

Quite simply, we had been shown the red card and there was going to be no volte-face by a malignant management. That's why I do not forgive and will certainly never forget the actions of our bosses during those appalling days.

Standing outside the back door of the old *Irish Press* these days is a bit like paying homage at the headstone of a lost loved one. I stand there and I'm reminded of the great men and the great women and the great stories they gave to the nation. Talented people who put flesh and bones on old Dev's dream of giving Ireland a truly nationalist paper way back in 1932.

Frank Gallagher was the first to carry Dev's news torch – and he was followed by a galaxy of fine editors and fine writers. Like the late Jack Smyth, who presided over the famous Berrigan baby rescue story, Tim Pat Coogan, who dragged the *Irish Press* into a new modern era, Mary Kenny, who changed the world for Irish women more than an army of feminists, Brendan Behan and Bobby Pike, the artist with magic in his long, bony hands.

Then there were those erudite and urbane gentlemen, Douglas Gageby and Conor O'Brien and Sean Ward. Indeed I can still see Conor O'Brien expounding his newspaper philosophies over a glass of gin and tonic in the Mucky Duck on Burgh Quay. And Con Houlihan, and the irrepressible Joe Sherwood, who got up everyone's nose with his beautifully scripted column on the back page.

The beginning of the end came when the Americans, under the baton of a gentleman called Ralph Ingersoll, arrived and swapped ideas with the Burgh Quay brains trust. On the surface the coalition of these great minds seemed plausible. Dream time had arrived, and the naïve amongst us saw it as a marriage made in heaven. However, wiser minds shared a different opinion. They saw it as a futile marriage of incomprehensible inconvenience, and told us so. They predicted bad, sad and mad days ahead.

Of course they were right. The marriage that was allegedly made in heaven hardly survived the honeymoon before both of them ended up in the High Court squabbling over *Irish Press* affairs.

So, what would old Dev say about the closure if he were to come back today and saw what happened to his dream? He'd see a poor down-and-out sleeping rough at the back door of what used to be his newspaper empire.

Racing Edition

The Middle Years

Garda six-packs, IRA six-guns and the hunt for Don Tidey

Don Lavery
(Reporter/Security Correspondent/Newsdesk Stand-In,
Irish Press, 1982–1988)

The man we dubbed 'Sgt Psycho' rammed his Smith and Wesson revolver into the side of my head through the open car window. I could see the gun was cocked and his finger was curled around the trigger. Inch by inch, I slowly moved the steering wheel as he ordered me to park the *Irish Press* Mazda 323 at the side of the country boreen.

I could see in the rear-view mirror that a soldier with an FN rifle was aiming at our back window. Another knelt in front of the car with a sub-machine gun levelled at the front window. My colleague in the passenger seat, Fergal Keane, waved a press card and shouted: 'We're press!' Fergal, later to become famous with the BBC as a war correspondent, managed to persuade the garda sergeant that we were from the media. It was just before Christmas 1983 in Ballinamore, Co. Leitrim, in the middle of the hunt for the IRA gang that had kidnapped supermarket executive Don Tidey with a demand for a £5m ransom. The man we called Sgt Psycho in a report for the *Irish Press* the next day left us shaken as he led a patrol of soldiers down the road.

A local motorist sped down the road, and I fully expected his car to be raked with gunfire. Instead, the man was pulled out of the car and spreadeagled on his belly with the sergeant's gun pointed at his head. He, too, was let go and allowed to drive back up the road towards us. He got out and told me, 'He's fucking mad!'

The security forces were angry and frustrated that the IRA gang had shot their way to freedom after their hideout was discovered in a forest. When the search party, made up of gardaí and soldiers, stumbled on the camouflaged tarp under trees, the IRA opened fire and threw a grenade. One soldier, thirty-five-year-old Pvt Patrick Kelly from Moate, Co. Westmeath, died, along with garda recruit Gary Sheehan, a twenty-three-year-old from Carrickmacross, Co. Monaghan.

Don Tidey escaped by rolling down a hill and found himself staring at a soldier's gun. To add insult to injury, the four-man gang of hardened terrorists captured seven gardaí and soldiers as they made their getaway, telling them: 'This is no time for dead heroes.'

Both Fergal and I, new to the *Press*, were sent down to the scene from Dublin with barely enough time to grab a change of clothes. We entered into what resembled a war zone with thousands of gardaí and soldiers backed up by helicopters, armoured vehicles, surveillance radar, and the newly formed Special Forces unit, the Army Ranger Wing, and also, I believe, by soldiers from the British Special Air Service. We heard soldiers with the Rangers talk in British accents. An army spokesman claimed they could be London Irish (and we came down in the last shower of rain).

With hundreds of armed personnel taking part in 'grouse hunts' across the wild countryside trying to 'beat' the gang towards hidden Ranger ambush parties, we soon learned to disregard the official spokesmen for the army and gardaí. Instead, we took it in turns to hang out near Ranger jeeps and listen to the radio traffic.

They would be called in to deal with the gang if they were spotted. On one mad dash I followed the jeeps at nearly 100 mph through armed checkpoints – and was mildly surprised we were not shot at. We were mistaken for a detective car.

We had checked into the local hotel and the *Press* had sent us £200 each to buy clothes and rain gear. With the influx of dozens of reporters, prices of items in the local shops skyrocketed. We heard the BBC crew drank the wine cellar in the local hotel dry. I thought of that when we came upon the BBC crew held under gunpoint in their white Mercedes at the side of the road by an army patrol. I got out of my car and approached a towering army captain and told him to let them go and that they were media. In response, he forcefully stuck the muzzle of an FN rifle in my chest and threatened to shoot me. His sergeant checked our credentials with Ballinamore HQ and he told us to go, apologising for his officer's actions.

We phoned in our copy regularly on the latest developments with me scribbling down my story in shorthand before phoning a copy-taker. Fergal, on the other hand, was probably the best reporter I ever saw at phoning copy off the top of his head. Cormac MacConnell also worked on the story, showing me how to keep the gardaí sweet by delivering six-packs of Guinness to checkpoints in the freezing, heavily forested terrain.

There was a certain amount of support for the IRA in the area, and after losing two men the security forces were nervous and edgy. Once I went out to look at Derrada Wood, where the kidnappers had their hideout, after talking to detectives I knew from my time in Mullingar. As I walked along dressed in boots, Levi's, a warm Iceland sweater and anorak, a detective car with six people in it reversed at speed and stopped opposite me. They jumped out and checked me out thoroughly. I appreciated that they were doing their job. But on another occasion on the same narrow road, a detective car driving towards me suddenly speeded up to 70 or 80 mph in an apparent game of chicken. He missed my car by inches, taking off the side mirror at the base, and sped on.

Despite a huge hunt, the authorities finally had to admit that the IRA gang had got away. We went back to Burgh Quay. British Prime Minister Margaret Thatcher congratulated the Irish government on Tidey's rescue, which was more then we got, although I believed we had beaten the *Independent* and *The Times* hands down. Instead, an editorial executive demanded that we hand back wet gear! I told him he could have the underpants too, called in the NUJ, and they backed off.

On occasions like these we often put our necks on the line to get the story – and it is mildly amusing today to see reporters who cover sordid court cases offered counselling!

The *Press* newsroom was seen as the best in Ireland at the time – best reporters, best news editors, best snappers, best NEWSpaper – the place to aspire to. It was cool, exciting, and sometimes dangerous. At my interview, legendary editor Tim Pat Coogan asked me what I would do to improve the paper. Before I could answer, another member on the interview panel said: 'If he knew that he'd be running the paper!'

At first I worked for all three newspapers, and then just the *Irish Press* on their 'A' team. The newspapers were full of some of the best reporters around: Gene McKenna, Tom Brady, Fergus Black, Jimmy Walshe, Gerry O'Hare, Ann Flaherty, Philip Molloy, Clodagh Sheehy, Tim Hastings, Denis McClean, Gerry Moriarty, Pat Igoe, Mick Sharkey … the list is endless. The news editors weren't bad either, and I learned quickly from men like Mick O'Kane, Paul Dunne, Michael Keane, and Dermot McIntyre of the *Evening Press*, who had a fearsome reputation and was said to leap over typewriters at reporters who were not up to his standard.

Coming from weekly newspapers I wasn't used to daily deadlines. One morning at around 7 a.m. I was reading the paper when I was asked by Dermott in his best Donegal brogue, 'What are you doing?' I said I was reading the newspaper. This was quickly followed by a bellow of: 'Do ye not know Shergar's been kidnapped?!'

I replied innocently: 'Who's Shergar?' To his credit, Dermot didn't implode. But while you could get a bollicking before the deadline, afterwards he would take a fatherly interest, sit beside you, and put his arm around your shoulders while he told some story about his beloved Donegal.

The *Press* worked you in all areas, agriculture, politics, industrial relations, education, and my interest: crime, security and defence. For a time I was security correspondent. And there was plenty of crime: kidnappings like those of Ben Dunne, John O'Grady, the death of Fr Niall Molloy, the disappearance of Philip Kearns, the activities of 'The General' Martin Cahill, and countless murders. Dublin was struggling with a heroin epidemic, and working-class estates were cordoned off with blazing barrels to keep drug dealers out, while groups like the Concerned Parents Against Drugs were prominent, with the IRA also involved.

I got a call one day to go to a housing estate where a group of about thirty men in balaclavas waited for me: the Concerned Criminals! As they encircled me and showed me their weapons, the snapper with me suddenly decided that he had another marking and took off. One of their men had been kidnapped by the IRA, and they stopped traffic as they marched to an estate where they believed he was being held. Locals came out of their houses, a van pulled up, and iron bars were handed out as the two sides squared off. All this was watched by local detectives, who had a good laugh.

Another night, I got a call to go alone to meet a notorious criminal in his home – he wanted me to take £10,000 on the table and act as an intermediary to get his friend released by the IRA.

I said: 'I suppose that is drug money?'

'Nah, I only do cigarettes,' he replied.

I told him to approach a local priest instead.

The camaraderie in the *Press* was always special, and I got a glimpse of it on my first visit in 1976. As a journalist with the

Westmeath Examiner I had reported a speech by Defence Minister Paddy Donegan where he called President Cearbhail Ó Dalaigh a 'thundering disgrace' for referring emergency legislation to the Supreme Court.

The president resigned, and I went home to my parents in Blackrock for the weekend, aware that the biggest political story of the year was underway. What I didn't know was that both the *Press* and the *Irish Independent* were trying to track me down for an interview. The late Sean MacConnell in the *Press* somehow found out who my landlady in Mullingar was and rang her. She didn't know my address, but knew my dad, an ex-army officer, who was national organiser of the Irish Red Cross. For security reasons he also had an unlisted number. With those titbits of information, Sean was able to get my address and telephone number. A taxi from the *Press* then arrived at my home to take me to the newsroom, about five minutes ahead of one from the *Independent*.

Sean interviewed me, my picture was taken, and the package was used on the front page. My fifteen minutes of fame was quite enough. Editor Tim Pat Coogan showed me around the newsroom and then brought me to the Silver Swan for a drink, stepping over one reporter splayed on the stairs. Tim Pat, while telling me Sean was one of the best reporters they had, escorted me home to Blackrock. I was immediately hooked by the professionalism, friendliness, and enthusiasm of the *Press* family.

But all good things come to an end, and after six years working there I was very reluctantly seduced by better conditions and stability in the *Independent*, as were many of my colleagues.

But that's another story.

An angry bishop, psychos, and a psychic theatre critic

Eoghan Corry
(Features Editor, *Irish Press*)

In his sports-themed memoir, *Over the Bar*, Breandán Ó hEithir paid tribute to an air of 'barely controlled lunacy that existed' in the *Irish Press* that he joined in January 1957.

When I joined nearly thirty years later, the barely controlled lunacy hadn't gone away. It might even have no longer been barely controlled. It appeared that the *Press* had become a refuge for a group of people who could probably not otherwise have ever found work.

There was the equivalent of a Las Vegas flashing light atop the building, relaying the message that anyone who suffered from an addiction (mainly, but not exclusively, alcoholism), severe mood swings, bipolar disorder or any other mental defects could come and WORK HERE. You will be WELCOME. We might even PUT YOU IN CHARGE.

Getting the newspapers onto the street took something more focused. The Irish Press Group could do focus as well. There was a small group of creative people, literate geniuses, who would inspire any conversation and would be welcome guests at any dinner party, who could be counted on to send out the sparks that illuminated the newspaper and made life in Burgh Quay a very special and rich experience.

They would occasionally come up with something so stunning that the rest of the country and the rest of the industry would sit

157

back in awe. There was a group of about two dozen people, solid and predictable, and not altogether as creative, but you got the sense that if there were a nuclear holocaust they would still get the paper onto the streets.

There was another group of hard-working enthusiasts who would finish the task to which they were put, and you could trust them to spell people's names half right most of the time. The sub-editors, or the sober wing of the subeditor craft, would happily translate what these people wrote into English.

Then there were the passengers, those who sat back and enjoyed the ride, living out life on their metaphorical sunbeds, or rather the all-too-real barstools in Mulligan's, the White Horse, Regan's, Kennedy's (the quietest in the pint-er-land of Burgh Quay, it was known as Dead Kennedy's) or any of the other nearby hostelries whose entire business seemed to depend on the alcoholic wing of the *Irish*, *Evening* and *Sunday Press*. Their company could be great fun. When it came to delivering anything of journalistic significance, it seemed as if they had nothing to offer, apart from their memories of past glories and their faded battle tunics. That would be a mistake. Occasionally something of genius would re-emerge from their sodden brains. It might be a rare occurrence, but it was always worth the wait.

Mulligan's, however, was NOT the *Irish Press*. Twenty years after its closure the legacy of the *Press* is not the air of lunacy but the pursuit of excellence and the values of its newsroom. Maybe it is romantic but I like think that the *Press*, to the end, remained true to the ideals of its founders, to what would probably be called a mission statement nowadays, represented in the famous cartoon on its first edition: 'We've got them on the list, and none of them will be missed'. The Old Order with its long beard, Social Pretension with her nose in the air, Hypocrisy in a top hat, Cant with an Adolf moustache and, surprisingly and appealingly, Long-faced Gloom all lined up for the guillotine by a grinning, youthful tricorn-hatted *Irish Press*.

The sixty-five-year history of the *Press* has been mythologised mercilessly, often by its own journalists (myself included, judging by the 400 words above), so it is worth dwelling on its achievements. There has been an undue emphasis on the morning paper and not enough on the other newspapers when the real story was one of innovation, of the remarkable market savvy of Press Group newspapers, of tough business decisions and radical changes in each decade. The distribution system the group developed, partly because it was under-resourced and partly because it was excluded from the rail system by their opposition, later served as model for other papers.

The morning newspaper became the second biggest selling daily newspaper on the island. Its two sister papers were even bigger and more immediate successes. The *Sunday Press*, launched in 1948, was outselling its rivals almost immediately (383,716 against 380,915). The *Evening Press* was a close second within eighteen months of its 1954 launch (103,377 against 118,844 for the *Evening Herald* and 77,747 for the *Evening Mail*, with the *Evening Echo* on 31,940). By the mid 1960s the *Evening Press* had reached 124,163, a record for an evening newspaper. The *Irish Press*, with 122,844 sales, had 40 per cent of the daily market. The *Sunday Press* hit 432,000 in 1973. Individual editions achieved remarkable market penetration, selling over 500,000 copies when promoting a major book serialisation or launching a competition, such as the Golden Key in 1971. The *Evening Press* peaked at 173,000 in 1981.

The circulation success was not replicated on the advertising side. Like all left-leaning and challenger brand newspapers, the Press Group could not uproot the advertising spend of the old order it had set out to dislodge, and this is the main reason why the *Irish Independent* triumphed and the *Press* failed in the end.

The two traditions that should be highlighted by any *Irish Press* retrospective are photography and layout. This was where the group excelled, and the tradition is poorly reflected in the archives, memoirs and the academic records. I first encountered this as a teenage reader anxious to become a journalist. For me the *Press* was a work of genius, capable of grasping the flavour of events ahead of everyone else (at the risk of a major generalisation, news stories were not *The Times*'s forte at the time; they picked over other people's news rather than breaking stories of their own, a situation not helped by Fergus Pyle's shafting as a result of their breaking the 'Garda Heavy Gang' story in 1976). They also presented things better, partly because of their amazing photographic department. Colman Doyle's 'Eggs for president Nixon' in February 1971, a shot that won him the 1972 Ilford Camera Award, was the start of a great decade for Burgh Quay.

On the day after Cearbhal Ó Dálaigh resigned the Irish presidency in 1976, their front page consisted of one elongated photograph of Ó Dálaigh looking thoughtful: CITIZEN Ó DÁLAIGH was the headline.

They were also brave, taking on issues and topics that put their journalists in danger. The Liam Cosgrave government of the time treated them with barely concealed contempt.

The literary heritage of the *Press* was richer than its competitors, evident from the roles played by figures such as M. J. McManus, Dorothy McArdle, Patrick Kavanagh, Brendan Behan, Ben Kiely, Aodh de Blacam, Breandán Ó hEithir, John Banville and David Marcus. It was a conspiratorial cadre of these literary geniuses that created a heart-stopping account of Ronnie Delany's Olympic victory in 1956 by the fictitious Tom Stanaway. This is one of my favourite *Irish Press* stories. The newspaper group could not afford to send a reporter to the Olympic Games, but they rewrote the wire copy in such an evocative literary style that it was the *Sunday Press* account of the victory that endured in popular culture.

Tim Pat Coogan's innovation, New Irish Writing, has itself been mythologised as a result of the number of writers who were ushered into print under its mantle. It perished because it was over-resourced and under-read. Most of the pressure to bring it to an end came from the caseroom, where the typesetting resources it was eating became entangled in a larger battle. Occasionally, short (?) stories of 7,000 words would be shoehorned into the page.

The *Press* titles were central to the development of business journalism as it evolved from lists of stock exchange prices to something more analytical, the hard questions at financial press conferences in the 1970s and 1980s were being asked by *Press* journalists while the Evening title developed the personal finance genre.

The paper's pioneering role in the development of a more literary style was even more apparent on the sports pages, led by figures such as Joe Sherwood, Pádraig Puirséal and Con Houlihan. There was also a strong tradition of minority sport coverage that has been discarded in more modern media. A separate mythology has developed about how the *Irish Press* invented the GAA: the emergence of the GAA as a mass market sporting organisation coincided with the foundation of the *Irish Press*.

Much of the vibrancy and energy of the three titles came from the fast-evolving features departments that had emerged in all three titles, and it was as features editor that I came to the *Irish Press* from the *Sunday Press* in August 1986. I knew there was a short window for implementing change before the entire process was brought to a halt. By the time the budgets were slashed the system was still able to operate – the most testing period came when the discretionary spend budget was reduced in 1993 to £170 a week at a time when

I was maintaining writing rates at £80 per 800 words and £150 for a double-page spread. I doubt if any team has produced as much for so little money as the *Irish Press* features department in the years between 1987 and 1994.

My new columnists were chosen for their writing skills, emerging from the colleges, undergraduate magazines (Michael O'Docherty), *Hot Press* (Declan Lynch, Liam Mackey as columnists, Kate Shanahan as the full-time writer) and *In Dublin*. I cleared out the existing columns and brought in Patricia Redlich as an agony aunt, Ruth Buchanan as food columnist, Declan Lynch on television and Liam Mackey on radio, Michael Sheridan and then Patsy McGarry as theatre critic, the very young Ian O'Doherty to write about the emerging drug culture, Carol Flynn, Patricia Murray, Cathy Dillon, Catherine Murphy, Muriel Bolger, the tragic Pam Nolan, who did the sort of socially engaged journalism that was treated with suspicion by newspaper editors at the time. Brenda Power departed for the *Sunday Press*, a bit of a blow as she was one of the best writers in the industry. Much of what we did was treated with suspicion by the elders of Burgh Quay, but it was generating some much-needed noise for the newspaper on the airwaves.

The *Irish Press* had an unusual relationship with its readership. They felt they owned the newspaper, and because of its convoluted share structure, many of them actually did. Editor Hugh Lambert was unrelenting in his support even when our readers baulked at our more irreverent moments. When Declan Lynch raised the ire of the Catholic Church with a reference to the pop star Madonna nobody got too cranky. Most of the letters of complaint seemed to have been orchestrated by Bishop Brendan Comiskey in a bid to raise his own profile before his ecclesiastical career went pear-shaped. One batch came from St John of God's Hospital. A complainant began his letter: 'As you can see from my address I am mentally unsound.'

I couldn't resist opening my letter in return (under the letterhead 'Irish Press, Burgh Quay'), 'As you can see from my address, I too am mentally unsound.'

One Friday evening in 1987, I was at my desk in Burgh Quay when I had a call from a man who was threatening suicide. A self-styled poet, from what I could tell from his coin-box call he wanted a guarantee that his poem would appear in the following day's 'New Irish Writing' or he would take his own life. He was apparently standing in a telephone box with the means of killing himself and wanted an instant reply. I did what my still-young mind could muster and stalled for time. I had no idea of what or where his poem was, but I knew that didn't matter. The page had gone to press, and on a point of principle nobody blackmailed me into putting anything into the paper, then or now.

I picked up a few letters and press releases from the huge volume of paperwork that is always around the desk of a features editor, rustled them loudly, thumped myself on the forehead with them a few times, opened and closed the large filing cabinet behind the desk, and then said to my suicidal poet: 'I am terribly sorry, I cannot find your poem. I will be sure to use it, but could you please send it in again as it appears to have gone missing?' I think it worked, but I read news reports and death notices with some trepidation in the following days.

I assumed the unofficial role of airwaves troubleshooter for the occasional storms that erupted around our coverage, putting out fires where they could be quenched. The biggest fire of all? Probably the review of a theatrical performance that had yet to take place. It was Theatre Festival opening night, and the *Irish Press*, true to our commitment to the arts, was the only publication to cover all eleven openings that night. One of our reviewers panicked when she came back to the office, abandoned the review of the play that she had (correctly) attended, and instead conjured up a review of another play that she imagined she was supposed to have attended. The night staff added to the series of unfortunate events by inserting the pre-prepared block for the wrong play.

That started a real drama because the second play had not even opened. I was alerted to the tragedy when Seamus Hosey telephoned me from RTÉ the following morning. It wasn't the easiest defence of newspaper practice I have ever fielded. I apologised to all concerned and told stories of other newspaper mishaps, making sure to keep the offending reviewer's name off the airwaves. It could have been a career crusher for her. I made sure it was not.

Some of the staff recruited in 1931 were still around when I worked in the *Irish Press* in the 1980s. Founding contributor Seosamh Ó Duibhginn, who had been interned in the Curragh with Máirtín Ó Cadhain, was still a columnist. Jimmy Kelly, who was the last of the original staff, was with the *Irish News* in Belfast and lived until he was 106. Maureen Craddock, the newsroom secretary, was still there. John Redmond, group news editor and father of John, the group sports editor, had recently retired. Frank Gallagher was a leader writer into the 1970s, as was Michael Mahon.

The early *Press* must have been an exciting place in which to work. The newspaper was condemned from the altar by the Catholic clergy and pilloried by the authorities. Founding Editor Frank Gallagher was put on trial by a military tribunal for seditious libel, the charge a relic of the devices used by Dublin Castle to persecute journalists since the eighteenth century. That was the *Irish Press* of my parents' generation, lively and pioneering, challenging the establishment and even running news on the front page when the opposition preferred advertisements.

Although we used to joke about whether certain writers were 'sound on the National Question', it is wrong to make assumptions about the politics of the *Press*. At times it was less supportive of

Fianna Fáil than other publications, and a lot of the analysis of the history of the group is dangerously devoid of context, including what was happening in other media and newspapers at the same time. There was certainly a time when *Press* reporters were regarded as de Valera's ciphers, but that applied to the morning paper, not the *Evening Press* and *Sunday Press*. There were subtle changes of policy after Walsh's tenure ended. Across the group the politics of the individual editors varied, and the *Press* always valued Protestant/Unionist input to its pages. I regularly commissioned the DUP's Sammy Wilson to write for our title.

Twenty years later, no paper has attempted to replicate the diversity of political and cultural opinion that the Press Group of newspapers represented. The ideals of the *Irish Press* were to become the paper of record and the international voice of Ireland, and it achieved this despite chronic underinvestment. If you want to get a snapshot of what was happening any day in Ireland from the 1930s to the 1970s it is to the archives of the *Irish Press* (now happily online) that you look, a role that was eventually achieved by an ex-*Press* veteran, Douglas Gageby, at *The Irish Times*, but not without a struggle on Burgh Quay's part that continued right up to the decision to change to tabloid.

The news coverage and its adherence to fairness was the source of pride to everyone associated with the publications. There are always two sides to every story, and sources were attributed rather than anonymous. Because of the accusation that it was a mouthpiece of Fianna Fáil (which it was through part of Frank Carty and Joe Walsh's era), there was a sense that we needed to have higher standards than other organisations in these regards.

That proud newsroom tradition continued until its demise. It may even have contributed to it. The best stories, and the *Irish Press* broke stories every day, no longer contributed to sales because they were paraded on the airwaves before people had woken up for work each day. It was a pity, because the values that the *Irish Press* espoused are as relevant in today's multi-platform media culture as ever. I miss those values, and the sense of accomplishment that we felt with every newspaper that was rattled out of those printing presses that shook the whole building.

I miss the camaraderie.

And yes, I even miss the barely controlled lunacy.

The Last Days of Dubliner's Diary

Helen Quinn
(Reporter/Diarist, 1984–1985)

'Helen at the Helm' – that little promo on the front page of the *Evening Press* said it all. After ten years in the newsroom, Dubliner's Diary was mine. I was the first woman officially to take on the mantle from the great diarists before me, Terry O'Sullivan, Joe Kennedy, Michael O'Toole and Kim Bielenberg. On Sunday 5 December 1994, I headed out on the new adventure with photographer Brenda Fitzsimons.

The gold metal page of that first diary takes pride of place on my wall. I am looking at a photo of *Fair City* actress Martina Flynn wearing a wedding dress. Not her own; she was opening a shop for 'once-worn' dresses with her mum, Marjorie, who'd been made redundant from Switzer's after fifteen years.

Later, at the Abbey Theatre seminar, one of Dublin's favourite sons, Roddy Doyle, came in for a bashing when panellist Damien Smyth described *Paddy Clarke Ha Ha Ha* as 'Glorified Disney, the Shirley Temple of the South.' Playwright Frank McGuinness, on his way in to chair a debate on the future of the Abbey, said that the national theatre had to survive. 'I don't know how anyone can contemplate anything else,' he declared. Isn't that what we thought about the *Irish Press*? That it would be part of the fabric of Ireland forever? Little did we know then that the three papers would cease production less than six months later.

Dubliner's Diary was a whirl of meeting and greeting, trying to get a story that hadn't been written on the press release. For example, at the launch of Maeve Binchy's hilarious book of unasked-for advice called *Dear Maeve,* a well-known RTÉ journalist told how she'd been expelled from the Holy Child Convent in Killiney, but Maeve was kept and went on to teacher training afterwards.

'Write that up carefully.' Maeve used her best school marm voice. 'I'll be reading it tomorrow.' At least I didn't have to write it out a hundred times!

The event was a roll call for Irish novelists: Deirdre Purcell, Patricia Scanlan, Rose Doyle, Vincent Banville, John Quinn and Liz Ryan, who had just published her first novel, *Bloodlines.* After the *Press* closed I brought a selection of their novels with me to the Seychelles, where I worked as a newsreader in Paradise FM. The vote went to Patricia Scanlan's *Promises, Promises.*

I loved being part of Team Diary. Features subeditor Paddy Madden's quirky headlines, captions and layout always made me look good. Nightly excursions on the town with photographers Brenda Fitzsimons, Tom Hanahoe, Cyril Byrne, Mick Slevin, Austin Finn and Ray Cullen, not to mention the patient taxi driver we left outside, were always fun. Reading back some of the diaries, it strikes me how some things have changed utterly and some not at all. Many of the people mentioned then are still vibrant in Irish society, still relevant, and best of all still standing despite the recession. Some like Boyzone and Michael Flatley found great fame while others like Charlie Haughey, Bertie Ahern and Michael Fingleton have fallen from grace, and sadly there are others who are no longer with us: Seamus Heaney, Cyril Cusack, and Boyzone's Steven Gately.

Here are some of the last Diary entries.

The Last Ha Ha

Roddy Doyle's mum says that he was a quiet child; he was quieter in her presence. He stood back so that I could chat to her. 'When he went to England and came home with an earring, my eyes rolled up to heaven. It was the same when he let his hair grow long, but then I thought if that's all he's doing then I've nothing to worry about,' said Ita Doyle. She picked Booker Prize-winner *Paddy Clark Ha Ha Ha* as her favourite work. 'People have come to the conclusion that it is about his dad, Rory, but they needn't think the story of Charlo's wife, Paula, is about me. It most certainly is not.'

Roddy's mother also put me right on the swearing in his books. 'He didn't hear that bad language in our house,' she said.

All's Well at the Abbey

The Abbey got to celebrate its ninetieth birthday. President Mary Robinson cut the traditional Gort cake after the performance of the *Well of the Saints*. As we examined the exhibition of theatrical photographs, former Abbey actress Eithne Lydon, the widowed mother of Hot House Flower Liam Ó Maonlaí, told me that she had found love again. Virginia Cole and Deirdre Purcell had a good giggle at the photo of Deirdre in high boots and 1960s miniskirt.

Virginia, ex-wife of Riverdance director John McColgan, was sixteen when she played Concepta in the first RTÉ soap, *Tolka Row*. Many roles followed on stage and screen including *The Irish R. M.*, *The Snapper* and Lee Dunne's long-running *Goodbye to the Hill*, before being Called to the Bar by Kings Inns. Virginia has recently taken early retirement from the Bar to go back to her first love with a cameo role in Sebastian Barry's *The Secret Scripture*, produced by Noel Pearson and directed by Jim Sheridan.

Talk to Joe

I've always said it: a baby won't make any difference in the house unless you are used to sleep. In April 1995, *River of Sound* producers

Nuala O'Connor and Philip King – parents of three-year-old triplets Molly, Juno and Ellen – were on hand to give advice to June and Joe Duffy, the proud parents of Dublin's newborn triplets. (No, they didn't call them Gay, Pat and Marian). Nuala had typed a manuscript of dos and don'ts for the new parents.

'Like how we organised everything on open shelves for easy access, the type of baby changers needed so that mam and dad's backs won't be broken, not to buy a triple buggy because nobody goes for a walk with triplets on their own. There'll be eighteen nappies and eighteen bottles …'.

Tribute to Austin Finn

Photographers are a mine of information; they can always put a name on a face and cover your back so you don't miss a story. One of the most poignant moments I experienced as a news reporter was at a Mass for organ donors. The families of donors and recipients were present. Austin Finn had been to this event before, and he introduced me to a man who had received the heart of a young father of two who had died in an accident. His young widow, her eyes still pained, was there with the two small children. She allowed us to take their photograph with the recipient's arms around them.

Austin died in an accident when freelancing for the *Indo* after the *Press* closed.

King Cole

Joe Dolan and Dolores Keane were at the Harcourt Hotel Party to celebrate Paddy Cole's eight-year residency, which had started off as a two-month trial. That same week the Paddy Cole Bar in the Blarney Park Hotel was opened. Paddy featured annually at the Cork Jazz Festival. Modest to the core, our Paddy thought that when owner Gerry O'Connor rang him he was going to lose the gig at the festival.

'So you can imagine my delight to hear that he just wanted my permission to call the bar after me!'

Bringing Down the Banks

Anne Bushnell was singing Piaf at Dobbins bistro attended by Noel Pearson, wine importer Kevin Cassidy, his wife, Clare, and Irish Nationwide's Michael Fingleton, who enjoyed great popularity with journalists. Many of us had our mortgages with him. Interiors owner Bob Bushell was there too. He supplied the lighting for Barings Bank offices in the IFSC.

'It's okay, it's okay, I've been paid,' he laughed as my eyes widened. How lucky was he? We all remember Nick Gleeson and his role in bringing down that bank. Did we ever think it would happen here? Who would have dreamed that Gleeson would find sanctuary in Ireland? Become the CEO of Galway United? Appear on reality TV?

There was a nice pic of Amanda Byram at the fashion trade fair at the RDS in 1995. Didn't she do well? Photographer Tony Gavin had an eye for talent, but we weren't to know that she would make it big in America with the reality TV series *Paradise Hotel, The Swan* and the rest.

No thanks, Mr Eastwood

The diary took a jaunt to Killarney for the Roaring Twenties festival, but skipped over to Millstreet to see Steve Collins beat Chris Eubank. There was no thanking Barney Eastwood that night. Steve was saving his breath for trainer Freddie King. Barney Eastwood had said that Collins would lose, that the champ Chris Eubank would take a beating, but would win.

'I was wrong,' he admitted.

Steve and his radiant wife, Gemma, were in happier times then. They hadn't seen each other for six weeks coming up to the fight. 'We are off to the Burlington for a few days and then on to Connemara, organised by Sean Bán Breathnach,' she told me.

Way back in the days of *Wanderly Wagon* I wrote a bilingual script featuring Sean Bán and Marian Richardson. RTÉ's Joe O'Donnell liked it, and it is through him that our three careers took off. SBB got his own show, and Marian and I moved on to Bosco, she as presenter and me as scriptwriter.

Sir Peter takes the Michael D.

Some headlines just write themselves. Sir Peter Ustinov was in Ardmore Studios in Bray where MGM announced plans for a multiplex cinema in Parnell Square. A wickedly funny impersonator, everyone he mentioned got the mimic treatment. But it was his affectionate take-off of then minister Michael D. Higgins that made us chuckle the most.

'I'm not really a minister, I'm a poet and I'll send you my books,' Sir Peter said with a familiar Galway *blas*. 'The books arrived yesterday, a year to the day, and Michael D. is, indeed, a poet,' he added, confessing that he loves Ireland so much he sometimes feels like signing his name '*as gaeilge*'.

Enjoying the brunch was film censor of the day Sheamus Smith, who was the Dubliner's Diary photographer in the days of the famed first diarist Terry O'Sullivan. To appear in Terry's column was a thrill. I still meet people who have yellowing cuttings in their wallets. I was in it myself at the opening of a launderette in Churchtown. In that life I was a glamorous Aer Lingus transatlantic air hostess.

Cock and Bull

January 1995 saw Jim Sheridan flying in from America to open sculptor John Behan's retrospective of his work in the RHA Gallagher Gallery. Edna O Brien, Placido Domingo and Pierce Brosnan each own a work of art by John, but he doesn't have one himself. 'I've always had to sell, even now,' he said ruefully.

Famed for his monumental bulls, birds and swans in flight, a sacred cow took pride of place. 'It's a statement on the Beef Tribunal,' John told me. 'The cow has always been an important symbol in Irish life, and it has been abused.'

Charlie Haughey's press secretary, P. J. Mara, was there with his wife, Breda. Big fans of the sculptor, they also had some of John's work: a *Táin Bó* bought years before, and more recently a rooster.

'I thought it would be nice to have the cock and bull,' teased Breda.

'Your Christmas present?' I said to P. J., nudging the story a bit further.

'Yes,' he agreed.

'No,' puzzled Breda. 'You bought it for me. I gave you a surprise.'

I hurried across the room, leaving them to work it out.

Jim Sheridan was in America to discuss a film project on the time he and his wife, Fran, spent poverty-stricken in New York. You read it in the Diary first, folks. That project, as he called it, was the highly successful *In America*, which hit the big screen in 2002. Another project on Brendan Behan written and directed by Jim's brother, Peter Sheridan, was screened in the same year. Overnight fame is one thing, but it took seven years to bring them to the big screen!

It was Peter who introduced me to music legend Carole King at the Project Theatre. She was with Paul McGuinness's wife, Kathy Gilfillan, and was staying in an apartment in Temple Bar. We had a lovely chat, and it all appeared in the Diary under the headline 'Dublin, You've Got A Friend.'

Put Away Like Parking Fines

Maurice Sweeney was features editor of the *Irish Press* when a young woman wrote in, looking for help in finding her mother. He gave this freelance mother of four the letter. I hit the ground running. Kristina, thirty-seven, had been in Banada Orphanage with her sister. Unknown to them they had another sister in a convent down the road and a brother, an Artane boy, in Dublin. At age sixteen they were all put out in the world to fend for themselves.

It's the stuff of films now, but we can only hazard a guess at how difficult life was for a single mother in the 1940s. Brigid was living in the Regina Coeli Hostel for young mothers like herself. The hostel was still there. Details of the residents were filed neatly on cards in tiny writing. The matron told me with a tut that she remembered Brigid well. When she had her first child, a boy, she kept him a secret from her family for three years, but duty called her to her dying father's bedside.

She placed Victor in an orphanage so that she could go home to the midlands and appear as normal. Although Brigid visited her son, she never had the wherewithal to reclaim him or her three girls. Brigid did find solace in a marriage ten years later, and was blessed with a son, but tragically he died in a motorcycle accident as a teenager.

In the 1940s, children were put away through the courts. A court clerk who checked on the details for me was shocked to the core. 'My God, they put children away then like parking fines,' he gasped. Although it took time, and there was some sensitive side-stepping involved, it was easy enough to trace the mother through the well-kept parish records, but it was too late:

she had died six years before Kristina wrote to the *Irish Press*. That three-part story got me my staff job, News Editor Mick O'Kane told me later.

Brigid's children were able to pick up the story afterwards. An aunt, who has since died, could not cope with their visits, but their mother's husband was very welcoming and filled in lots of background details. Bringing them together in London was a deeply moving experience, and watching them look at a photograph of their mother for the first time is a memory I'll always cherish. Carlo Gébler took the photographs.

The girls were lucky in later life and each had a loving husband and family, but Victor, who has since died, had a difficult life in Artane and a lonely life in London. However, his sisters loved him at first sight – the best Christmas present he'd had in his life.

Spirit of Christmas

The thought of Sonia O'Sullivan cooking turkey and ham for six Kenyans on Christmas Day in London gave her parents the best laugh they'd had in a long time.

'I think it's a tactic: they'll all be running against her in Durham on New Year's Eve,' chuckled her dad, John.

'I can't imagine it,' said her mother. (It was easy to see where Sonia got her gamine looks from.)

They were in Jury's Hotel, and accepted the Irish Athlete of the Year Trophy on her behalf. Other guests included Bertie Ahern, with his lady, Celia Larkin, Lord Killanin, FAI President Louis Kilcoyne, and Ronnie Delaney. Back from London was Olympian Michael Carruth.

RTÉ's Brendan O'Reilly told me he once missed an Olympic high jump chance through lack of financial backing.

Riverdance: the show

Backstage, beautiful Beata Flatley poured champagne for guests crowding into the dressing room of Michael, her husband, and next door Jean Butler was smiling happily as she had her hair put up for the after-show party. Everybody was radiant. The *Riverdance* spectacular had raised the roof. There were hugs and handshakes for producer Moya Doherty and director John McColgan. Charles Haughey said it left him breathless.

'It's like nothing I've ever seen; words cannot describe it.' Máire Brennan had 'goosebumps', and actor Gabriel Byrne wished he had kept up the Irish dancing. 'All that stuff we were ashamed of for years, it was joyful.'

American Ambassador Jean Kennedy Smith was escorted by former *Irish Press* editor Tim Pat Coogan; Celia Larkin accompanied Bertie; and actor John Hurt, his hair shoulder-length and wearing a cloak, said that he did not consider himself separated from his wife, Jo. 'It's just a different way of living,' he reasoned.

All eyes were on Eileen Murphy, chic in black. 'I've had letters from people from all over the country wishing me well,' she said, referring to her recent break-up from her husband, Mike Murphy.

Promoters from England and America were at the show. 'It's up to Moya, but we are hoping it will travel,' said composer Bill Whelan.

Casting Michael Collins

Casting agents, film directors and resting actors turned out in force for the first night of the Field Day Theatre Company's production of *Uncle Vanya* at the Gate Theatre. Seamus Heaney was also there for Frank McGuinness's version of Chekhov's play.

Backstage, Stephen Rea looked serious. 'I never smile,' he said. He had been cast in *Michael Collins*. 'I don't know yet what part he'll play, but he's not cast as Harry Boland, and Liam Neeson is in the title role,' said director Neil Jordan.

Well, we know now that Aidan Quinn was Harry, Rea was Detective Ned Broy, Julia Roberts played Kitty Kiernan and Alan Rickman was a phenomenal Éamon de Valera. Mary Coughlan got the job of helping Julia with her song in the film. It seemed the Hollywood beauty hadn't a note.

In the Zone with Louis

Long before he became a showbiz story himself, Louis Walsh was always good for a tip-off, so I knew Boyzone were to get the New Entertainer award before I arrived at the National Concert Hall for the Telecom Awards. They were smashing young lads; their run-through rehearsal with the RTÉ crew brought a round of applause from the floor technicians who appreciate no-nonsense artists.

Dressed to kill with mountain boots, shirts hanging over their trousers and the obligatory baseball caps worn backwards, they were revelling in their fame.

'It came so fast,' said Stephen Gately. He was eighteen at the time, and told me he got a CD and a big remote-control truck for Christmas. And have they made any money? The boys held back their answer.

'Not a lot, not yet,' said Louis, 'but I'm going to take them all to England and "Love Me for a Reason" will be released in Holland and Germany, and that should do it.'

From the Irish Crèche to Prime Time

David McCullagh
(News Reporter, 1989–1993)

I got a job in the *Irish Press* because my Dad fixed Éamon de Valera's glasses.

Not *the* Éamon de Valera, I have to admit, but his grandson, who was then (the late 1980s) running the newspaper group. On a plane to London, they got chatting after my father managed to fix a screw on Major Minor's glasses (he was known as Major Minor as he was the son of Major Vivion de Valera, who had been in charge of the *Press* before him). I was advised to send in a job application, and after an interview and an initial rejection I was offered a job, to my great surprise.

Six of us were taken on in a batch in December 1989, with the idea that we could be trained – perhaps 'moulded' is the word they used – in the *Press* style and ethos. I was by far the most inexperienced of the bunch, with no practical experience and just three months in journalism college to my name. Frankly, I wouldn't have given me the job – and I would have been right. Perhaps my employment was a sign of how badly things were going wrong in management at the time.

Some unkind people around Burgh Quay called us the *Irish Crèche*; others referred to us as the Zodo Club, after the paper's page for kids. But we didn't do too badly – three of us have ended up in RTÉ's *Prime Time* programme (programme editor Donogh Diamond, senior researcher Paulette O'Connor, and me); Michael O'Kane is editor of *News at One*, also in RTÉ; Caroline Lynch has

178

had a range of roles in public relations and communications in the charity sector; and Donal MacIntyre has had a sometimes hair-raising career in investigative reporting.

We were quickly inducted into the ways of the NUJ (Gerry O'Hare instructing us always to claim our expenses, as otherwise it would make everyone else look bad – sound advice). While my five colleagues had at least the experience of working in newspapers before, it was all completely new to me, though of course by today's perspective it was terribly old-fashioned. Typewriters, for starters. Copyboys ripping off sections of copy as you typed, running it down to the subs, and then to the caseroom. 'The stone', where the paper was laid out. The rumble as the presses started to roll. Damn, but it makes you nostalgic!

After the Great Unpleasantness of summer 1990, when the papers came within hours of closing, computer 'technology' was introduced. Even by the standards of the day, the machines were horribly outdated. They came from some UK newspaper that was finished with them. I presume we had to pay for them, though legend had it they were found in a skip.

The *Press* was, in many ways, a wonderful place to work. It was also at times a bit odd, to say the least. Partly that was due to the drinking culture that was then widespread, but has since died out in my experience. Hacks still drink of course, but nowadays they usually wait until *after* they've finished work. That wasn't a huge problem in the *Evening Press*, where I worked most of the time, because we finished at 4 o'clock. The same could not be said of the *Irish* or the *Sunday Press*.

Another oddity of the whole group was its history as the house journal of Fianna Fáil. Again, links with the party were no longer strong by the time I started working there (whether that was more to the detriment of the papers or the party is a matter for debate). But there was still a knee-jerk approach to certain issues – when writing an obituary of some former Republican foot soldier, or a story about some dead hero of the Legion of the Rearguard, it was not the done thing to say that they had 'opposed the Treaty', or even that they had 'taken the Republican side'. Oh no. They had 'remained' on the Republican side – the other lot deserted us! There was also the sight, come election time, of the aforementioned Major Minor picking out an editorial on a manual typewriter to ensure that the paper founded by his grandfather stayed true to the party he also founded.

The parlous state of circulation and finances were constantly in everyone's mind, particularly those with mortgages and families to support. Like any sinking ship, though, it created a certain camaraderie, and over coffee in Bewley's in Westmoreland Street, or pints in Mulligan's, we dissected the latest twists in the never-ending crisis surrounding us.

Among the memories that stick with me is the Saturday-morning run after the first edition to the local café to get five or six takeaway fries for breakfast, to be eaten while listening to *Scrap Saturday*.

Or the sinking feeling when news of a murder, a fatal fire or a tragic car accident came through, and news editor Mick Sharkey's gaze fell on you and you realised you'd be the one knocking on the door of some poor unfortunate, looking for a few lines and perhaps a photo of the victim, hoping you'd be there before the *Herald* arrived.

The climb up the back stairs at seven in the morning, arriving though the empty caseroom into a quiet newsroom, Gregg Ryan at the 'day-town' desk, making check-calls, while Sharkey or Niall O'Flynn or Aindreas MacEntee sat at the newsdesk scouring the morning papers for anything that could be turned into an *Evening Press* lead. The mobile phone, then the size and weight of a brick, was the last word in modern technology in 1990. There were two of them in the newsroom, and if I remember correctly they had to be signed out as they were so valuable a part of our news-gathering operation.

Copy-takers – the lovely ladies who typed the stories we read to them over a crackling phone line when out of the office. Nowadays, we complain if we can't access Wifi to work on – back then, it was all about the hunt for a phone box that worked.

I was there for four years, and it gave me a lot. Apart from a grounding in journalism, a good contacts book and a lot of friends, I met my wife, Anne-Marie Smyth, there. Well, we actually met in the Children's Court in Smithfield when she was working for the *Tribune*, but we got to know each other in Burgh Quay. For that, and so much else, I'll always be grateful.

And all from a chance encounter and a broken pair of glasses.

Drunk with Power

Brenda Power
(Reporter and Feature Writer, *Irish Press*, 1981–1993)

It was around 9.30 on a Saturday morning, which, when you're twenty, practically counts as the crack of dawn. The telephone in the corridor outside our bedsit woke the whole house at that ungodly hour. Half asleep, my flatmate and I agreed that it couldn't possibly be for either of us, so we let it ring until one of the girls in the flat upstairs eventually cracked and answered the phone.

A few seconds later, there was a knock on our door. The call *was* for us – well, for me. I jumped out of bed, fearing the worst. Actually, as it turned out, not fearing the worst at all, since the worst I could have imagined was that somebody had died. And it was worse than that. It was Dermot McIntyre, the news editor of the *Evening Press*, and the single most terrifying human being I knew. Ringing at 9.30 on a Saturday morning. With a spelling lesson for me.

'L,' he began. 'A. Z. Y.' I think he may have repeated it for good measure. It's a shame it wasn't 'excavate', a word I can never spell without putting in a 'g', for some reason. Because I was never going to forget how to spell 'lazy', not ever, not after that.

What happened, he explained after our brief spelling bee, was that I had been sent to cover Bray District Court the previous day. I had filed a couple of no-account stories of minor offences committed by nobodies, and I had bailed out at lunchtime and gone home. After I'd been on to the copy-takers, I'd asked to

182

be put through to the newsdesk. There was absolutely nothing stirring in Bray District Court that day, I told them. I think I may have been mildly miffed at being sent to such a backwater in the first place, since my normal beat covered the far more prestigious environs of the Special Criminal Court and, at a push, the marvellously unpredictable District Justice Robert O'hUadhaigh's reign of terror in the Bridewell. By comparison, this place was dead as a doornail, so I folded up my notebook and caught the bus back to town.

But that very Friday afternoon, for the first and quite possibly the last time in Bray District Court, Something Interesting Happened. The internationally renowned author of *Manchu* and *Dynasty*, Robert Elegant (that was actually how Dermot described him, clearly reading from the *Herald*'s report – you can see where this is going, can't you?) had been brought before Bray District Court on a charge of drunken driving.

Which would have been perfectly fine, and needn't have cost either Robert or me a moment's sleep, if some unsportingly diligent *Indo* stringer hadn't hung about for the afternoon sitting. The story made the late editions of the *Evening Herald* that Friday, and was front-page news on Saturday's *Independent*. And either Dermot or I may have invented this bit, but my recollection is that he was driving a Bentley at the time. In Ireland of the early 1980s, you can understand how that detail would have sexed the story up even further.

I have never forgiven Robert bloody Elegant for not observing the relatively permissive drink-driving limits of the time, or for not having the foresight to hire a chauffeur for his bloody Bentley (if he had a Bentley at all). Or for not getting caught somewhere other than Bray.

At the time, I wouldn't have appreciated that summary tutorial in journalistic thoroughness, nor realised how lucky

I was to be a young journalist learning my trade in the *Irish Press* in what would turn out to be its final decade. I am pretty certain I didn't hang up the phone that morning thinking that I was so fortunate to be training in a newsroom where passion and commitment and integrity and sheer dogged pride in the product drove grown men to apoplexy in the face of sloppiness and apathy, and, worst of all, being scooped by the *Herald*. I probably didn't go back to bed giving thanks for the lesson I'd learned (not the spelling one, obviously). But I should have done.

Because the *Press* took seriously its reputation as the country's best-ever school of journalism, the one that could claim just about everyone of consequence in the media of the day. People really did shout at you if you screwed up; the sloppiness that you see in some papers these days was not tolerated – a judgement much feared by modern journalists. But, equally, they praised you if you did well. You didn't need pull or connections or even a college degree to get on in the *Press*, and none of those assets could save you if you weren't up to the job. I joined the *Press* as an eighteen-year-old trainee straight from Rathmines College of Commerce, and left twelve years later after my first baby was born, and like every other veteran I've got my share of mad, bonkers and largely unprintable anecdotes about the place and the people and the times that were in it.

But mostly I've got the very fondest memories of a newspaper that didn't just have a character all of its own – it WAS a character, it was a living, breathing, huffing, puffing, churning, clanking, smelly, steaming hulk of a creature, insatiable and inexhaustible, with a noisily beating heart that had clattered into life long before most of us were born, and would clatter on, so it always seemed, long after we'd gone. As you walked out the back door into the first light of a summer dawn after a 'night-town' shift, with the heat and the smell and the thunder of those giant rolling drums shaking the building as you left, it really did feel like a living thing. Once or twice when I've found myself on Poolbeg Street late at night I have heard it again, surprisingly clearly: the ghost of the presses. In a time before twenty-four-hour takeaways and all-night revelry on the city's streets it was the building that never slept – like most of the hacks, in fact, or maybe they just looked that way.

It's hard to tell the difference between a modern newsroom and a busy estate agents' office, with their flat screens and their paperless desks and their low, industrious murmur, and, most of all, their journalists dressed like evangelical Christians trying to look casual. But when you finished a shift in the *Irish Press* newsroom, back when I started in the 1980s, there was no doubt that you had just done a proper day's graft. You'd have blackened knuckles, filthy fingernails and the smell of ink and grease and smoke in your hair and clothes. Firemen regularly finished their duties around the corner in Tara Street in neater nick than the average *Irish Press* journalist after a night-town gig.

I know that I asked lots of times, but nobody ever really explained why all the typewriters had been stripped down to their bare skeletons, the covers prised off and the bony fingers of the keys exposed. It was certainly not for hygiene reasons – whenever you picked one up to carry it to your desk, the oil and ink and accumulated dead skin cells of your colleagues left your nice white blouse looking like a first sketch for the Turin Shroud. The naked typewriters were one of the many eccentricities that made the *Press* probably the most unforgettable place in which most of us have ever worked – the rest of the eccentricities were on the staff.

And more than the anecdotes, more than the architecture, more than the smell and the noise and the shudder, it's those

---

people who come to mind, in fleeting cinematic glimpses, whenever I pass Burgh Quay now: John Banville in one of his multicoloured knit waistcoats, taking a puff of his pipe before he'd deliver a verdict on a queried headline; Sean Cryan doffing his homburg when you'd meet him on the street; Con Houlihan holding his nose in the same circumstances (couldn't blame him, we all probably stank); George Douglas taking a fistful of coins from his pocket to demonstrate how he'd throw them in the face of a mugger in New York (it'd have to be a life-or-death situation, the others agreed, for George to part with a fistful of cash since he'd famously reclaimed his contribution to the whip around for Michael Conway's second wedding).

Colum McCann, on crutches for some reason, checking the roster to see if he'd got any freelance shifts that week; Noeleen Dowling, always a delightful, smiling presence, and always a reliable source of teabags if you were stuck; Éanna Brophy and myself returning to the *Sunday Press* office after a particularly boozy lunch and Éanna announcing he was 'drunk with Power'; Jim and Tommy in the library, fiercely guarding their little envelopes of cuttings from awkward people wanting to consult them; Freda and Roma on the phones correcting your prose as you went along; and Liam Hayes turning purple with embarrassment the day somebody in the *Sunday Press* thought it might be a good idea to hire a stripper to come INTO THE OFFICE on the day before he left to get married – I can still see him obediently pulling her red garter up the leg of his jeans.

Paul Muldowney sauntering down the newsroom one night to tell us there'd been a bomb threat phoned in, and the protocol was that we could leave if we liked, and the copy-takers had already fled the building – nobody else left, but it was a tense few hours all the same; Colman Doyle persuading a furious Charlie Haughey to let me into Abbeville during a photo session when he had specifically banned print journalists (back in the days when a Fianna Fáil Taoiseach could literally call the shots); the general mystification as to how Terry Keane's photo byline could have ended up in the *Sunday Press* TV pages over a preview of a new BBC series called *The Mistress*; Emmanuel Kehoe's on-the-spot ditty about the next social diarist's request for a pay increase ('Oh, Maureen Cairnduff / Is not paid enough / For writing her stuff / Please pay her enough / Or she'll leave in a huff'); Mick O'Kane delicately picking up a colour piece I'd written on one of my early shifts and 'filing it' on a lethal spike of metal protruding from a wooden block.

Michael Keane taking the time to sit down with a very green student hack and talking through some effort of mine in the middle of a madly busy newsroom with real patience and encouragement; Willie Collins leaving a handwritten note in a brown envelope (I thought it was my marching orders) about some piece that had caught his eye; and I think I may already have mentioned Dermot McIntyre.

I had left the *Press* and moved to the *Sunday Tribune* two years before the big metal drums finally stopped rolling and footage from inside the newsroom began appearing on the *Nine O'Clock News* each night. From what I could see in the reports, nothing much had changed since I'd left, apart from the fact that journalists were now openly sleeping in the office. The weird skeletal typewriters were still there, since you still had to queue to input your copy into one of the banks of Ford Fiesta-sized computers at the subs' end of the newsroom, and the night-town box and the picture desk piled with camera bags and the pigeonholes for post. And the same faces were still there – amidst the hubbub I could see copy-takers and caseroom men and correspondents and copyboys and former colleagues against a background so familiar I could still navigate it in my sleep.

And I did, again last night, probably because as I was writing this piece I was back in the *Irish Press* newsroom, in my dream, trying to find a free desk and looking for a functioning typewriter and searching for a roll of copy paper with the carbon in the middle because I had a cracker of a story to write. I'd been out in Bray District Court, you see, and you'll never guess who turned up on a drink-driving charge....

Garvey

Patsy McGarry
(Political Reporter and Theatre Critic, *Irish Press*, 1987–1995)

You will read elsewhere in this collection about the geniuses, the eccentrics and misfits; the prodigious drinking; how reporters thumped typewriters hard so each key registered on the long double-sheeted spools of paper.

Sounds primitive now. (Did you know that Jack Kerouac wrote the entirety of his book *On the Road* on a single such spool that went on for 120 feet?!) And the noise in that huge open-plan newsroom, etc, etc. You might well wonder how a daily newspaper could emerge from such chaos and how that newsroom also had a reputation for being the best in Ireland.

From my experience at the *Press* I would attribute such achievement to a well-managed news team and one rock-solid man in particular: 'Garvey'. I don't think I ever met a newsman like John Garvey. The occasionally gruff Newry exterior masked a finely tuned news instinct, high intelligence and a sensitivity rare in the business, and that made him the backbone of the *Irish Press* in my time there through the late 1980s and early 1990s. He was deputy editor then, but the title was only that. He had been effectively the paper's editor for years. He wrote most of its leaders and determined much of its news content on a daily basis.

He died aged seventy-six on 24 November 2011, my birthday also. As his obituary in *The Irish Times* said: 'John Garvey had black ink running through his veins. That was what his colleagues said. He understood hot metal newspaper production so well.

'The world of inky galleys, clattering manual typewriters, even louder Linotype machines, the smell of molten lead, reading type backwards on the stone before the big old printing press roared into life, spitting out papers hastily gathered into vans speeding off through the night....

'Garvey – he was Garvey to those who worked with him, said with a mixture of respect and affection – had something else. He had an intuitive grasp of what would interest readers, a good story. He could smell news, one said. It used to be unkindly said that *The Irish Times* wouldn't know what news was, but could tell people what to think about it afterwards, and the *Irish Independent* only knew news when it appeared in the *Irish Press*.'

I have reasons to be ever grateful to Garvey. When I left pirate radio in 1987 after being fired for the third time in a row over low wages – I was Father of the Chapel (shop steward) there – I went to him with ideas for stories, and he was supportive from day one. For someone like me, that was hugely important then. I had no formal training as a reporter.

In those days the only journalism course in Ireland was at Rathmines College in Dublin, and it didn't accept applications from graduates like me. In 1982, while teaching at Bolton St. College, I had been to every single one of the three major papers in Dublin – the *Press*, *The Times*, and the *Independent* – offering ideas, but each told me I must be a member of the NUJ before they could accept work from me. I went to the NUJ offices at Liberty Hall and was told there I had to be earning 60 per cent of my income from journalism before they could accept me as a member. I was snookered.

Then, in the summer of 1983, an opportunity arose to work part-time in the newsroom at Sunshine Radio in Portmarnock, Co. Dublin. I began work there then and, believing that independent radio was around the corner, went full-time at the end of that year.

We cleaned up the newsroom practices immediately and began the long haul for admission to the NUJ in the face of fierce resistance from the chapel at RTÉ. But we got in. When I left Sunshine I began working on a freelance basis for *Magill* magazine and the *Irish Press* – Garvey, really, at the latter. We just got on from the beginning. I just liked him and always had the deepest respect for him. I also recognised almost immediately the sensitive soul behind that Northern bark.

At a time when I most needed it he was very encouraging, gave me some fine opportunities, and helped greatly to build my confidence in this new world, which could be so intimidating. Finding yourself working alongside national names and being treated as an equal by them took getting used to. You see, I had arrived at my journalistic equivalent of a holy of holies; I grew up on a diet of the *Press*.

Ours was an old-style Fianna Fáil household, and my father wouldn't allow any of the other national dailies inside the door, believing them inherently hostile to his beloved party. He paid some deference to the gospels of Matthew, Mark, Luke and John, but the only one he put his faith in was the gospel of Dev: the *Irish Press*. So to find myself working there was, initially, something of an out-of-body experience, even if my beliefs and those of my father had long parted. But to be welcomed, as I felt I was by John Garvey, was very heaven.

In 1990 his faith in me was severely tested, but he stood solid. I have often wondered what I'd have done in similar circumstances had our roles been reversed. I came across a story of a plot to unseat Alan Dukes from his position as then leader of Fine Gael and how this had been foiled by Dukes himself. I named the four ringleaders as then senior Fine Gael figures Jim Mitchell, Michael Noonan, Sean Barrett and Maurice Manning, who had met seven times that summer to plot Alan Dukes's downfall. However, he outmanoeuvred them by appointing most of the quartet to head up Austin Currie's campaign for the presidential election that year.

The story appeared on the front page of the *Irish Press* on 19 September 1990 under a huge banner headline: 'Dukes foils plotters. Rebels put in charge of Currie bid'. Inside was a full-page story on the 'plotters' with names and photographs.

There was murder. Jim Mitchell denounced the story publicly as 'a new low in Irish journalism' inspired by Fianna Fáil. I, frankly, was very shaken by the vehemence of this response, despite trusting my sources. What if they had got it wrong or misunderstood? Would Garvey still believe me? That, really, was my main concern. I needn't have worried. His editorial the next day dealt only with the Jim Mitchell denunciation, of which he wrote: 'We reject this utterly and comprehensively.'

He said: 'We fully accept Mr Mitchell's right to make such a statement. We recognise our duty to publish that statement, which we do elsewhere in today's issue. After that our paths must diverge. Our report was not published lightly.'

To say I was heartened by this would be a great understatement. But it got better. The following November Alan Dukes was deposed as leader of Fine Gael. John, bless him, penned another editorial on the matter. It read: 'Two months ago, when this newspaper detailed a plot to topple Alan Dukes, Fine Gael spokesmen denounced the report as "a new low in Irish journalism." Now the plot is front-page headlines, with those who denounced this paper and the journalist concerned leading the campaign to oust the leader. Fine Gael made great play about truthfulness and integrity in the recent presidential election campaign, most notably some of those leading the current coup. And some people wonder why there is such widespread public cynicism about politicians!'

Of course the prominence of the late Jim Mitchell in all of this led even more stories about his role in the Dukes downfall plot to wing their way to me. One, which I reported after Alan Dukes had been deposed, concerned a meeting of the plotters at Jim's house in Rathfarnham when his brother, and staunch Dukes supporter Gay Mitchell, called. Consternation. Gay was shown into the front room. He asked to use the phone. It was in the room where the visiting plotters had gathered. Jim excused himself, rushed the plotters out the back door, brought his son downstairs and seated him in the room with a paper in his hand before inviting brother Gay in to use the phone.

To top it all, one of the first interviews Alan Dukes gave after being ousted was to me and the *Irish Press* in July 1991. I should say that he had nothing to do with how I had accessed the original plot story.

Only once did Garvey ask me to do a story for which he had any sort of agenda himself. That was in May 1988. The Ombudsman, Ireland's first, Michael Mills, was being punished for perceived sins past by then Taoiseach Charles Haughey. Haughey hated Mills, who had been political correspondent for the *Irish Press* and was close personally to former Taoiseach Jack Lynch. In 1984 Michael Mills had been appointed Ombudsman by the Garret FitzGerald-led coalition. Charles Haughey became taoiseach after the 1987 general election. At the beginning of that year the Ombudsman's office had sixteen investigating officers, four senior investigating officers and a director.

By the end of 1987, and following the return of Haughey to power, seven investigating officers and one senior such officer had been removed from the Ombudsman's office. The director had left and wasn't replaced, while three administrative staff were also removed. The Ombudsman's budget was cut by £100,000 in 1987, with further cuts of £125,000 in 1988. It was widely believed that Haughey was deliberately screwing the office to get at Mills or even to get rid of him as Ombudsman. Michael Mills was under severe pressure.

John Garvey's sympathies lay very much with Michael Mills, and I was dispatched to do the interview, which was given a full page and prominently displayed in the paper. It was clear from the statistics alone what was being done to Mills. Things improved for his office thereafter, something he never failed to mention to me. But his gratitude was misplaced. It belonged to Garvey. Like so much else.

I knew the Lenihan family from Roscommon. Brian senior was a friend and sometime boozing buddy of my father's. He gave me his first interview (for the *Press*) after his liver operation in the US and again after he lost the 1990 presidential election campaign. But it was Garvey's idea that I accompany Brian Jnr on the canvass during the 1989 general election campaign. Brian Jnr was canvassing in Dublin West for his father, then in the US for that operation. It was a revealing experience concerning the younger Brian, who then had the air of an academic going door-to-door. That would change in the years ahead.

Among others I then interviewed for Garvey was Shane Ross, who had recently joined Fine Gael after ten years of being an Independent, having realised in October 1989 that 'a politician can be more effective in a party.'

And there was PD TD Geraldine Kennedy, whose ambition in February 1988 was 'to sit at the Cabinet table where the real decisions are made.' And Michael McDowell, who in July 1991 revealed he had become so disillusioned with the FG/Labour 1980s coalition he considered voting Fianna Fáil.

There were so many more, and all thanks to Garvey and his faith in me. A young journalist could not have asked for a better mentor. It was my great good fortune to know him. But I was not alone.

This is how the 2011 obituary in *The Irish Times* put it: 'As the Press Group fades from memory, the roll call of talented people whose careers began or was advanced there is often overlooked. It is too long to recite here. Many household names had good reason to remember good advice, gruffly given, and the skilled editing of their copy by the man they called Garvey.'

May that good and decent man rest peacefully.

Charlie and the Press factory

Lucille Redmond
(News Subeditor)

Every second Thursday, in that giant factory floor that was the newsroom, a man would sidle in and slide past the specialist writers, past the *Irish Press* features desk, through the reporters' desks, by the *Evening Press* feature writers in their alcove. Charlie Gannon had the look of the older men of the *Press*, from the days when they all belonged to the Movement – a belted trench coat, a quick glance left and right, a slouch hat pulled down over the eyes.

Charlie would walk through, the floor shaking from the printing presses thundering a floor below us as the paper ran off, the thunder rising to a roar now and then as someone opened the door at the far end of the caseroom to the walkway over the presses. He'd edge past the front desk, giving a nod here and there to the editor and his chiefs, past the back desk, and finally he'd go around the sports subs and past the E-shaped subeditors' desk, and go around past the stone and into the canteen.

He carried bunches of supermarket bags in each hand, and as he edged into the canteen, that place of Burko boilers and filthy mugs dark brown from years of tannin, men would rise silently from their desks and drift after him. Charlie was a retired comp. His passion was plants, and all through spring and summer and autumn he appeared with glorious plants: cranesbill geraniums, rare roses, dahlias, penstemons…. He would leave after a few minutes, and the men (and occasional woman) would come out with precious bags of beauty for their gardens.

When I first worked in the Irish Press Group, freelancing in the 1970s, it was a place of ferocious noise. The open-plan newsroom, around fifty metres long, with telephone wires coming down from frames in the ceiling and chunky Formica desks crammed together, thundered with men beating manual typewriters and shouting the most private secrets of the country into the phones. 'What you say, Minister? Bribes? You're joking, Jim – g'wan?' and furiously taking shorthand notes.

I'd chosen subbing over reporting because subbing finishes when you go home, while a reporter expected calls at all times of day and night as stories broke. Unless you had a wife behind you, a reporter's work was impossible for anyone with children.

I worked in all three of the papers for several years: the *Evening Press,* with its lackadaisical attitude, two-inch headlines, sparkling writing and Austin Finn's fabulous photos; the bestselling *Sunday Press,* whose staff knew well that it was the financial heart of the group, and whose financial editor, Des Crowley, broke the stories that are today making the news; and the flagship *Irish Press,* which took itself more seriously than the others, as the news core not just of the group but of Irish journalism.

In those days journalists served a seven-year apprenticeship, and virtually every reporter and editor in the major newspapers and broadcasters and the country papers had been trained in the *Press,* in its stringent school of grammar, fact-checking, contact-building, networking and ruthless truth-seeking combined with occasional merciful blindness.

I worked three nights a week during most of that time for the subs' desk, captained by John Banville, who said nary a word for most of the night, but would break out in occasional literary discussions with Mary Morrissy or others of us. Banville had been a surprise choice for the job, and I was told that the newsroom watched tensely on the night he came on first as chief sub. There had been a long-running turf war between the reporters and the subs over who owned some obscure piece of daily news – not the tides, but something equally inessential. According to the legend, that first night, a news editor shouldered over to the subs' desk and said, 'We're taking the …' whatever the heck it was. Banville looked up. 'Fine,' he said, and, according to the legend, again, the news editor's face registered triumph, followed by swift dismay at the realisation that he now had to find someone to do the job every night. After that, Banville was master of the ring.

To my astonishment, in interview after interview in which I was rejected for a staff job (once, apparently, because I was carrying a copy of *The Satanic Verses*), I was suddenly staffed one day on the *Evening Press* subs' desk on the orders of group second-in-command, Vincent Jennings.

This was a place of deep and sometimes cruel enmities and friendships, controlled and calmed by chief sub Jim Carwood, whose passion was the racing pages. Jim had an unprecedented ability to pass work to people and make them feel that they were particularly valued for being able to do it. I was the one given the difficult phone calls – the outraged parish priests shocked at too plunging a neckline in a photograph (now that Bean de Valera was no longer on the scene to demand that these be inked in to more modest levels).

Jim was a darling, and the ultimate source on news values. His sight had deteriorated gradually over the years to the point where he could only read copy by holding it a couple of inches from his eyes, raising his glasses and squinting, so if he had any doubt he'd lean over to one of his more trusted staff and mutter, 'Read that, could you, and tell me if it's all right?' A couple of times when a sub or a reporter became unable to do the work properly due to bereavement or illness, Jim would simply draw a sub aside and mutter, 'I'm going to give you all so-and-so's copy to redo for the next couple of months.' The person whose work was being kindly minded never knew.

Con Houlihan produced his work in the old-fashioned way – not on double rolls of newsprint with a carbon between, rolled into a typewriter and typed off in long scrolls, but as separate one-page takes of newsprint. Each page held a single paragraph, with 'm/f' for 'more follows' on the bottom right, each paragraph numbered and named at the top right 'All-Ireland Final 1' with at top left 'EP' for *Evening Press*. This was the old method for news writing, and is the reason that every newspaper in the world has a house style – because in the old days ten takes would be rapidly set by ten separate linotype operators; the style had to be consistent or the piece would read as nonsense.

But Con's handwriting was so dreadful that only two people – subeditor Shane Flynn and typesetter Harry Havelin – could reliably read it. The takes would be brought over to Shane for subbing, then passed to Harry by an overseer squinting at the hieroglyphic copy and shaking his head.

Con was beloved of the caseroom. One birthday the compositors brought him to Mulligan's to celebrate and bought him so many brandy-and-milks that he came back, heaved himself into the sacred overseer's desk and slept there for the afternoon, the overseer calmly working around him.

Every now and then, 'Major Minor' – de Valera's grandson, now the owner of the group – would come through and inspect the work. I particularly remember him appearing one night when we had one of the many bomb threats of the time, and printing had been delayed as the firemen swept the building and we waited in Mulligan's....

All gone now. If the management had known the upturn that was coming for newspapers the group need never have closed in May

1995, and could have been a profit-maker and a happy workplace through the Celtic Tiger years. They didn't know, nobody did, and so it closed.

But if you ran a DNA test through Dublin pressmen's gardens, you would find a strong Charlie Gannon strain. I thought I'd killed the Hansa rubus rose I got from him when I cut it back drastically this spring, but up it came again and it's in fine leaf. I expect a warm summer of that wafting deep-scented rose on my windowsills this year.

Our eyes met across a crowded Dáil bar

Gerry O'Hare and Anne Cadwallader
(Gerry O'Hare: Reporter/Travel and Tourism
Correspondent/ Deputy News Editor, 1997–closure.
Anne Cadwallader: Political Reporter, 1987–1989,
Northern Editor, 1991–closure)

We can't even agree how we met. Gerry says it was in the Dáil bar. Anne says it was in Mulligan's. What is certain is that Gerry was working as a parliamentary reporter in Leinster House and Anne was Dublin correspondent for the BBC.

What is also certain is that Anne was intrigued by all the stories she heard about Gerry's IRA past and that, although he was the *Irish Press* travel and tourism correspondent, he was barred from both the USA and Britain.

A few weeks after we had crossed each other's path for the first time, the 1986 annual Oireachtas Press Ball came around. We both went. Gerry sat at the 'top table' along with, amongst others, P. J. Mara (then government press secretary), Sean Duignan (then RTÉ political correspondent) and Mick Hand (then editor of the *Sunday Tribune*), while Anne sat at the lowly 'Foreign Press' table.

It was Joyce Buggy, herself a long-time freelance at the *Irish Press*, who dared Anne to ask Gerry for a dance. What a scandal, she opined, if the BBC Dublin correspondent was seen dancing with the former IRA man. Anne can't turn down a dare – and the rest is history.

GERRY: In 1978, after several years freelancing at Burgh Quay, I was offered a staff job, but before it could be confirmed I was told I had to see Major de Valera in his grand office in O'Connell Street. At the time, Conor Cruise O'Brien was regularly ranting about Republican 'sneaking regarders' in Irish journalism. Major de Valera said the only place he wanted to see my name in his papers was on a byline. I took the hint.

Rising to become deputy Father of the NUJ Chapel, I did, however, become a different kind of thorn in the *Press* management's side. If there were insufficient typewriters or chairs in the newsroom, it was 'down tools' and into Mulligan's until satisfactory arrangements were made.

The move was less convincing, however, when I called the newsroom out after complaints that the atmosphere was too muggy. Having an 'air break' in the notoriously smoke-laden Mulligan's lacked a certain credibility.

As part of my multifarious duties during the 1980s I was asked to cover Irish interests at the Epsom Derby and kitted out in top hat and tails. My mug duly appeared in the paper, superimposed upon a picture of Her Majesty shouting encouragement at a past race to a royal gee-gee. This witty little collage didn't amuse chief executive Vincent Jennings, who baulked at the idea of a Belfast proletarian being provided with such a wardrobe at the *Press*'s expense. Jennings, however, was peremptorily informed that the offending threads were merely on hire from a local company.

One story that, thankfully, never made the paper was the outcome of a house-sitting event in the early 1980s. I was minding the home of a rich American on the Hill of Howth and returned early one morning from night-town duty at the *Press*, filling the washing machine and leaving a note for the cleaning lady (whose husband, coincidentally, worked in the *Press* caseroom) reminding her to turn it on.

I retired to bed, only to be woken by ear-splitting screams. In the kitchen, I discovered the poor woman in hysterics, surrounded by a pile of wet laundry and the constituent parts of a very dead cat. The unfortunate creature had climbed into the machine after I left the note. I administered a large Cognac and dispatched her home.

On my arrival for duty the following night, it quickly became obvious that the entire caseroom had already heard the sad tale. The sound of hissing and miaowing as I made my Walk of Shame through that cavernous room lives with me still.

In the 1980s, press trips abroad were plentiful. As travel correspondent I was invited on many (despite the USA and Britain being *hors de combat*). One year, Morocco beckoned and I was regaling friends in Mulligan's about the upcoming trip, amongst them one Maurice Sweeney, a noted Arabist, who enquired if I would be kind enough to search out a particular tome in Morocco that he was anxious to obtain. Ever obliging, I agreed, and Maurice inscribed in his best Arabic the name and author of the book on a scrap of paper.

In Marrakesh, in Casablanca and in Agadir, I enquired at various booksellers. Each and every time the bookshop owner would read the note and quickly explain that, regretfully, he was unable to supply the required volume, while suggesting another location in the bazaar or souk. Towards the end of the trip we were discussing our failure to obtain the elusive book, at which point our tour guide kindly offered to intercede.

'What is this mysterious and esoteric book?' he enquired, upon which I handed over the scrap of paper that had passed between me and Maurice Sweeney in Mulligan's. A frown quickly appeared on his forehead that grew into a deep blush.

'Do you know what this means?' he asked me.

'No,' I replied, 'it's just the name of the book.'

'No it isn't,' breathed the tour guide. 'Indeed not. The words on this paper read: "Can you find me a little boy?" '

Needless to say, the bold Sweeney was unaccountably absent from his usual haunts upon our return to Dublin. He had, so we heard, been widely entertaining friends in various hostelries with speculation as to my fate. On my return this focus of conversation changed to the ways in which I intended to end his miserable life. Some years later, however, Maurice apologised. Apology accepted, but the story might have ended differently had I ended up in a Moroccan jail. Very differently.

ANNE: I joined the *Press* from the BBC in 1987 as political reporter, becoming the only female at that time in the 'pol corrs' room (and the only Brit!) working alongside the paper's political correspondent, Sean O'Rourke (now of RTÉ).

In 1989, the Fianna Fáil leader and Taoiseach Charles Haughey called a general election. Sean had, by then, departed for RTÉ, and I was acting political correspondent. After three weeks of exhausting campaigning came Polling Day, Thursday 15 June. As is usual, the press corps, after long hours on the campaign trail, was left bereft of news to cover on the day of the vote itself. Like my colleagues in the *Cork Examiner*, *The Irish Times*, RTÉ and elsewhere, all we could do was keep in touch with the various party headquarters throughout the day to try and judge the turnout.

A low turnout would have been deemed bad news for Fianna Fáil, as it would have meant that some of the faithful had stayed at home. Conversely, a high turnout would have been deemed excellent news for Mr Haughey and the elusive clear majority Fianna Fáil so ardently desired.

I spent the day in the party headquarters, chatting with Peter White of Fine Gael and P. J. Mara and others in the Fianna Fáil HQ. Then most of the pol corrs returned home to their newsdesks, and finally their homes. Being of a stubborn inclination, however,

I decided to stick it out in Lower Mount Street, where both of the two major parties had their HQs, until the polling stations had closed.

Having established that the tally-men for both parties agreed the turnout had been lower than expected, I penned a story claiming this was bad news for Haughey before heading to bed at around 3 a.m.

Waking to hear the 8 a.m. RTÉ news and 'What the Papers Say', my blood ran cold when I heard the general consensus that the turnout had been high and good news for Haughey.

This was confirmed on the 9 a.m. news, by which time I was out of bed and on the phone.

The news from Burgh Quay was not good. 'Mick O'Kane is going to hang you,' said one colleague. 'You're finished,' said another.

I crawled, white-faced and stunned, around the various party HQs again. Nothing had changed. But what would the turnout actually be? Who had got it right? I screwed up my last vestiges of courage and slunk back to Burgh Quay. The bustle of the caseroom was quiet as the grave as I walked through to the newsroom where Mick O'Kane was waiting for me, speechless with fury.

Blushing, exhausted and stiff with stress, I walked to my desk and gazed glumly out upon the River Liffey to await final judgement. The first few results began to trickle in. Most, but not all, seemed to indicate a slightly lower turnout, but not enough yet to reach any firm conclusions.

After lunch, between twenty and thirty results had come in. The general story was that the turnout was, after all, slightly down. I walked to where the group financial editor, Colm Rapple, was busy with his calculator.

'Colm, what do the figures say?' Ever cheerful, he opined, 'Well, we have enough results in to say the statistical chances of a high turnout are virtually nil.' Relief flooded through me. Utter and blessed relief. I had been right, and so had the party HQs. The next day, a cut-out 'slasher' in the *Press* read 'We got it right!' Later, Haughey went into coalition with the Progressive Democrats.

Was it worth the agony of waiting? Probably not. Eaten bread is soon forgotten, and within three months I had been supplanted as political correspondent and departed Burgh Quay for Century Radio and RTÉ, only to return two years later in January 1991 as Northern Ireland correspondent.

This was before the IRA ceasefire, and Belfast was still a frightening, albeit exhilarating, place to work. I heard no fewer than fifty explosions that first year, nearly becoming a statistic myself.

More than once, after an eighteen-hour day, I retired to bed only to hear the unmistakeable sound of a car bomb in the night. I would immediately phone the newsdesk, whose invariable first question was 'Any dead?' How one earth could I know at that stage?! It was always infuriating.

An immediate priority on my arrival back in Belfast was to make contact with 'P. O'Neill' , the soubriquet by which the IRA's rotating spokesmen were known. Living in the Republican heartland of West Belfast, as various 'P. O'Neills' and I did, I frequently became the first journalist to receive many official IRA statements. On several occasions the door rapped in the wee hours and, bleary-eyed and pyjama-clad, I found 'P. O'Neill' on the doorstep.

On one occasion he arrived at the house and entrusted me with a cigarette paper upon which were inscribed the words of an official IRA statement. I was instructed to transcribe them onto a new sheet of paper, destroy the first scrap and its forensic evidence immediately, and broadcast its words to *The Irish Times*, the BBC, the *Guardian* and RTÉ.

I had a brainwave. Just that week I had taken possession of a fax machine (a technological innovation), which doubled as a photocopier. I placed the cigarette paper on the platen and pressed the photocopy button. The platen turned. The photocopy duly arrived. But the cigarette paper remained stubbornly unseen within the machine's interstices. Imagining the RUC turning up in force and bludgeoning their way into my home, I toyed with the idea of throwing the fax machine out of the first-floor window to recover the paper. Wiser counsel prevailed, and by dint of a darning needle and tweezers I recovered the paper. Rejecting the idea of tearing it up and throwing it down the lavatory, I placed it on the empty fire grate and lit it. The scrap went straight up the chimney. After long minutes of hacking away at the flue with fire tongs and a poker, I retrieved it. The lavatory was, after all, its final destination.

On my forty-third birthday, 26 May 1996, both Gerry and I lost our jobs. We had mortgages to pay in Belfast and Dublin, and life was hard for a long while. We both have very fond memories of our days in Burgh Quay. They were golden years for us. But we survived. The closure should never have happened. Ireland and its democracy are the poorer.

Hey, kid, get into your car ... and vamoose

Ken Whelan
(News Reporter/Father of the Chapel, 1979–1995)

They never really carried out an autopsy on how the three titles died, although news editor Ray Burke did a really efficient forensic job on the demise of the papers in his book *Press Delete*.

We all have our own theories about the passing, and for the record I believe Burgh Quay unravelled the moment the Ingersolls arrived in Dublin in the late eighties with their junk bonds and junk money and junk editorial ideas, and then just junked the whole commercial underpinning of the group by splitting the company into a property venture and a newspaper group. But what the Ingersolls couldn't do, even to the end, was destroy the great news ethic that permeated the old building and ensured that the *Sunday Press*, *Evening Press* and *Irish Press* whipped the opposition every a.m., p.m. and Sunday throughout the eighties and nineties.

And how we loved doing it.

'Hey, kid, there's a fella hanging upside down naked from a tree in Fairview Park. Get out there and find out what's going on.'

'I don't believe you.'

'It's true, Ken. Just heard about it as I was driving in. Get going.'

Another Saturday 6–2 a.m. shift in the *Sunday Press*, and another 'Hey, kid' story to bring back to news editor John Kelly. The Fairview Park story (the victim thankfully survived) was the first in a series of homophobic attacks in the suburb during the eighties, and was a typical Kelly news story that he just happened to hear about while driving into the office.

'Hey, kid, there's some big stuff going on with agriculture officials down in the docks. Get going.'

And what do you know, when I arrive on the scene there's a huge hullabaloo outside the Eirfreeze plant, a Larry Goodman affiliate, with officials and vets shifting tonnes of well-travelled beef from the stores. That 'Hey, kid' story was the straw that broke the camel's back for a government then under huge pressure to investigate the imaginative commercial practices within the Irish beef industry. It partly led to the setting up of the Beef Tribunal under Mr Justice Liam Hamilton the following week.

I still have the missive from the good judge himself, asking me, politely, to cough up the details on how the *Sunday Press* got the story and advising me to retain legal counsel. I should have replied, 'Hey, judge, ask Kelly. Or better again, ask his car.'

That's the way things were in Burgh Quay, and if you didn't get a bizarre story to chase up when you arrived at six bells on a Saturday evening, you certainly got one when you returned back to the office from the 11 p.m. cutline in Kennedy's. By then, the chief sub, Willie Collins, had trawled through the Country editions of the alternative 'Sundays' searching for his beloved 'follow-ups'.

The calm, urbane, pipe-smoking Collins was a master of the 'follow-up', and the one that always stays in my mind was the great Roderic O'Connor art forgery rumpus.

A *Sunday Indo* art critic had opined on page forty-eight, or somewhere even more remote in the newspaper, that one of the paintings in a retrospective exhibition of the artist was ... wait for it ... a forgery. Jesus wept – to the power of two – a forgery. Collins was probably the only man in Burgh Quay at the time with the patience to read the *Sunday Indo*.

'The *Indo* have thrown in the ball, Ken, and we're going to run with it,' he puffed.

Within half an hour we had gallery owners and leading Trinity art historians fuming and blackguarding about the claim and, with words like 'outrageous, scurrilous, baseless and shocking' bandied about liberally, the story took on the beauty of an O'Connor painting by city edition time.

A great *Sunday Press* 'follow-up' and a four-day bawling match between the opposing factions followed, culminating in an *Indo* apology on some obscure page near the greyhound racing results.

I have had some great Saturday nights in my life – and I intend to have many more – but few will compare to a 6–2 a.m. *Sunday Press* shift with Kelly and Collins.

The unlikely hero overseeing this *Sunday Press* news culture was none other than Vincent Jennings – an aloof, polite, slightly patrician and unstreetwise sort of guy who wound up as one of the chief pall-bearers for the deceased newspaper group. What a dreadful personal calamity.

But if the *Sunday Press* had galloping news-driven culture, the *Evening Press* brought this culture to epic shout-in-your-face proportions.

'Are you free? Hi. Don't take off your coat, there's a murder out on the southside.' It's the news editor, Dermot McIntyre, on a roll, and I am saying to myself, 'Ah, fuck it, not again.'

The Donegal man had every news obsession in the book, even down to the vagaries of the seasonal retailing of the humble spud. Without fail, every new potato season, Dermot would arrive back from his lunchtime shopping in Moore Street and rage about the fact that the Molly Malones were selling new spuds from Cyprus. Jesus wept to the power of three.

'Get on to north Dublin growers and find out what's wrong with their harvests. We're importing potatoes from Cyprus for God's sake. Never heard the like of it,' he would fume.

McIntyre was formidable when it came to the rights and wrongs of things, and even had me convinced during the eighties that the newfangled microwave ovens caused cancer. I was so convinced that even today – thirty years later – I wouldn't touch one with a forty-foot bargepole.

Microwave ovens aside, news accuracy and big, in-your-face headlines were the stock in trade of McIntyre and his commandants, Mick Sharkey and Paul Dunne, and when you put all this well-directed a.m. mayhem together – alongside Con Houlihan writing elegantly on page one on a good sports day – you had an unbeatable magic formula.

But God protect you if you had an inaccuracy in your copy.

I remember doing 'day-town' one bright morning and hearing from a usually reliable source in Pearse Street Garda Station that the drug squad had lifted nineteen kilograms of heroin from a van on O'Connell Bridge the previous night.

'How much is nineteen kilograms of heroin worth on the street?' I asked Tom Brady, our ruthlessly efficient security correspondent back then – and a great man with a calculator.

'£420,000, Ken,' he replied.

Brilliant – a lovely 'lash it out' story ('short takes, please') – but sometimes some things are too good to be true. It turned out that the '19k' the garda source was talking about was old pound notes and not kilograms. 'Fuck it.' So I had to make the long walk into the editor, Sean Ward's, office to tell him that the story was wrong. I said I had cocked up the figures, adding, to ease my pain and his, that I was never good at maths at school.

'Is that a fact, Ken? Look it, you could work out the takings from a winning yankee in less than a minute,' he replied gruffly, before telling chief sub Jim Carwood, in no uncertain terms, what to do with my heroin story. Monkeys and places where the sun doesn't shine were the gist of his instructions.

Pure mortification followed, and a temporary absence from the serious *Evening Press* cutline prognostications between Jim Carwood, literary editor David Marcus, Paul Dunne and me about the best handicapped horses running at exotic locations like Catterick Bridge in the afternoon.

Where would you get it? By the way, you can say what you want about David Marcus (and it all will be good), but he was some guy with the form book.

Over in the *Irish Press* the same news culture prevailed, but with much more politics, and mostly not of the Fianna Fáil variety, much to the annoyance of the Soldiers of Destiny. Yes, Fianna Fáil always got their great words reported. They had to since the paper was founded by the one and only Irish Machiavelli, but it was run on the old Tim Pat Coogan maxim that there was a 'huge difference between being a friend and being a lackey.' Certainly, the newsroom never came under any pressure to hack it out for FF, and if the truth be told, the Fianna Fáil party had a greater affection for papers than the journalists had for the party.

The friendship element of this indefinite relationship certainly worked to the advantage of the papers on numerous occasions. Late one night in Government Buildings, the trade unions steamed out from national pay talks, spitting venom about a total breakdown in communications and negotiations. They were on fire. As the industrial reporters raced to the phones to tell the story, I was quietly called back into the Taoiseach's office for a parlay.

Taoiseach Haughey, with a wave of his hand, simply said: 'You can tell the good readers of the *Irish Press* that a national pay deal will be signed at lunchtime tomorrow and it will be 3 per cent with a six-month pay pause.' And so it transpired, at noon the next day, much to the annoyance of the newspaper opposition, who were reporting industrial Armageddon. Thank you very much, C.J.H.

The other side of this coin is best exemplified by a routine story I was sent one Sunday in Sutton about the effect the construction of the Dart line was having on property prices in the area.

The FF government sent out a cabinet minister to allay the bank balance fears of the local population, only for the great intellectual to meander off-script and tell the gathering that the cabinet was considering taxing children's allowances. Jesus wept to the power of four.

Splash in the bag, and four days of denial from the every government minister who wasn't at the meeting, before the inevitable announcements in the Dáil that the words reported in the *Irish Press* were true. It was just that the minister was merely thinking and speaking aloud in the wrong place.

And at no point during this kerfuffle did Tim Pat Coogan question the accuracy of the story. He was certainly no lackey.

When Coogan left the *Irish Press*'s editorial chair, some of that old news spirit left with him. You'd have days when a Labour Party walkout at cabinet ('We're here looking for a head, Albert') was relegated to page three because some row between would-be TV personalities was deemed more important. There were also days when the credit for killer political stories by Emily O'Reilly would go to the *Indo* and *The Times*, who merely lifted her reports verbatim from the *Irish Press*'s Country edition.

By the early nineties I was elected Father of the Chapel and witnessed first-hand how fractured the management relationship between the de Valeras and Ingersolls had become. It was inevitable that everything would end up in the courts. The Ingersoll faction always chose the nuclear option when it came to industrial relations, and on a good day simply goaded the trade unions just for practice.

On the one side you had Vincent Jennings trying to keep the show on the road, and on the other the Ingersolls, who cared more about their junk investment than the institution. It was ugly.

I remember Colm Rapple, the group business editor, and a member of the chapel committee, questioning the Ingersoll valuations on *Irish Press* property one day, only to be threatened with the door for his truthfulness. The commonsensical intervention of Niall Connolly, then the editorial manager, halted this stupidity. When he was asked by the Ingersolls what the journalists would do if they fired Colm, Connolly bluntly told them: 'Whelan and the chapel committee will go into Mulligan's and have a gin and tonic, and then close the place.' 'But what if we discipline him?' asked the Ingersoll man. Niall replied: 'Oh well, they will have two gin and tonics and close the place.'

The Ingersolls came close to closing the place on numerous occasions during my two years as FOC, and probably would have were it not for the restraining influence of Jennings, Connolly, *Sunday Press* editor Michael Keane and other FOCs like Kate Shanahan, John Kelly and Ronan Quinlan, and, undoubtedly, Colm Rapple himself.

Looking back on it now, the real tragedy was that everyone should have known that junk bonds and Republican bonds don't mix, and the experiment should never have been attempted. The whole place fell apart twenty years ago, and the only traces of what was a great national treasure that you will find around Burgh Quay these days are the few newspaper mementos that still hang on the walls of Mulligan's of Poolbeg Street.

But if you are ever having a pint in that fine place, and you listen hard enough, you may hear the raucous banter of long-gone reporters, photographers, subs and printers all arguing the toss about everything under God's sun. But if you hear a loud 'Hey, kid' while drinking the best pint in Dublin, best get into your car and vamoose.

Our Lady of Fatima Mansions who was blessed by the Pope

Isabel Conway
(News Reporter)

It was an early morning of chaos at the *Evening Press* long table in Burgh Quay. Each potential front-page lead resembled last night's congealed greasy takeaway.

The 'huge blaze' at a Wicklow factory, phoned in by the local tip-off man (given to exaggeration) turns out to be a minor fire instead of an inferno. One of the wizards of the *Evening Press* permanent news team, the late Brendan Burke, could be relied on to produce riveting fast copy if all else failed about a major disaster (a filling station down the road in danger of exploding) averted by the speedy arrival of the fire brigade.

There were many 'ifs' and 'could haves' on slow news days when every traffic accident, fire or pub brawl took on earth-shattering proportions. Big and sometimes massive stories broke, and the *Irish* and *Evening Press* newshounds and snappers were on the scene quickly, priding ourselves, whether true or not, on delivering more accurate and less sensationalist accounts than the competition.

Wild goose chases were par for the course. A fracas between quarrelling neighbours in Fatima Mansions could easily become 'all-out war' after a delinquent minor was caught carving 'fucking bastards' with a razor blade on the adjoining front door.

The clock was ticking away and tension was mounting fast on this particular morning when deliverance came clothed in tragedy. A woman's 'sympathetic approach' was needed, muttered the newsdesk, dealing me the short straw. A photographer and I took off in a cloud of exhaust, tearing the innards out of the office Mazda, to the wilds of a tough Dublin suburb to 'call on' the family of a pre-teen killed in a joyriding accident. The hostility you met on doorsteps on tricky and sensitive house calls was offset by the misfortune of the *Herald* getting there first to elicit enough quotes for a spread and, far worse, to 'be let in'.

On this freezing winter morning we broke every speed limit to beat the opposition to the stricken house. A line of beaten-up cars were drawn up outside a thrashed terraced home. I was more than halfway up the path, walking hesitantly as befits this kind of call (which most of us hated doing), as the blinds moved. The door flew open, a stream of four-letter bugger-off-like sentiments were shouted, and then a huge snarling dog like Arkle on speed galloped out.

In utter terror I made for the side wall and cleared it, falling on top of a bunch of nettles next door. Some might say we were getting our just rewards for intruding on a family's grief and privacy. I was not looking forward to phoning in. Evening paper (and tabloid) news editors, as we in the business know, have an aversion to failure, and the doorstep is no exception.

In the pre-mobile-phone days of the early 1980s you could never find a public telephone box that had not been vandalised. We often knocked on people's doors, trying not to look like Jehovah Witness callers – picking houses with well-kept gardens and snowy lace curtains – offering whoever answered a handful of coins and pleading for the brief use of their phone for a local call – this was a big *Press* emergency and we could be sacked if we didn't ring them. That generally worked.

'I am not always right, but I'm never wrong,' *Evening Press* news editor, Dermot McIntyre, was fond of saying. Short-tempered, tense and often unreasonable as deadlines approached, he was a bit of a softie underneath. Dermot could be a hard taskmaster, but his eccentric ways won me over and he didn't hold grudges. As the editions got away he unwound by telling fantastically tall, long-winded stories that qualified for Ripley's 'Believe it or Not', generally involving himself, claiming they were 'the honest truth and all' . Hardly listening as I described almost being savaged to death by Coolock's Hound of the Baskervilles, he barked, 'Go on to copy and file, then talk to the picture desk.'

To prove we were there, I duly dictated a few paragraphs to a bored copy-taker. The psycho dog reception had morphed into 'traumatised family too upset to talk'. The frantic nature of evening paper journalism meant that, even though desks were side-by-side, proper communication could pass them by. A persuasive voice on the picture desk, in all seriousness, was now asking: 'Can you go back and ask nicely through the letterbox if they've a picture, like a first Communion photo, and we'll return it?' The long route back to Burgh Quay with a leisurely coffee break on the way calmed our frayed nerves.

Looking back, sometimes there was a lot to be said for not having mobile phones at times like this, being instantly contactable, under pressure to tweet and blog, though my video link that day might have gone viral on YouTube.

A news reporter vacancy was coming up at the *Irish Press* in 1978, and I would have every chance of getting into Burgh Quay according to one of the matinee idols of the day, Martin Daly. We were working hard at pulling a bit of controversy out of a teachers' conference in Sligo. Now and then I have bizarre nightmares related to my job interview for the *Press*. They usually involve Tim Pat Coogan's bushy eyebrows. I imagine that he was unimpressed by what he saw. I had none of the feistiness or opinionated confidence of a future Mary Kenny, his muse in the 1960s. Chief news editor Mick O'Kane – a fantastic newsman, fair and out to give his reporters, regardless of their sex, a chance to shine – did his best to put me at ease.

I didn't get the job, but the one who did left after a week, setting a record, it was said, in non-staying power at the coalface of Burgh Quay. The sudden vacancy was conveyed by telephone, and I was offered the senior reporter position without having to endure the longest half hour of my life again in that editorial conference room.

Most of the greats of Irish journalism had worked at one time or another in the *Irish Press*, many talents staying on despite the lure of higher wages elsewhere because they truly loved the place. The previous woman journalist (we were in a minority back then) to occupy my desk at Burgh Quay was the legendary Diane Chanteau. She would be a hard act to follow, I was warned. So I tried that bit harder at wedging my foot politely in doors and at least returning with a story. As a Dutch-based stringer for UK tabloids and broadsheets later, the *Irish Press* courteous-firm-foot-in-the-door approach would prove useful.

Seconded from the *Press*'s London office on Fleet Street, Diane Chanteau was outrageous, charming and fearless. Recognising and pinning down stories, she bucked the status quo, ignoring anything that got in the way of her pursuit of the truth behind the waffle. It is no wonder that, after leaving journalism, Diane (she is a great friend – we first met through our shared admiration for Aidan Hennigan, *Irish Press* London editor whom we see regularly) was a natural as a QC prosecutor.

Luck is essential in journalism – getting to a vital source a few minutes before they are due to leave for the airport or the handlers take over, being in the right place at the right time as a momentous event occurs. In recovery mode after a late night's partying in the mid 1970s, Diane – who had stepped out for a ciggie and some downtime – came up with the *Evening Press* lead as a human torso floated past in the river below.

Seven and a half months pregnant, I was sent to Tralee to try and interview the (also heavily pregnant) wife of a key figure in the Kerry Babies drama, a strange saga involving alleged police cover-ups and enough lies and red herrings to cover the entire Wild Atlantic Way. The team of T. P. O'Mahony, Fergus Black and me were based for weeks at Benners Hotel, Tralee. Here we knocked back the G & Ts late into the night in the company of the likes of Nell McCafferty, Dr John Harbison (state pathologist) and a smattering of junior and senior counsels.

The 'wronged wife' on whose door I knocked, who had not spoken about being at the centre of a national 'scandal', allowed me inside and put me sitting on a chair as I half fainted on her doorstep. We were Comrades in Bumps. Her front door was closing when the *Irish Independent* got to the gate. Being clearly male and not pregnant he had no chance in the world of qualifying for a cup of water and a sit-down in Mrs Locke's kitchen.

'Miss' Betty Hooks, editorial secretary and keeper of the markings book that dictated our working existence from the power house of the chief editor's filing cabinet, told me years later that she remonstrated with Mick O'Kane about sending me off down to Tralee because of my 'advanced' state of pregnancy. O'Kane replied: 'If anyone gets in that door, she has the best chance' – a shrewd assessment, and one that worked.

The vast newsroom at Burgh Quay had pockets of calm and introspection as well as emergency wings and haemorrhaging pockets of mayhem. The *Evening Press* features area was an awfully nice place around the corner, with an air of privileged endeavour impervious to the mad world on its borders.

If you were not working at the long news table, you embedded yourself safely into cosy corners on the periphery. But you could never be sure that someone else's notebooks, dirty teacup and stale biscuits would not be ferreted away in the unlocked drawer assigned to you. And after a few days off, an unfamiliar face – freelance casuals came and went a lot those days because they were cheap, willing, and had hopes of being staffed – might have squatter's rights to your desk.

We wrote our stories on dilapidated office typewriters that regularly seized up. There were far too few of them, and some staff, notably the industrial correspondent, George Douglas, worked off their own portable typewriters. We could be typing away crazily with seconds to spare on deadlines when keys blocked and ribbons broke. Copy-boys (some of whom are household names in Irish journalism now) stood by ready to dart off with 'takes', paragraphs at a time ripped away from the carbon blacks.

Mulligan's was a second home for some. We knew the ones whose first pint coincided with the rolling of the presses for the first edition. So, in an emergency, the search team headed for Mulligan's, or even the White Horse. Occasionally we held chapel meetings of our union in Mulligan's backroom. Leave-taking sessions were always held there, and you always met colleagues, morning, noon or night. Nine times out of ten, the great, late Con Houlihan – absent-mindedly opening his tattered atlas and pulling out a tenner to pay for a drink, or putting it on his tab – could be found in deep thought or conversation in Mulligan's.

Some of the characters were dying off by the time I reached Burgh Quay, but the place continued to be hugely entertaining, peopled by kind and immensely talented professionals. We used to say that if they stopped paying us we would still turn up. Some of us regularly called in on days off to meet friends in the newsroom, catch up on the gossip or lend a hand on a story.

Among the cuttings and photographs I cherish in memory of a decade at the *Press* are the type-written arrangements for coverage of John Paul II's historic visit to Ireland. It was the biggest story most of us had ever covered, or would be part of again. The *Press* schedule of coverage, the culmination of weeks of planning by newsdesk man Andrew Bushe at the Phoenix Park is classic. Equipment: two pairs of binoculars and three sets of radio contact equipment, two telephones for the entire news team located in the *Press* Centre. Emmanuel Keogh writing the colour story for the *Sunday Press*, the late Sean McConnell and Stephen Collins sharing a pair of binoculars to observe Pope and altar, reporting on the ceremonies and participants, Fergus Black, Tim Hastings and Philip Molloy placed like snipers covering the crowds, others observing the build-up of excitement. Then there was the late Sheila Walsh – doyenne of the diplomatic circuit – circulating among the VIPs at a party in the nearby American Ambassador's residence, to tell the world about the view, what they ate and drank, and who was there.

My own instructions were the following: 'Isabel Conway positioned among the sick, main job to try and get close to the Pope should he stop to talk to individual people who are ill.' Luck was with me. I got to shake the Pope's hand, not once but twice, after borrowing a child to push into his arms to bless.

The best of days during the best of times.

Let sleeping subs lie
(under the desk)

Fred Johnston
(Sports Subeditor, 1972–1973)

During the Burgh Quay interview, it became apparent that my desire to be a reporter was about to be dissolved. It was 1972. I thought I had followed the correct course, from writing features for the old *Woman's Choice* magazine to carrying through an 'apprenticeship' in court and general reporting for the *Drogheda Independent* for a year.

Indeed, Mary Kenny had published my very first effort some time before, a piece on the hairdressing industry. But things had rather overtaken me, and I sat for the *Irish Press* interview sans the now requisite certificate from a school of journalism.

It was a subs' desk for me. The *Evening Press*, sports. Apart from being competently able to proof a page, I was unacquainted with the mystical geometry of page layout and its arcane arithmetical architecture. The subs' desk was a long altar flanked by high priests of the art whose expertise mesmerised me. Paddy 'The Flynner' Flynn held court here, flicking typed pages over the bench at me, and sometimes, in those days, hand-scrawled parish sports results, accompanied by a lightly barked instruction on column length and typeface size. Seán Diffley sat adjacent, at The Flynner's side, and John O'Shea flitted back and forth, full of information.

It came to me quickly that some of the subs were extremely knowledgeable about, and even practitioners of, the various sports upon which they subbed. Consequently, there were languages spoken here daily that I had some difficulty interpreting, an intimacy with the vagaries of the champions and assorted players of myriad sports that I could not penetrate. The sports subs' desk was a foreign country. I was helped and coaxed along, however, with a tolerance I scarcely deserved, and my blunders corrected. Subbing the racing results was a particular tedium.

On occasion, I had to learn by rough experience. One day, sent up to the stone, I was leaning precariously over a set page, reading back to front and upside down quite fluidly, when a roar over my shoulder informed me that there would be consequences if I so much as attempted to rest a probing finger on any of the type. Nonetheless, it was a strange adventure later to wander around the print room, closely supervised, up over walkways where the metal railings were drenched in black ink-dust and the whole place resembled the cavernous engine room of a ship.

Curious customs lived around the subs' desk. Arriving early one Saturday morning, I sat at my place and felt my feet collide with something soft. And it moved, but not much. A sub was asleep there, quite contentedly, on the floor, and under the protecting shade of the massive desk. One by one, other subs arrived and sat. Once he had been identified, no further attention was paid to him. He was left to surface under his own steam.

On a particularly frantic Saturday morning, I found myself donning a pair of headphones in a booth along with a row of young women, our task being to take down the half-comprehensible screeching of sports reporters or stringers in, I imagined, freezing and windy phone-boxes in deepest rural Ireland. It was as close as I would ever get to dealing with foreign correspondents.

Stricken with an attack of migraine that left me half blind for an hour, I stumbled one day down the stairs and into the neo-Victorian lavatories and consequent reduced light. This was a place of confessional calm, into which the convulsions of the great newspaper could not intrude. In those days, smoking heavily and anywhere was the norm. Yet there was a peculiarly illicit pleasure in having a quick puff in these dribbling lavatories. Back, then, and up into the smells of printer's ink and the tap of typewriters. Being unable to see things properly did not, apparently, inhibit my subbing duties.

I was not suited to the job. I hadn't too many sports bones in my body. So my days at the hallowed sports sub shrine were numbered. Looking back from this distance, I realise that, almost in spite of myself, I learned a lot there, about deadlines, about coherent writing, about decent editing. It has all stood me in good stead. Tired, gritty-eyed, the big windows behind me stern and tall over the River Liffey, I sometimes imagined myself seated in an ancient and exotic church, waiting for small but vital mysteries to unfold.

A blueshirt girl among the Northern media mafia

Mary Harte
(Freelance Reporter/Feature Writer, *Evening Press* and
Irish Press, 1982–1983)

I should never have crossed the threshold of the Irish Press Group. My political profile was all wrong; I was the enemy. I grew up surrounded by portraits of Michael Collins in his army regalia and was nurtured, even indoctrinated, by two staunch pro-Treaty grandmothers who both grew up amidst the internecine violence that pervaded the borderlands of Donegal and Derry during the War of Independence and the Civil War.

My grandfather and grand-uncle were among the first recruits to the Free State Army. Neither shied away from doling out their political opinions, which, while overtly anti Fianna Fáil, were in truth anti de Valera. 'Up Dev, free beef' was a phrase I heard frequently. And then there was the small matter of my father, a Fine Gael TD. So, in the great scheme of things, Burgh Quay was the last place I should have begun a career in journalism. But that is where I headed, and I'm very glad and proud that I did, because it's where I learned the rudiments of sharp reporting and met some of the most creative, witty, charming, abrupt people, whose energy and dedication never ceased to amaze me, and who worked as hard as they played.

My time as a freelancer at the *Press* was fleeting. I left newsprint for a full-time job in broadcast journalism with the BBC, yet the experience was long enough to engrave forever a special place in my heart. I have only fond memories of those heady days but that's not to say the lot of a cub reporter was easy – it was anything but.

So why in the summer of 1980 did I turn my sights on Burgh Quay and not Abbey Street and the *Independent,* the perceived propaganda machine of Fine Gael? Simple. I happened to know someone in the IP, an RTÉ reporter I'd met some years earlier during an election campaign in Donegal. I'd had a hankering that I'd like to be a journalist for some time, a sort of *All the President's Men* Woodward and Bernstein kind of hankering: starry-eyed, I saw myself as an investigative reporter who could rid Ireland of all manner of corruption.

Seán Ó hÉalaí had moved to the features department at Burgh Quay and agreed to meet me, in hindsight I believe more out of curiosity than any potential he saw in me as a feature writer. I was a young graduate with a stint in the EEC in Brussels under my belt, but little or no writing experience. I'm not sure what I was expecting to find that day, possibly a glamorous scene akin to the *Washington Post.* I was disappointed. Through the mayhem that was the newsroom, the haze of smoke and the din of typewriters, I arrived at features to meet my contact. Seán didn't mince his words: 'So you want to work in the *Press* do you? Well, you know there's no money in features and you'll have to learn to type and take shorthand?' I quickly realised that I was pretty useless without the tools of the trade. This was pre-media-degree Ireland, pre laptop computers. In fact, telephones didn't even have keypads: in Dublin they had the rotary finger wheel, in Donegal it was a wind-up handle.

My first assignment was a test as much as a need to fill a page. Seán, a Derry man, wanted a two-page feature on his native city's economic downturn – no pressure there, then. Two weeks later, and even more in debt after my bus trip over the border, my first full-page feature was published and I got my first byline. It's hard to describe the elation I felt the first day my name appeared in print. I still have my copy of the original article. It was probably the first time the *Irish Press* found its way into my home in Donegal.

There was certainly little money in freelance writing, and I fed myself with what money I made as an all-night waitress in Jury's Coffee Dock, but it was the only way I could build up a portfolio to become a member of the National Union of Journalists. Without an NUJ card it was nigh impossible to get any work in the newsroom, which was virtually controlled by the union. I sauntered in and out of the features department, avoiding the hacks in the newsroom who rarely lifted their heads from the typewriters (and if they did it was to snarl at someone who happened to get in their way). To be honest, they terrified the wits out of me. On the other hand, they seemed a much more benign bunch in features: Seán, Campbell Spray and Damien Kiberd, although I know some would venture to say they were really the wolves in sheep's clothing.

On occasion the features department assigned me a pseudonym because I could glean information on my visits to Leinster House to meet my father for the free lunch. Once my byline was 'Mary McGoldrick', my mother's maiden name, but my cover was blown by the late Ted Nealon, who told me it took him a few days to figure it out.

As the author of *Nealon's Guide to the Dáil and Senate* he knew the maiden name of every TD's and senator's wife. On another occasion I met Albert Reynolds, who jovially greeted me with the words, 'It was you, wasn't it?' The previous Saturday night I had been in the Ashling Hotel in Parkgate Street and spotted a huddled group at the back of the restaurant. It was during one of the many purges against Charlie Haughey's leadership. I tipped off John Kelly at the *Sunday Press* newsdesk. The picture of the 'gang' scurrying away in a Merc made it onto the back page the next morning, and into the annals of clandestine Haughey stories.

Then there was the time when I ended up on the front page of the *Press* and it wasn't a byline – no, it was the off-lead headline. I answered the early morning knock on my front door to be greeted by a *Press* reporter whom I knew to see, Tomás MacRuairi. He was accompanied by Eric Luke, the photographer, and greeted me with the words, 'Congratulations, Mary.' I was baffled. I hadn't entered any competition as far as I knew, not even 'Spot the Ball'. Tomás handed me his copy, fresh off the printing press: 'Government minister's daughter gets top job'. I found myself plunged into a political storm in a teacup and a media hunt to track me down. I quickly learned what it was like to be on the other side of a story and, more importantly, that all political leaks have an agenda. This one had to do with a dispute between the minister for justice in the new Fitzgerald-led Fine Gael/Labour coalition and the civil servants at the Government Information Service.

Jim Mitchell wanted a press officer in Justice, but the GIS informed him that it was not advisable because of the sensitivity around national security and Northern Ireland. So he sounded out a few journalists, including me, about the merits of appointing his own press officer, something that is the norm nowadays. Tomás left with my version of the story, but Eric didn't get his picture. Afterwards, the journalist who wrote the story apologised to me; he had no idea that I was the same person he'd been tipped off about. Like John Boy Walton, I learned a lot that summer.

I eventually got my NUJ card, thanks in no small way to a mighty battle waged by FOC John Kelly with the Dublin Branch, which had much to do with party politics and little to do with journalistic credentials. It's a long story, but suffice it to say that John and I have dined out on it many times.

I was now on the next rung of the *Irish Press* corporate ladder, or, more precisely, I could now apply for freelance shifts in the newsroom.

This time the interview was a bit more daunting. Again I was led up the creaking stairs to the real editor's office. Tim Pat Coogan put the fear of God in me, but I don't know why because he was one of the most polite and charming editors I have met in my long years in journalism – and I have met plenty. Then out into the madhouse that was the newsroom, and the first person to welcome me was the news editor, Dermot McIntyre. 'Your father and I were in the same class in primary school.' I knew I was in safe hands. It wasn't long before I discovered that the newsroom in those days was actually under the control of a Media Mafia from my bailiwick, Derry, Donegal and Tyrone.

I realised that I was among my own. I would like to think my two grandmothers would have approved, regardless of the de Valera banner. They had both passed away by the time I secured my first reporting shift.

My introduction to the rigours of accurate reporting was in the Children's Court under the watchful eye of the diminutive Ann Flaherty, who seemed way too young to be showing me the ropes – which she did expertly. Many years later I worked with her husband, Fergal Keane, in the BBC. Dublin Corporation and Planning Appeals were also on the initiation list. On my first posting to City Hall to a Planning Appeal, the two seasoned reporters from the two other dailies asked if I would join them in the pub across the road. When one of them became a little worse for wear, we proceeded to agree that we would agree the gist of the story and the sober senior would write it up and we'd copy it. Far be it from me to break with a long-standing tradition.

Generally, it was like that when you worked a freelance shift, be it a press conference, council meeting or community event – there was always a kind reporter if you got into difficulties, regardless of which paper you represented. There were many occasions too when the *Evening Press* was the only paper at an event, one of the reasons, I believe, for its success.

Then there was Mull's – for a young reporter like me it was like nothing I'd ever experienced. It was the office without the office, a safe haven from whatever deadline was lurking around the corner. In later years when I worked abroad I would invariably find a press club and think of Mulligan's, because it, too, was an exclusive club: the 'cosy' where great raconteurs perform with their peers, the urban myths grow and escapades get re-enacted. The drink was only an excuse.

I'm extremely proud to have played my part in the *Press* gang at Burgh Quay. The men and women I met during my time there were dedicated to the cause of journalism. And, for the record, no one in the *Irish Press* ever asked me about my political persuasions or what I thought of de Valera. I never asked them either. After all, we were reporters first and foremost.

Have change for the phone box, but don't mention the wages

Ann Cahill
(Reporter)

When Tim Pat Coogan asked me, an eighteen-year-old journalism student in Rathmines, what I thought of his newspaper, I followed the precepts I was being taught and put honesty first: it looks like a mortuary card, I told him earnestly.

He didn't seem to appreciate my candour, but I'd finished my interview with him for my thesis and thought no more of it.

I didn't get one of the three jobs promised to the three top students at the end of the year-long Rathmines course. The strict intake limit of no more than 25 per cent girls apparently applied to the jobs too, and despite coming second in the end of year exams, I took the traditional route of provincial papers for a few years.

Chatting to the deputy news editor a few years later after phoning in some court copy from a phone box in Edenderry, he offered me a job. 'Right,' I said. I was deeply sceptical after having various applications ignored, and told them so at my interview (what was it about Burgh Quay that forced one to risk candid remarks?)

A few weeks later I turned up for my first day at work at the *Irish Press* after my bank holiday weekend honeymoon, only to get a frosty reception and be asked, 'So what do we call you?'

'We'll hardly be swapping exclusives as pillow talk, we're just married,' I said, or thought I said, as I realised that they feared there was a spy in the camp; my husband worked across the river

232

in the *Indo*. (I did lend him a Biro once when we met on a job for the *Evenings*.)

I just loved working for the *Press* (and the *Evening Press* especially), and soon remembered never to leave the house without change for the public phone box. I also quickly learned to shout a story from my meagre notes to the copy-taker, and loved those who would remind you when 'you said that already,' or sighed when it was becoming boring. And I loved Dermot McIntyre shouting 'hai, hai' down the room, tearing the copy from the typewriter and rushing up to the subs. It drove some people to distraction, but it made me giggly and happy.

One of my first breaks was when George Douglas, the industrial relations correspondent, was going on holidays and I was asked to fill in for him. He even let me use his typewriter, which surprised most people as he reverently locked it away when he was not using it. When he returned from his holiday, to my surprise, he told me I did very well. But I was dumbstruck when he said that, in future, when doing stories about wage increases, I mustn't include the actual sum that workers got; I should mention only the percentage increase. 'Otherwise their wives will know how much they are earning,' he told me.

I may have been the first journalist in the country to take maternity leave, as it had just been introduced. I did my best to fool everyone for as long as I could, wearing tight clothes one day and loose the next. However, I do remember Michael Sharkey asking me if I'd robbed the curtains for my dress one day! I took a four-week holiday during the sixth month, and there was no denying my bump when I returned, so I made the official announcement.

'Do you want to be in or out?' Well if it was going to be like that, I decided I had better choose 'out'. Which turned out to be a near-permanent marking in the Special Criminal Court. Judges falling off their perches; superintendents' word taken as law;

no jury – which would have been an all-male affair at that time anyhow. But my main job, I realised quickly, was to make it up the stairs to the reporters' room first to take control of the solitary typewriter. My colleagues were almost always senior reporters, legends, with impeccable copperplate shorthand and a habit of bickering over intros that usually began with 'At the Special Criminal Court yesterday.' I nodded as often as I remembered as they read out their paragraphs, and got on with writing my 'modern-style court report', though relying totally on them for correct quotes.

Quite often, by the end of the day, the boys had had a very good liquid lunch across the road and needed a hand getting back to HQ. Sometimes it meant leading one or more safely inside the door of their office and handing them over to the porter, having tucked their copy into their pocket. There was the occasional phone call from a fretful news editor in another publication asking for the whereabouts of the person or the copy, which meant they had managed to escape the guiding hand of the porter to some other watering hole.

And then one morning, with the papers full of the story of the man who was sentenced to hang for the capital murder of a garda, I was dispatched to Co. Kildare to talk with his mother. I found her home faster than I would have liked, and walked past it a number of times wondering how I could do this. I got the bright idea to call to a neighbour. To my surprise and relief, the lady who answered the door said it was a great idea and the family would like me to call.

I still relive that walk to the cottage and the less-than-strong knock on the door and the shock of the welcome, immediately being brought in, sat down and handed a cup of tea, and then brought upstairs to the mother's bedside. I can see a tiny, elderly lady, her rosary beads in hand, some morning newspapers on her bed and a cup and saucer on the bedside table. When it was explained to her why I was there, she took my hand in hers and thanked me for calling. I didn't ask her one question. She talked about her son and his wife – she blamed nobody, and regretted the way things turned out. She understood that they all had a job to do, was sorry for those who had the difficult task of deciding that her son should die, and wasn't I good to call? I couldn't take notes through the tears. And then I remembered I was working and needed to get to a phone box and ring over copy for the *Evening* before I missed another deadline.

The story, of course, was quickly overtaken by appeals and pardons, and tomorrow's shift was another day in the *Press*.

Despite Diane Chanteau's advice to 'bung the baby on the bottle and come back to work', I didn't, and it was quite a few years later before I wrote again for the *Irish* and *Evening Press*. I was freelancing in Cork, back writing news for them when T. P. O'Mahony left, and wrote the splash for one of the final editions of the *Irish Press*.

It's hard to believe that it's twenty years since it closed.

One minute we were safe as tethered goats...

Mary Moloney
(News Subeditor/Deputy Chief Subeditor/Feature
Writer/Film Critic, *Evening Press*, 1979–1995)

OMG.... It was the angst I'll never forget, the years of shifting emotions and sifting rumours about asbestos, takeovers, cutbacks, even robots who would one day replace us. Twenty years is a lifetime, and after death and loss there is closure, only we had it the other way around. The end, when it came, was a shock, but an unhappy – not a happy – release, of sorts.

After months of unrelenting tensions, it was capitulation without condition; in any war, the losers are goners.

We were mad to last the course, to hang on, hang out, assume we'd have manna, if not from Heaven from some tycoon intermittently wheeled in to assess what remained of the still-writhing carcass as we held our collective bad breaths in what might now be deemed mindful contemplation. Two decades ago it was a gasping last grab at a get-out-of-jail card.

For years we paddled like hapless ducks through flotsam, unaware it was dragging us down, thinking we were at any time free to fly away, take flight and head back to Herbert Park.

By the time conditions had got really bad it was too late to leave. We were institutionalised. Our united psyches contorted. Instead of escaping the leaking canoe, we'd spent Friday nights subsidising going-away parties and pressies for Pressites heading to safe and more strategically well-paid berths. We were daft. It was scary to leave, and just as scary to stay.

Were lives lost due to the stress? Did relationships crumble, ill health take a foothold? As morale faltered in that last year, sick days multiplied, pressures mounted, even the freelances ran for cover. Not everyone went on to prosper. Names and faces have become shrouded in a mist of false hopes. It had been edgy for ages. No fun any more. That's what I remember.

We had all become used to leading a kind of schizophrenic existence because the *Press* was that sort of place – nothing was ever certain, nothing obvious…. Reality seeped into disbelief. We never had a clue what was really going on, didn't always care, had become used to disrespect as hierarchy ruled. Colleagues picked us up when we fell, switched desks when coffee splashed onto keyboards. We had all the trappings of family intimacy, but inbreeding was wont to create even more havoc among us.

Were we counselled? Consoled? Not at all. The weak just drifted and the tears were shed in private. It wasn't always easy to get a grip. We were always like two halves, torn apart by the wanting and the waiting, signing up for something, not realising it had become something else. Like one day we worked for Irish Press Limited. Next it was Irish Press Newspapers. Our Father of the Chapel was just that – then blink, and he was representing management on the other side of the table. We had years of rising circulation figures followed by a slump. We relearned the alphabet – meaning the ABC of the ad guys, dismissing an older readership we knew how to chase in order to woo the pimply cohort of youth who hadn't money to spend on anything at all, least of all on newsprint.

And when we couldn't sell news, or as many small ads, we had the promotions bods like Lucy Gaffney on the floor with holidays, shopping sprees and baked beans to give away. Well, almost. The late *Evening Press* editor, Sean Ward, was instrumental in starting the Women's Mini-Marathon (cringe-cringe was that Run Girls Run slogan), although maybe, had we just concentrated on sports events like this, we might all now be working for the likes of Rory McIlroy.

We had our glory days, great conditions, short hours, long holidays, good wages – and we were actually paid a work-through allowance for chomping sandwiches at our desks, or hot dogs when the Americans came if we were clever, which we weren't. It wasn't all just jam tomorrow. But the *Press* couldn't sustain the recession of the 1980s; the company was forever in some kind of trouble, and us with it. If it wasn't Tony O'Reilly who was attempting to strangle us, he was supposed to be taking us over, then he wasn't allowed. We gritted our teeth. We'd survive. But, like a lot of addicts, we were of course in denial.

Those Yanks tried to bail us out. The original shareholders were then passing on to the next generation their portfolios as worthless pieces of paper. But the second coming never really came – it was another illusion called Ingersoll. Their chief sidekick, Chazy de Wallaby, famously once asked me why I went swimming in the pool around the corner at lunchtime. The things they wanted to know ... was it corporate curiosity, or was she sizing me up for work as a bikini correspondent? Those times were mad. We weren't on the Ingersoll wavelength – not any of us – but you had to be on the ground to really know it. We were out of the loop. All of us.

I came to the *Evening Press* subeditors' desk in late 1978 on the heels of a UCD degree, a postgraduate journalism course in London, and a short stint on a local newspaper. This is a route lots of people take now, but back then I was twenty-one, suspected, and at my very first union meeting the issue arose as to why I, as a junior, had been appointed to a senior post. I nearly fell through the wooden floorboards, and later a union officer wrote to apologise: it wasn't really about me but about them – and anyway I was in, so untouchable.

Thus I took on the same mantle of paranoia as everyone else, watching for the glint of knives before they hit our backs, not sure if it was day or night as we trundled in at dawn to stir coffee with our pens, recycle teabags and poison ourselves with some of the souring milk left behind by the *Irish Press* shift. We didn't talk for the first hour, but grunted, scanned newspapers, surveyed the wires for explosions, murders or celebrity divorces, edited fast-moving copy from frenetic reporters. We all had visions – attempting to be people other than the ones we appeared to be, moonlighting as writers, poets and wannabes. We had to do something between takes when the Iraq War fizzled out, and saw ourselves as a throbbing heap of creative genius. A pity no one else did.

I was officially a news subeditor, but also a film critic, so I could fly to London to meet the stars on my days off, and became Arts Journalist of the Year for a series of literary interviews. Heady times. Sometimes I was on the *Sunday Press* Saturday night shift waiting for social diarist Terry Keane's copy to land, and then out on my break avoiding the druggie pimps on Burgh Quay. More of the confused existences we led. And there was Adrian MacLoughlin writing books about trains and towns; Aodhán Madden had plays going on in the Peacock Theatre; Brian Lynch wowed with TV drama and poetry; Jack Hanna with a memoir about the life and poetry of his precious son, Davoren.

But we were cutting edge really only because we used scalpels and glue and blades and paper clips as we hit deadlines and carved headlines by cutting out letters with scissors. We rotated in seats away from spiralling cigarette smoke and hangover vibes as the

Evening Press newspapers poured into the backs of the waiting vans outside, dictating increasingly early times off the stone in order to avoid the traffic jams to which they would later contribute. And so the mad circus continued.

We had bomb scares, and ran out of the building fearing for our lives as the Troubles spilt into the south. And we took it all in our stride, or pretended we did. Just how many death threats can an average telephone operator take? Bravado was our middle name.

Despite the intimacy of the *Evening Press* subs' desk, we were part of a big open-plan office, witnessing daily drama – from Sheila Walsh's weekly wedding column victims being wheeled in, to Vivion de Valera (and later his son, Éamon) checking figures on election day as if we were still part of a political machine propping up a fading dynasty. Budget day was bonus day with drinkies locally, or was that All-Ireland GAA Monday when we put Con Houlihan on the front page and sold out?

We were a thriving newspaper for a time, as I've said, but in an industry facing oblivion or change. These high jinks were mentally distressing. As soon as were trained up on a new technological system it was already out of date – but we did pass from hot metal to computers and online files and email.

I had been the only woman on the desk when I joined – Mary Dowey had already come and gone, to write about wine. Others were signed up, such as Helen MacGarry, Lucille Redmond, Helen Rock, Alva MacSherry, Deirdre Falvey and Fionnuala Mulcahy. Our chief sub was Alan Wilkes, who also wrote the best motoring column in the business. He was promoted to the back desk, to be replaced by Jim Carwood, gentleman and racing boffin.

The roll call included Stephen Dixon, Pat Chatten, Brian Phelan, Mick Morris, Liam Scott, Dick O'Riordan, who became editor, Eddie McGuire and Roderick O'Connor. We worked closely with features – John Boland, Paddy Madden, Noeleen Dowling and Patricia Murray – and the newsdesk, finance and sports.

The *Press* was neither staid nor dull. The late, never-to-be-forgotten features editor, Sean McCann, mentioned disappointedly one day that his son, a rookie reporter called Colum, was turning down a contract with the paper to go cycling around the States. Of course he went on to write a book about the trip, and kept on writing to stratospheric heights. I actually recall sympathising with Sean ... was I off my rocker?

Psychologically, those of us left behind were increasingly up against the wall, but didn't acknowledge it, clinging to our outside worlds to keep sane – or trying to. Our wage packets contracted and hours lengthened. We had endless hassles and rows about differential payments, pensions, allowances for picking our noses. We risked getting piles from sitting through union meetings as the management took chances on industrial relations while supposedly stalking the world for backers, so we walked out, walked back in, changed typefaces, redesigned logos. We were glad to still have jobs, fortunate not to be sleeping by the front door of Clery's.

Other newspapers opened, and stayed open, like the *Tribune*, or closed more quickly, like the *Daily News*, and every time the screw tightened and the building seemed to get sicker. We had fire drills. No kidding. And then it was over – the three newspapers in the group were off the streets, and the anguish evaporated into a summer of unrelenting sunshine with nearly all of us convinced we'd be back in the autumn – more useless hopes; more of that unflinching failure to truly grapple with real life.

Our minds were used to the seemingly never-ending series of rescue attempts that would give us steady ground. But in time we went to other places, drifted and prevaricated. I even had a job-share in *The Irish Times* for a time with a former *Press* colleague. Happy families indeed. One minute we were as safe as tethered goats. Maybe. Then we were gone.

City Final

The Last Days

Superquinn vouchers and a superhuman effort to save our bacon

Ronan Quinlan
(Staff Photographer/Father of the Chapel, 1967–1995)

It was a very hot summer in 1995, in more ways than one. I was travelling alone on the Dart from Sutton, heading for the city and enjoying the views from a carriage window on that scorching day. On my knee was a flimsy plastic bag with £20,000 worth of supermarket vouchers for the locked-out journalists of the Irish Press Group of newspapers.

Although it had been expected for a long time, the closure of newspapers came as a huge shock to everyone. For many years the papers had been produced against all the odds by a workforce that tolerated inferior conditions, enforced pay freezes and few resources for the product. On 24 May the management summarily fired the business editor, Colm Rapple. The journalists called a mandatory meeting on the premises, halting production, and demanded his immediate reinstatement. The management refused to countenance any talk of Rapple, saying that he was a 'former employee and would never work for the *Irish Press* again.' It was not untypical of the management's style of negotiation. Within hours of the stoppage we received a missive from the management ordering us to clear the building. The journalists decided to stay, and so began the occupation.

The NUJ called me as Father of the Chapel (shop steward) to Dún Laoghaire, where there was, coincidentally, an Irish

Delegate Conference in progress and Deputy General Secretary Jake Ecclestone handed me written instructions to stop the action forthwith. We knew the NUJ had to take this course to protect itself from a damages suit, and we ignored the instruction. The NUJ gave financial support to members who had just been stripped of their livelihood, and also assisted with legal costs in the months that followed.

The occupation of Burgh Quay only lasted for four days (we stopped it to facilitate talks), but it was to be pivotal in getting support for our actions. Almost immediately the phone calls began and cards and letters started to arrive at the back door of the building, wishing us well in our efforts to revive the papers. Within hours there were unsolicited supplies of food and drink from local shops and pubs to sustain the twenty-five self-incarcerated journalists inside. Then began a steady stream of people calling to the back door on Poolbeg Street to offer support: TDs and senators, government ministers, actors and singers and sports people, too numerous to mention without leaving too many out. There was support also from colleagues in rival publications, from RTÉ and the BBC, from the Garda Press Office and from workers everywhere. Two days after it began, the Irish team were playing at Lansdowne Road and, afterwards, Jack Charlton brought them all in the team bus to the back door to meet the besieged hacks and offer their support.

But the besieged hacks weren't resting. Within a day they decided to do what they did best: to print a newspaper. They called it the *Irish X-Press*, but almost immediately the management threatened legal action if we used the titles and an alteration of them. We had intended to ignore that legal letter, but it inspired a redesign of the masthead and a new name, and so the *X-Press* was born.

This tiny publication was to grow and spread our message and gather support for us from the four corners of Ireland and farther afield over the next few months. The first edition appeared the day after the last *Irish Press* was published, and it never missed an edition until it was finally wound up in August. It was produced with a minimum of facilities using a variety of technologies and printers, with assistance from the most unlikely quarters, and against all efforts from others to stop it. At times it was prepared in living rooms and garages in the dead of night, but it was always produced. It even carried our message worldwide on the fledgling internet.

The *X-Press* told the world what was happening and helped to raise funds for those who, at the time, had no income. It was sold in pubs and shops and on street corners in towns and cities across the country. Our reporters travelled to matches all over Ireland, stopping to sell a few papers before heading back with their reports. There were special editions for the NUJ, for the ICTU conference and for Fianna Fáil, a *Wheels X-Press* and specials for the Irish Open Golf, for the Galway Races and for the All-Ireland GAA Finals and even one for the creditors at the company liquidation in September. The *X-Press* became the flagship of the embattled journalists in their fight to keep the papers going.

The closure of the papers was engineered by the management to shift the blame to someone else, anyone but themselves. I said this on the RTÉ television news on the very first day the papers stopped. The management denied it in statements (they would not appear in any media outlet to answer questions), but within ten days they filed for liquidation and admitted that the Rapple incident had no bearing on the decision. It had clearly been their plan for some time; preparations were well in hand.

The final blow for the *Press* had come on the same day Rapple was fired when the Supreme Court set aside an award of £6m in favour of the *Irish Press* against former partner Ralph Ingersoll and instead awarded costs of £4m against the company. Effectively, this was a further £10m loss on top of the crippling accumulated debts, and was a terminal blow to the very sick entity. The management could see no option but to liquidate the operating company and save whatever assets they could in the holding company and its other subsidiaries. They had long since prepared for this in 1999 when they split the company into separate subsidiaries and thus were able to separate the titles from the papers. Their plan was to dump the operations company, Irish Press Newspapers Ltd, and its 600 staff, and to start again with reduced staff numbers and the backing of Tony O'Reilly and Independent Newspapers, to whom they were already heavily in debt. It was to be yet another failure in a long line of doomed plans.

The company started the process of liquidation, blaming the Supreme Court decision, the government, the Competition Authority and anyone else for their woes. They admitted that the closure had nothing to do with the action taken by the NUJ in defence of Colm Rapple. Labour Court talks on that matter had been adjourned to allow the management to 'consider their conciliation options'. Instead, they used the opportunity to announce liquidation with immediate effect. It was in keeping with our expectations of this devious management.

We opposed the liquidation and applied to the High Court to have an examiner appointed, becoming the first group of workers to use this process. Initially we had the support of the other unions in this, but they unexpectedly and inexplicably pulled out on the night before the hearing. We spent that night and into the next morning rewriting affidavits in the names of three NUJ members, and we arrived exhausted before Mr Justice Frank Murphy. It was ironic that our senior counsel in the case against Éamon de Valera was called Michael Collins! The judge granted our application, which had the backing of creditors like the Revenue Commissioners and the Minister for Enterprise, Trade and Employment. On 26 June, the day before a creditors' meeting was to take place in the Point Depot to liquidate the company, Hugh Cooney was appointed as examiner.

Cooney produced potential investors within ten days of his appointment (we had supplied him with an extensive list), and in the end built sufficient investment to relaunch the three newspaper titles. But the management had no intention of going away, and blocked all external efforts to revive the national institution that was the *Irish Press* by threatening potential investors with protracted Supreme Court appeals. The liquidation finally went ahead in September. Shortly after that, Éamon de Valera and Vincent Jennings announced plans to republish the *Sunday Press*, but this plan, unsurprisingly, and like most of their plans, came to nothing.

That summer of 1995 was the worst of times, with 600 people thrown out of work for all the wrong reasons. But it was also in many ways the best of times. The camaraderie that was always present in the *Irish Press* flourished during that fight, for the *Press* was always a kind of family – with all the usual domestic rows! That summer the spirit of Burgh Quay shone through like a beacon of hope in the efforts of all concerned. There was the immediate problem of having all these people suddenly deprived of income, and so began the fundraising.

There were concerts and quizzes and golf classics and football matches and all sorts of events for the cause. There were famous singers and poets, playwrights and writers, sports people, politicians, business people and public servants, all gave their support free of charge. Pete St John even wrote a special song for the cause, and our current president, Michael D. Higgins, gave us a poem to publish. Columnists like Jack Charlton continued to write for the *X-Press*, again without charge. There was even a world exclusive interview with U2 about their new album in our humble publication, their first in two years.

Our members travelled the country to festivals and fairs, to matches and races and all kinds of sporting events, raising awareness and much-needed funds for the cause. There was also support from government ministers and opposition parties, from TDs and Senators from home and abroad – we even got a message of support from the Ulster Unionist Party! The goodwill messages and offers of support were from ordinary readers in their thousands from all over the country and from all over the globe.

And so I found myself on the Dart that summer day with the £20,000 of Superquinn vouchers. That strange journey came about after a businessman, whom I didn't know and who did not want his name used, rang me and asked to make a personal donation to the fund – I nearly dropped the phone when he told me how much! We decided on supermarket vouchers, and so I travelled to Superquinn HQ in Sutton to collect the prize.

Some years later I met that same businessman and he told me he got a great bargain that day: 'They gave me bulk discount,' he said; 'they only charged me £19,000!'

The reporter who broke his leg in two places, and the ex-IRA man who outranked his English father-in-law

Ray Burke
(Reporter/News Editor, *Irish Press*, 1984–1995)

After the congregation led by President Michael D. Higgins had prayed for the repose of the soul of the eminent financial journalist Colm Rapple in St Kevin's Church, Harrington Street, off the South Circular Road in Dublin earlier this year, a group of Colm's former colleagues walked together to a nearby public house.

The group was made up of former journalists from the *Irish Press*, the *Evening Press* and the *Sunday Press*, and most of them had been in the same church two and a half years earlier for the funeral of another much-loved and respected former colleague, Con Houlihan. What was different about this occasion, however, was that the group left the hostelry and dispersed after consuming no more than two drinks each.

The unspoken thought of all those present was that if any combination of them had entered a public house on any early evening twenty or twenty-five or thirty years earlier, none of them would have left the premises before closing time. Pubs played a big part in the working life and the social life of the people who worked for Irish Press Newspapers between 1931 and 1995.

There were two pubs within twenty paces of the front and back doors of the newspapers' Burgh Quay offices and printing works: Mulligan's and the White Horse. Mulligan's was so popular among journalists that they used two synonyms to refer to it that were only slightly inaccurate: 'next door' and 'the annexe'. Several other pubs were a mere stone's throw away: Kennedy's and Reagan's on Tara Street, The Regal on Hawkins Street and Finnegan's on Townsend Street. A reporter who fell on thick ice and broke his leg one January as he walked to his late-night bus was said by colleagues the next day to have broken his leg in two places: Mulligan's and The Regal.

Such was the proliferation of pubs in and around what Con Houlihan called 'our village' of Burgh Quay and Poolbeg Street that it was never necessary to go elsewhere for alcohol or company, but in the late 1980s some journalists began to venture a little south-west of O'Connell Bridge to Temple Bar – an area that was being transformed from a bohemian quarter to a trendy tourist spot. The pubs there began to attract huge crowds to watch Republic of Ireland soccer matches on big TV screens.

One night a famed *Irish Press* reporter, Gerry O'Hare, one of the last great characters to work in the Burgh Quay newsroom, fell down stairs and cracked his head after watching a Republic of Ireland match in a Temple Bar pub. In a previous life Gerry had been incarcerated in Mountjoy and Portlaoise prisons for IRA offences, but this was the first time that he had actually shed blood for Ireland, observed the more callous of his colleagues back at Burgh Quay.

Despite the head injury he sustained while on active service in a pub armchair, or maybe because of it, Gerry was shortly thereafter selected to accompany another brigade, 'Jack's Army' of Republic of Ireland supporters who travelled to Italy for the 1990 World Cup Finals. When the team unexpectedly reached the tournament's quarter-finals in Rome, the demand for copy for the three *Press* titles was insatiable and another reporter was assigned to augment Gerry's reporting.

This assignment went to Chris Dooley, now foreign editor of *The Irish Times*, but then a young *Irish Press* reporter who had gone to Italy at his own expense as a fully fledged member of Jack's Army, but who was fast running out of Lira and glad to be offered free accommodation on the floor of Gerry's hotel room in the centre of Rome. Sharing the same room was Gerry's lifelong friend Stephen Rea, the Abbey Theatre, Field Day and Hollywood actor who would later star in the movie *Michael Collins*, which was produced and directed by Neil Jordan, whose artistic career had begun when a number of his short stories were published on the *New Irish Writing* page of the *Irish Press* in the early 1970s.

Gerry forgot to tell Stephen that a third person would be sharing their hotel room, albeit on the floor, and when Stephen stepped out of bed in total darkness in the middle of the night to go to the bathroom he tripped over Chris's prone and slumbering body. In the commotion that followed, Gerry awoke, switched on a bedside light and intoned in a voice that was more west Bengal Colonial than west Belfast Republican: 'Stephen, don't you know I always keep a boy at the foot of the bed!'

Gerry had joined the *Irish Press* as a freelance reporter at the end of the 1970s after serving an apprenticeship on the IRA weekly *An Phoblacht/Republican News* (moving from the contemporary *Gunman's Gazette* to the former *Gunman's Gazette*, as it were). At the time he was involved with a woman who was not his wife, nor even his former wife, and, like all freelance journalists, he was insecure and uncertain about his employment prospects.

In Mulligan's one evening he asked a news editor if the executives were happy with his progress. Told by the news editor that the bosses were satisfied with his work, but not happy about his 'syntax', Gerry was crestfallen, thinking that the bosses were unhappy about his 'living in sin', which was still an unusual domestic arrangement for any *Irish Press* staff members who were preparing to cover the impending visit of Pope John Paul II to Ireland.

When Gerry remarried he chose as his bride his 'English Rose', Anne Cadwallader, an *Irish Press* journalist who later became a human rights activist. On being introduced to his future father-in-law, a retired British Army major, Gerry is reputed to have declared: 'I had a higher rank in our army than you did in yours.'

Another Mulligan's habitué in the 1980s and early 1990s was the last *Irish Press* GAA correspondent, Peadar O'Brien (or 'Tommy Fitzgerald', to use the alter ego he employed when moonlighting for the *Irish Sun*), who had begun his *Press* career covering boxing and cycling. One of his early annual assignments was to cover the *Rás Tailteann* round-Ireland cycle race. His practice was to drive to the city or town where that day's race stage would finish and talk to the winners and race officials before filing his copy that evening. One Sunday he ensconced himself in the Great Southern Hotel in Galway and went for an afternoon swim in the leisure centre on the top floor, where he enjoyed panoramic views of Galway Bay, Lough Corrib, the Twelve Bens, the Clare hills and the Slieve Aughty Mountains while the cyclists were still sweating their way over Corkscrew hill in Co. Clare. He was alone in the swimming pool when a door opened and in walked the editor of the *Sunday Press*, Vincent Jennings, who had just checked into the hotel for a mini-break with his wife.

'Is that you, Peadar?' asked Jennings. 'What are you doing in there?'

Still supine and slowly treading water, Peadar replied: 'I'm covering the bike race, Vincent.'

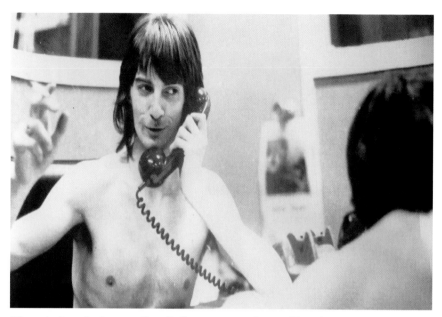

The naked truth: Snapper Ray Cullen gets something off his chest in the newsroom. Ray was later one of the 'Burgh Quay Eighteen'

Best part of the day: Enjoying two different types of scoops...

Sheila, take a bow: Sheila Walshe's farewell party. The picture includes some of our contributors: Michael Keane, Des Nix, Michael O'Kane, Tim Pat Coogan, Liam Flynn, Denis McClean, John Brophy, John Kelly and Seán Ó hÉalaí

Major Event: Major Vivion de Valera (third from left), who loomed large over the *Press* until his death in 1982. On the far left and far right are Sean Ward (*Evening Press* editor) and Tim Pat Coogan (*Irish Press* editor)

Two princes from the Kingdom: Kerry's legendary scribe Con Houlihan and former GAA county manager Mick O'Dwyer share a moment

Best of mates: Racing pundits Jim MacNeill and Cyril Byrne return from a 'meeting' in Mulligan's. Both were much-loved colleagues (photograph by Cyril Byrne Junior)

Sign of the times: The *Evening Press* signage was an integral part of the Dublin landscape

Hot metal: Tim Pat Coogan (second from right) runs his eye over the paper's 50th anniversary supplement on the old 'stone' (picture courtesy of Brian Barron)

Stone Age: Hugh Lambert, Éanna Brophy, Emmanuel Kehoe, Pat Chatten, Sam Battle, John Masterson, Sean Donnelly, Noel O'Neill, Eugene McHugh – and Willie Shakespeare's head in the background (photograph by Michael Morris)

Cheers: Michael Cronin, Niall Connolly and John Kelly raise a glass to happier times (photograph by Ronan Quinlan)

Hard Pressed: Vincent Jennings fields questions from Ken Whelan and Pat Cashman
outside Mulligan's. Also in the picture are Chris Dooley and Colm Rapple
(photograph by Ronan Quinlan)

Glum: editorial staff learn of management's order to vacate the premises in May 1995
(photograph by Ray Cullen)

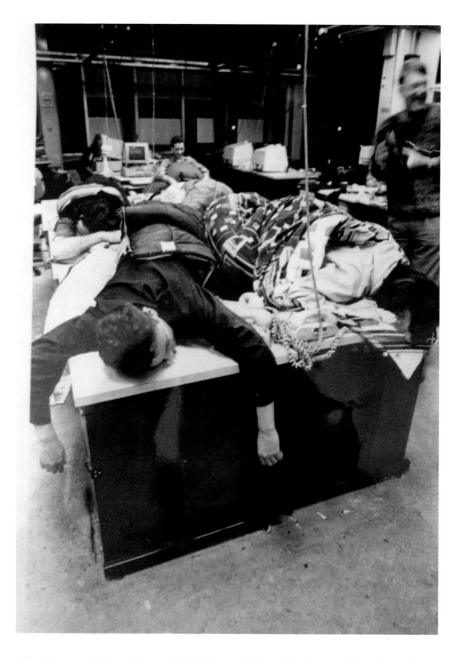

Sleeping rough: Dave Kenny, Enda Sheppard, Karen Doyle, David Lawlor and Pat
Cashman during the sit-in on Burgh Quay (photograph by Ray Cullen)

Simply Red: reporter Richard Balls and subeditor Dave Kenny busk on Grafton
Street to raise funds for the locked-out *Press* workers

The *Rás Tailteann* and the *Sunday Press* belong to a century that ended more than fifteen years ago. Twenty-first-century newspapers have less and less in common with their counterparts in earlier eras. A former *Sunday Press* correspondent noticed huge changes in the digital-era newsroom to which she returned in the 1990s after taking a lengthy career break.

The newsrooms she knew in the mid 1980s, she observed, had been mostly full of men clattering away on noisy typewriters on desks covered with telephone directories, reference books, landline telephones, overflowing ashtrays, notebooks and half-eaten bags of burgers and chips. When she returned less than a decade later, she said, it was to a near silent, carpeted newsroom full of as many fresh-faced women as men, working at desks that held nothing but a notebook and bottles of still or sparkling water, and on which the only chips were the Intel microchips that powered the silent processors of the desktops or laptops.

A few years later a former *Irish Press* journalist walked into a national newsroom early one morning to find the reporters in a state of near panic because a prominent politician had died during the night and they could not find any biographical information on him because, they said, 'Google is down, Google is down.' They had no option but to resort to using the tools that were indispensable to twentieth-century journalists on Irish Press Newspapers and elsewhere, and that are not yet redundant: the telephone, the pen and the notebook.

Getting locked in the newsroom and sticking it to The Man

David Kenny
(Copyboy/Sports Subeditor/ Feature Writer, *Irish Press*,
1985–1995)

'The bastards are trying to get in!' The former Republican prisoner raced through the caseroom and down the back stairs, cursing and puffing.

His voice trailed away as we sat, nerves flickering, in the light of the night-town reporter's TV. I lit a fag, convinced that I wouldn't have a chance to finish it before the SWAT team of security guards swarmed into the newsroom.

'They'll never take us alive,' someone remarked, drily.

'Oh yes they bloody will,' I replied, fully intending to be the first under a desk when the baton charge kicked off.

It was Saturday 27 May 1995, and the presses had stopped rolling at one of the country's most popular newspaper groups. Founded by a former IRA man, it seemed fitting that former Republican prisoner Gerry O'Hare had gone down fighting at the back door. That's the last we'll see of him, I thought. I was wrong. Gerry re-emerged a few minutes later. The management had not ordered a storming of the building. It had, however, been sealed off. We were now fully committed to what would be one of the most bizarre sit-ins in Irish history.

My memory of those four days is hazy, but images still poke their head through the fug of cigarette smoke and takeaway curry steam. On Thursday 25 May our NUJ chapel went into a mandatory session over the sacking of Colm Rapple. The finance journalist had been fired for comments he made in *The Irish Times* about the management of the paper, which had been set up by Dev in 1931. We laboured in a Dunkirk atmosphere, producing newspapers with meagre resources and poor pay (we hadn't had a rise in ten years). Loyalty to the titles and to each other was what kept us going. Rapple's sacking was the final straw. No paper was produced that day.

Management ultimately refused to engage in a meaningful way. They wanted to liquidate the business, clear their debts and carry on as a company that no longer produced papers. They succeeded in this, but we weren't going to give up without a fight. We would find an examiner and force the management to talk and walk.

On the day after Rapple's sacking, we were ordered to leave the building. Naturally, we ignored this instruction. Technically, we would remain at our desks, available for work.

That evening I took my 'cutline' break in The Regal on Hawkins Street. I was depressed and scared. I had joined the paper as a copyboy aged eighteen in 1985, working my way onto the sports subeditors' bench. I had no contacts in other newspapers and I knew no other way of life or work. I was genetically preprogrammed to be a hack. Newspapers and publishing go back five generations in my family. My dad had worked in RTÉ and the *Indo*. My great-great-grandfather was a bookbinder, and my great-grandfather, Matthew Walker, was the first Master Linotype operator in Ireland. He published the *Irish War News* under fire for Pearse in 1916, and printed the 1917 version of the Proclamation (which is rarer than the original). He also discussed taking over the *Indo* building with Connolly during the Rising. Fighting and writing was what my family did. No blood would be shed during our impending sit-in, but ink would definitely be spilled, I reflected as I morosely sipped my pint.

I started in the industry just as hot metal was ending. I remember the smell and the noise of the old caseroom, with its snarly overseer and inky men sitting behind tall, elaborate Linotype machines.

It was a world of archaic work practices where you could be reprimanded or 'chapeled' for touching a page proof without permission. The paper was 'made up' on 'the stone' – a long table where frames of print were assembled. These were back to front, which meant that the printers/compositors had to be able to read backwards at speed. The stone subeditor had a worse job: he had to read and edit stories back to front and upside down as he wasn't allowed to stand on the printers' side of the work area. It was, frankly, mental.

Printing also had had its own language. There were nonpareils, picas, ems and ens. There were also widows, orphans, galleys and dragon's blood (which sound like the ingredients of a Tolkien novel). There was a block clerk (who looked after advertising logos) and the occasional 'knock down'. This was the ultimate accolade from the printing fraternity and was reserved for departing colleagues. When someone retired they would say their farewells and the stone would be banged with metal rulers, hammers, fists and mugs as a noisy salute. It was always very moving to witness and is a practice that is now gone. Try banging a PC with a metal ruler and see how long you keep your job.

There were great characters on the stone, most of whom were erudite and well-informed, sometimes more so than the preening scribes whose work they laid out. There was the magnificently monikered Willie 'the Shake' Shakespeare (real name), who was one of the best comps in the business. I recall being very impressed by his extraordinarily rotund beer belly (he looked like he was smuggling a beach ball down his jumper). Then there was 'Lazarus'. I loved him, although he could drive you insane with his tall tales. Once, on cutline, Laz described taking the engine of his car asunder to root out a problem with the starter motor/carburettor/wheedle valve/

whatever. 'I laid out every piece,' he told his yawning colleagues, adding that his probing had revealed that he needed a new starter motor/carburettor/wheedle valve/whatever. 'So I jumped in and drove straight away to the garage. The mechanic agreed with my diagnosis.' His triumphant bubble was quickly burst by one of his more observant colleagues.

'That was some achievement, Laz.'

'What was?'

'Driving to the garage with no engine in your car.'

Lazarus climbed mountains. Or hills. Or both. Perhaps this stressful pastime was the reason for his preternaturally shaky hands. When the era of paste-up arrived (pages were printed on paper, cut by scalpel and pasted up on boards), Laz became a serious threat to everyone's health. He wielded a scalpel like a drunken, epileptic, blindfolded samurai warrior with a live electric cable stuck up his posterior. I used to count my fingers after a night on the stone with him. He never cut me, although he did occasionally slash through columns of print just as the paper was about to be put to bed.

He was always kind to me, and I was grateful for that. Others were not so patient with the greenhorn 'Glenageary yuppie', but I won't settle scores here. I wish them well now. Okay, and bad haemorrhoids as well. I'm not THAT forgiving.

Three months after I joined, the papers closed and reopened after a dispute involving the introduction of new technology. Thanks to editorial secretary Maureen Craddock, I was reassigned in 'teleads' (telephone advertising) as the night messenger. Teleads at night was a nuthouse. There were four of us: a team leader, two input men and me. Undertakers would call up and dictate death notices and the boys would input them on green-screened computers. They would then be printed off, and I would deliver them to the caseroom to be typeset. Most of the time the undertakers, being lazy sods, would request that a copy be sent to the *Indo* across the river. This was where I came in. Four times a night, in all weathers, I would traipse past Burgh Quay's tragic gay red-light area, across the bridge and down to Prince's Street with the latest stiffs. I was human 'email'.

I ran the gauntlet of muggers, gay lorry drivers thinking my bottom was for rent, junkies and assorted weirdos. I learned to blend in and frequently walked through pitched battles between groups of skangers with what I believed to be my '100-yard stare'. I reckoned that if I didn't look left or right, and believed I was invisible, then I would be impervious to trouble. Only once in three years did I get mugged, and that was from behind. The reality, looking back, was that the skangers probably thought I was a bit 'special needs' (judging by my stare) and just couldn't be bothered mugging/raping/whatever me.

I met my first serious girlfriend in teleads, and would often grab her in an inappropriate manner when the undertaker was prattling on about so-and-so being 'sadly missed by relatives and friends' etc. I slowly went *Lord-of-the-Flies* mad in teleads. I sought new ways of making the inputters laugh while dealing with death: dropping my trousers, dancing provocatively etc. I also changed the preprogrammed phrases stored in the computer system. 'Missed by grandchildren' became 'That's a grand cake, Nora' and 'RIP' became 'RIPe and ready for plucking'. Somehow, the changes never wound up in print.

I also got smacked in the face by a clerk from another department who was unimpressed when I wouldn't take a pile of coppers to buy him a sandwich. This was one of my unofficial duties for the teleads staff. My protestation that he didn't actually work in teleads fell on hungover ears. For the record, I didn't hit him back. I didn't even report him. I was nineteen, skinny and painfully lacking in self-confidence. It would have been pointless anyway, and might have cost him his job.

To be honest, I might have done him a favour in that regard. His job was one of the most boring gigs in the entire group, so boring that I can't even remember what it entailed. My brain used to shut down whenever he tried to explain it to me. There were logos involved and Zzzzzzzzz. Sorry, my brain just shut down again. In hindsight, I SHOULD have hit him back – repeatedly – just for having such a crap job.

The only thing of (relatively minor) note that I achieved in teleads was saving the life of the team leader. Each night he sent me out for ever more bizarre meal requests, culminating in dinners from a local restaurant that he wanted served on a plate. I wanted to strangle him. Carrying a steaming plate along Burgh Quay at night was not fun, especially if it was dripping with gravy. One evening he swallowed a chicken bone. My colleagues ran around like headless poultry while I watched him go puce. They smacked and whacked him, and I may have smiled a little inside. Eventually, I got up and performed the Heimlich manoeuvre on him. The bone shot across the room.

'You saved my life,' he said, and I was the hero of the night. The next evening I was sent back out for more dinners on plates. Perhaps I should have let him choke.

Shortly afterwards, I had a meeting with the editorial manager, Niall Connolly, requesting a move to the newsroom copyboy desk. I told him I wanted to be a journalist and couldn't work my way up from where I was. I did my best to impress him. I wore a sports jacket and carried a copy of Richard Ellman's biography of Wilde under my arm (to show how literary I was). By all accounts I must have looked a total tit, but it worked. A few weeks later I was invited to attend an interview for the job of sports subeditor. The sports editor was looking for a design man to lay out pages. I had told Niall I'd won a prize in the Texaco National Art Competition as a ten-year-old. Somehow, this had morphed into Dave Kenny is a Graphic Designer.

For the next seven years, I worked in sport. My lack of knowledge about sport was matched only by my complete lack of interest in it. I was quickly found out and treated accordingly by my colleagues. It was only when the direct-input computer system was introduced that I found my feet, helping older colleagues with the new technology. People who had barely talked to me for years now joked with me about my lack of sporting knowledge. I was a 'whizz-kid' in their eyes. It made life a lot more pleasant for all concerned. I'm glad it did. There were some good men on that desk: Cyril Byrne, Gerry Greene, Peter 'The Aussie' Bradstreet, Shay(s) Smith and Keenan, Jim McNeill (a phenomenal writer), Eamon 'Gibbo' Gibson and others.

Those same editorial direct-input computers that saved me from being constantly wedgied by my colleagues unfortunately negated the need for the Irish Print Union. The IPU was all-powerful, and a compromise was eventually reached where stories were written on the computers, printed off and subedited by pen. They were then sent to the caseroom to be retyped back into the system. It was an untenable situation. It was also one fraught with danger, depending on the time of the evening and the amount of alcohol consumed.

On one occasion, a story about the English soccer team included the following line: 'They wore the shite [white] shirt with pride'. There was also the tale of a knocked-out boxer who was 'out for the cunt'. The madness of this 'compromise' was not out of the ordinary in Dev's national institution. And it really was an institution ... in the nuthouse sense of the word. The *Press* heaved with insane characters who couldn't have worked in any other industry.

Most of the milder nutcases self-medicated in Mulligan's of

Poolbeg Street. The loopier ones opted for the White Horse, which was an early house. Booze was central to everything. My 'interview' for newsroom copyboy had been conducted in Mull's, and consisted of me buying the chief sub a pint.

Levels of inebriation varied throughout the week, peaking on a Wednesday evening when we were paid in cash. Work started at 4.30 p.m. with our first break at 9.30 p.m., which meant nipping to Mulligan's to pay off the previous week's 'slates'. I had enough slates to reroof the Pro-Cathedral.

Work would be resumed at 10 p.m., and the drinking continued at closing time in Mull's. That was when the real boozing began....

When I joined, the next stop after Mulligan's was Finnegan's. There was a special knock to get in, and the door would creak open to reveal a Guinness-black interior. We would then slip inside and drink in semi-darkness in hushed tones. I still don't see the attraction of it. A crowd of half-pissed men whispering to each other in a gloomy room? It almost sounds homoerotic now. Almost.

We would then sneak out and head to the Irish Times Club on D'Olier Street. This was, to be strictly honest, a shithole, where pints could be bought until 4 a.m. It was run by a nice man called Bernard who was always trying to get me to buy an annual membership for £20. This would entitle me to bring in a guest and get my own key. I always fancied the idea of having my own key, but wouldn't have inflicted the Times Club on any prospective guest of mine.

The key meant that you had 'arrived'. The club was several flights up, and if someone heard you ringing the bell they would throw down a key in a matchbox. It was an ingenious, if primitive, way of gaining entry long before text messages were dreamed of. And if the guards caught you fumbling around, half cut, on the pavement at 2 a.m., you could say you were looking for your matches. Mind you, at that hour of the morning half of Dublin's cop fraternity were inside skulling pints.

Guards and journos had a strange relationship. Both groups were wary of each other, but the Times Club often resembled the First World War scene where German and English troops climbed out of the trenches to play soccer on Christmas Eve. It became a no man's land where old enmities were set aside to drink and, when the club moved to the quays under new management, play pool. I remember one night searching for my coat in a pile of tunics and an Uzi clattered to the floor. The ERU were in the back playing pool against the sports subeditors' desk.

I also (barely) remember leaving the Irish Times Club at 4 a.m. and waking up on a cliff ledge on Killiney Beach, eight miles away, several hours later. A drinking companion was asleep and snoring happily on the sand below.

There were other bizarre occasions too, like the time we had to rescue a messenger friend from drowning in the canal early one morning. He had decided to go skinny-dipping. Egged on by some smiling Arab gentlemen, he disrobed and jumped into the canal … and was dragged under the weir. He was eventually pulled out and, although clearly in need of hospital assistance for shock, was brought for a fried breakfast in the Manhattan followed by more drink. He survived the ordeal. The breakfast, that is.

Another time, the same colleague ignited a street battle with some gougers after his jacket was stolen in Jaeger's Nite Club. Jaeger's was to glitzy 'nite life' what coddle is to fine dining. It was unbelievable. Once inside its velure-lined walls, one could buy bottles of premixed 'rum and blackcurrant' and watch the local ladies batter the bejaysus out of each other on the dance floor. It was during one such bout that my colleague's leather jacket was stolen. It was his pride and joy, which he had bought at a leather flea market in Turkey. The memory of it pains my synapses. It was tan, with piping at the Joan Collins-wide shoulder pads and down the sides. Michael Jackson would have barfed at the sight of it. To my friend, though, it was the bee's patellae. Best of all, he would tell us, the sleeves were removable (he would then unzip them to reveal his milky white arms). I was incredibly fond of this man, and still am, and never had the heart to ask him why anyone would want to wander around Dublin on a winter's night in a leather singlet unless they were gay and looking for a smack in the head.

The jacket had been stolen by Ireland's Most Stupid and Sartorially Challenged Thief Ever. He actually stood outside the nightclub wearing it. I remember feeling a mixture of anger at his nerve and embarrassment for him as he looked like a bad, anaemic, Turkish Michael Jackson impersonator. A crowd gathered, and one of the most pathetic street fights Dublin has ever witnessed ensued. No one was badly hurt, and the jacket was relinquished. My friend wore it with even more pride after that.

This was the world I knew. A world where Wellington's retort had been amended to 'Drink or be damned!' A world that was ending while I sat in the bar in The Regal on the second day of the dispute. At around closing time I went back to the office. I had suggested the previous day that we do our own newspaper. Those present, including Liam Mackey, began to write and to assemble the basics. I raided the caseroom looking for a masthead and other 'blocks' (graphics).

The *X-Press* was born, and continued to be published until after the All-Ireland Final of that year. It raised funds and kept us in the public eye. The paper cost a penny, but the public were generous and money poured in to support the workers' families. It was sold in bars and on street corners, at the Fianna Fáil *Ard Fheis* and the races. Celebs queued up to be photographed in it: U2, Norm from *Cheers*....

Household names were quoted in it bemoaning the IP's fate: Mick 'Miley' Lally, Liam Clancy, Joe Duffy, Dave Fanning, Neil

Jordan, Bono, Eamonn Coghlan, Gerry Adams (when he wasn't fashionable), the current president, members of the UUP....

Politicians of all hues lent their support, except for one 'socialist' TD who told our chief sub that we 'couldn't organise a piss-up in a brewery'. This was interesting as he was walking into a piss-up at the French Embassy for Bastille Day at the time.

P. J. Mara dropped in a cheque for £250 (not in a brown envelope) and Tim Pat Coogan donated £200, made payable to Mulligan's. Mackey's *Hot Press* connections came in handy. He got a world exclusive interview from U2 for the *X-Press*. It's still being read online today. He also brought Jack Charlton's team to the back door to lend support. Boxer Steve Collins was with them, looking slightly confused – as was Jack. Brendan O'Carroll arrived too.

'I've come to get the solution to yesterday's crossword,' he said. It may not seem funny now, but it was hilarious at the time.

Looking back, it's hard to believe the support we got. Sky News came to the back door and our protest went international. There was even a letter of support from one of Russia's leading dissident poets, Yevgeny Yevtushenko. Perhaps he was a fan of the farming pages, who knows?

The reaction to this unprecedented dispute was equally unprecedented. What made this different to other industrial rows was that, although the papers were ailing, they were still woven into the fabric of Irish life. They had the power to challenge at a time when politicians and the Church still held sway.

We were white collar workers occupying a landmark building. Journalists are an inert bunch. We report on other people's actions. Now we were taking direct action – and the public loved it. I did too: I was twenty-eight and sticking it to The Man.

Even Con Houlihan – venerated as a demi-God – was manning the barricades, albeit at street level. He was committed to the *X-Press* cause and wrote three columns a week for us. He also sold copies on O'Connell Bridge, retreating to Mulligan's whenever a gale blew up the Liffey.

The eighteen occupiers would have given anything for a refreshing Liffey gale. The roof had been closed off, so there was no access to fresh air. The place stank of cigarette smoke, curries, farts and BO. We were manky, and one of our number had to be treated for septicaemia after cutting his leg in the canteen. The joke was that he got foot poisoning where others might have got food poisoning.

Hot water was cut off. I showered only once, descending into the deserted machine hall to use the facilities. I lost certain parts of my anatomy when the freezing water hit me.

We worked on the *X-Press* and were kept busy with various tasks allotted by the beleaguered Mother of the Chapel, Louise Ní Chriodáin. I wrote a spoof piece called 'Crisis Cooking', which included recipes for stuffed baked beans. It later provided me with a template for my first satirical book: *The Little Buke of Dublin*.

Gifts flooded in, and the newsroom resembled BBC's *Swap Shop*, with tables groaning under the weight of food, booze, toys, clothes.... There was a steady stream of smokes arriving too. Tom Kitt TD even got off a flight from South Africa to drop in duty-free cigs to the hacking hacks.

Cork looked after us too: Murphy's made a special delivery to keep us hydrated. We ate well, but sleep was always elusive. The ramshackle newsroom was horrendous as a communal bedroom. It was filthy, and there was always the fear of rodent activity. I had worked with a few rats; I didn't want to sleep with them too. The phones rang throughout the night and there were 5 a.m. fire alarm 'calls'. The lights flickered non-stop.

The fatigue bred giddiness and irritability. I know I must have annoyed people in there as much as some annoyed me. Friendships were forged. I have always looked up with affection to Mackey as an older, cooler brother in the business.

On day four we were instructed by the NUJ to vacate the building as Labour Court talks were beginning. That night, as Sky News broadcast funereal reports from the back door, we decided to barrel into the beer. We were knackered, and it kicked in fairly quickly. Despite our depression at the impending evacuation, we did a chariot race on swivel chairs around the newsroom.

Republican 'head of security' Gerry O'Hare played all sixty verses of 'SAM Missiles in the Sky' (an IRA lullaby) on the newsroom tape recorder. Friends and colleagues left Mulligan's and serenaded us from the street below the canteen windows. We sang back. I think I croaked 'The Rare Ould Times'. Yvonne Judge sang 'Something Stupid'.

The following morning we assembled in the canteen and waited to be 'liberated'. I expected a few friends, my girlfriend (now my wife) and others to attend. Then I heard the drumming ... a 1,000-strong parade was marching up to the back door. I walked down the steps and was absorbed into a crowd of people who would never reassemble under such extraordinary circumstances again.

The *Press* closure was a coming-of-age thing for me. It taught me to stand up for myself. I went on to work for RTÉ, the *Herald* and the *Trib*. It seems like a million years ago, considering how the industry, and society, have changed. There were no mobile phones, email or social media. News was hard-won.

I often dream about the *Press*. I am walking past Sean the security man who always expected to be greeted with 'You're only a bollix, Sean,' (to which his reply was, 'It's MISTER Bollix to you, sonny') into the lift, which a legendary boozer once mistook for a toilet – much to the dismay of an ageing female copy-taker.

Then across the dimpled metal gangway above the machine hall with the presses rumbling beneath my feet. I can still smell the Major and Carroll's in the newsroom and hear the incessant buzz and clack of telephones and typewriters. I see my deceased friend and former *Sunday Press* sports editor, Mick Carwood, and slag him about his flip-flops. Mick died tragically young on a golf course. He was one of the most interesting, kind, gifted and beautiful human beings I've ever met. He got me back on my feet after the paper closed, giving me the job of deputy sports editor on the short-lived *Evening News*. He had a twinkle in his eye that never dimmed – even when I was being a monumental pain in the arse.

I also see the late Hugh Lambert – the last editor of the *Irish Press*. Hugh was a lovely, gentle man too, with a constant smile, like Mick.

I miss the place terribly, even after all these years. That said, I often wonder if we exaggerate the importance of newspapers. Our work influences and entertains while the presses are rolling, but once a paper has gone the earth continues to spin and governments continue to misgovern.

The *Press*, like the *Trib*, isn't even toilet roll at this stage. Once upon a time, those papers afflicted the comfortable and comforted the afflicted. Would the public now care if the entire industry vanished overnight?

You needed to be slightly unhinged to work in the *Press*. It was a glorious madness though.

And thoroughly uncurable.

U2's War story and Bob Dylan's Battle of the Boyne

Denis McClean
(News Reporter)

One enjoyable aspect of being a general news reporter in Burgh Quay during the 1980s was the sheer variety of the markings. The Dáil and the courts had to be covered, and there were a lot of routine follow-up phone calls, but there was always the prospect of something unusual popping up and getting out of the office.

Occasionally the courts did lead to some interesting opportunities to get out and about. One such was the relationship I developed with 'The General', then Ireland's most notorious criminal, which landed us both on the front page of *The Phoenix* on the occasion when he showed off his Mickey Mouse boxer shorts to the gardaí while his ghetto blaster played 'I'm Gonna Sit Right Down and Write Myself a Letter.'

Every morning I would call to his house in Cowper Downs looking for an interview, but to no avail. I sat down and wrote him a letter saying that I was the guy with him on the cover of *The Phoenix*, any chance of a chat etc? We met, and the result made a nice lead for the *Evening Press*.

Bono agreed to an interview about the *War* album and its hit single, 'New Year's Day', but only if I came out to Howth immediately. While the taxi waited we talked for a few hours, but the *Evening Press* subs' desk in its wisdom buried the story as the single dropped out of the charts.

I spent a week covering every aspect of Ireland's first world boxing title fight in decades, featuring Barry McGuigan. I even phoned in copy on the fight itself, though it was the first time I ever attended a boxing bout. I hung around for hours before McGuigan emerged from his dressing room looking like someone whose eye sockets had been used to hold pints of Guinness. Barney Eastwood shepherded him towards the waiting press and kept repeating to hangers on: 'Don't touch his hands, don't touch his hands.'

It was always nice to be sent somewhere by the sea. I spent an idyllic few days in sunny Howth waiting for any developments in the Jennifer Guinness kidnap case, a saga that ended up with me spending the night under a car on Waterloo Road listening to the gardaí negotiating her release with the kidnap gang.

The Rose of Tralee was my first marking outside Dublin. I quickly got into the swing of things, to the extent that I prevailed one evening upon my good friend, the late Michael O'Toole of Dubliner's Diary, to phone in my neatly typed copy prepared the night before as I anticipated that I might be indisposed the following morning.

Dick Hogan of *The Irish Times* played a cruel trick on me. I heard my name being called over the public-address system in the Mount Brandon Hotel one morning. I picked up the phone to hear a voice enquire: 'Is that you, McClean? Do you seriously expect a national newspaper to publish this shite you've sent us?' A reasonable question, I quickly thought. 'Give me a break, it's the Rose of Tralee, not Watergate.' Hogan got great mileage out of that.

My favourites for light relief, though, were the occasional opportunities to mix music and work. This reached its nadir when I took off on the train to Galway with a brand new bike to make my way to Lisdoonvarna. I hit a stretch of newly laid gravel on the hill into Clarenbridge and ended up with two flat tyres. There was no photographer with me to repair the punctures, so I left the bike in a convent and hitched my way to Lisdoon.

That night my sleeping bag was stolen. I emerged cold, tired and slightly hungover from my tent at dawn to observe a column of black smoke rising from the middle of the field. On investigation I found three young men in various states of undress staring disbelievingly at the burnt-out remains of their tent, destroyed by a runaway Hiace van propelled downhill by the impact of an explosion from a gas cylinder.

They were delighted when I identified myself as a reporter from the *Evening Press*. 'Nobody would ever believe us,' said one, as I anticipated correctly that this narrow escape from death by a stolen van driven from Belfast would make a nice lead for the Country edition.

My joy at finding a replacement sleeping bag abated that evening when I found that my tent had mysteriously collapsed. The following morning my neighbours informed me that I was lucky not to have been in it as the fireworks display following Jackson Browne's appearance had started a stampede of cattle from the next field, with predictable results. It was too late to file for the *Sunday Press* so I went to bed. Penniless, I was ferried back to Dublin courtesy of a group of prosletysing Hare Krishna monks.

I came very close to seeing Bob Dylan play a huge outdoor concert at Slane Castle in 1984, but work got in the way. Let me digress. My enthusiasm for Slane as a venue was ignited by my attendance at the inaugural concert in 1981 featuring my then favourite band, Thin Lizzy, supported by U2 and Hazel O'Connor. It was a great day out, attended by a smaller crowd considering the mega events that were to follow.

I joined the *Irish Press,* and the following year volunteered/insisted that I be assigned for the week to cover the Rolling Stones' gig in Slane and the build-up to same. It was too late to get one of the twelve or so rooms in the Conyingham Arms Hotel on the main street of the tiny village, associated hitherto with the poet Thomas Kettle, some rich fucker living in a castle, good farmland and the River Boyne.

Such was my enthusiasm for my assignment that I negotiated with a local housewife to be allowed to pitch a tent in her front garden, close to the castle entrance, should I feel the need to stay overnight anytime during the week. I got on famously with the rough-and-tumble promoter Bill Graham (RIP) until I did a story featuring the rather harmless but confidential backstage demands of the Stones: nine female dwarves, two transgender uileann pipers, an ample supply of Flahavan's oatmeal porridge … I wish. It is a pity the *Irish Press* archive is not available online, but I think that, apart from the booze, the height of their excess came to a couple of pinball machines.

I really pissed off burly Bill when he came across me trying to engage Mick Jagger in conversation on the eve of his fortieth birthday (I thought at the time that he looked tiny and ancient) as he surveyed the stage in the making from a vantage point on the green, grassy slopes of the Boyne (a phrase used a lot that week). However, Bill was delighted to give me an interview on his own exploits in the music industry, regarding which there was a very limited interest on the *Irish Press* newsdesk, I have to say, but I took notes.

So, when 1984 came around, I had booked my room in the Conyngham Arms several weeks in advance. I moved into the village a few days before the Sunday gig and was feeling quite at home with the locals, and in that glorious summer I tested the waters of the River Boyne, swimming behind the backstage area in the furtherance of my research.

I was tasked over the weekend with filing copy for the *Irish Press*, the *Evening Press* and the *Sunday Press*. On the Saturday afternoon I phoned Andy Bushe on the *Sunday Press* newsdesk to advise him that I would be extremely surprised if there was no trouble in the village given the formidable quantities of alcohol the gathering hordes were consuming in the summer heat.

I remained quite sober myself, and spent most of the day chatting to concertgoers. I was fascinated to meet people from the North who told me that they had never been south of the border before. As I had not yet had the pleasure of working out of the *Irish Press* Belfast office, and as a rather innocent Free Stater, this struck me as very odd indeed.

As the drunken, sunburnt but happy crowds milled about the main street, I became more aware of the potential for mayhem as local farmers drove up the street on their tractors hauling trailer loads of golden dry hay, which seemed to be crying out for some joker to toss a match or flick a cigarette butt, just for the craic like.

There were no street fighting men on the streets of Slane for the Stones, who sensibly played on a Saturday. Dylan's disciples seemed to be made of sterner stuff as they staggered towards the Sabbath in the mood to protest at the first available opportunity.

Darkness had not yet fallen when a disturbance broke out in front of the garda station on the main street. A rowdy, drunken crowd of youths took umbrage at an attempt to arrest one of their number and sought to retaliate by attempting to set fire to the garda station, an event the like of which had not been seen in the village since the War of Independence.

It has become common practice in many trouble spots across the world to drive vehicles packed with explosives into buildings of public importance, but in small Irish villages in 1984 it was still quite a novel idea, even if the explosives were only a few molotov cocktails to set the vehicle alight once vacated by the driver.

And so began a long day's journey into night.

I nipped in and out of the battle lines on the main street to phone my copy over to Burgh Quay, thrusting my NUJ card into the face of anyone in or out of uniform who looked like they wanted to beat the shite out of me.

Gardai came from all over the country to stem the tide of violence as cars were burned out, poor boxes stolen, windows broken, northerners fought southerners, etc. It was difficult at times to understand what was going on, but the gardaí definitely had their work cut out as they tried to clear some very experienced rioters from the roads leading into the village from the northern approaches.

Eventually, as a hotel guest entitled to after-hours bar service, I found myself in the lounge area of the Conyingham Arms, listening to first-hand accounts of the battle for Slane. The bar was packed with exhausted gardaí enjoying a few well-deserved pints.

The cosy scene disintegrated upon the arrival of a chief superintendent, who exploded with rage to find so many of his troops wetting their whistles while on well-remunerated overtime.

The *Sunday Press* had long gone to press. I went to bed, figuring that Sunday would be a busy day, but with any luck I would still get to see and hear Mr Dylan. Alas, it was not to be. The real tragedy of that weekend unfolded on the Sunday when two young men drowned, foolishly trying to swim across the Boyne to see the concert.

I spent a lot of time in the rather bare press room in the basement of Slane Castle sorting through my notes and communicating with the *Irish Press* newsdesk. As the only reporter present throughout the whole debacle, I was getting ready to do the mother-and-father of a wrap-up for Monday morning.

I remember reflecting on the 1980s equivalent of 'the digital divide' that afternoon in the form of the unfair advantage people like Charlie Bird had in terms of instant, almost real-time, access to his audience via radio.

My work nearly done, I was relaxing with some comrades over a full Irish breakfast on Monday morning when the concert promoter, Jim Aiken, popped in to wish me well, or so I thought.

Instead, he flung a copy of the *Irish Press* onto the table in front of me with the raging headline: 'Slane Says Never Again'. Jim, being from Belfast, seemed to be of the view that Saturday night's events were a storm in a teacup exaggerated by fellas like me who would do anything for a story.

He was right. I would. We would!

Before the Fall

John Moran
(News Subeditor, *Irish Press*, 1987–1995)

'The Yiddish Sons of Erin' was the first story of mine ever to appear in a national newspaper. I could hardly believe my eyes when I saw it, and felt a strong sense of achievement and no little pride. At the time, I was a mature student journalist in the National Institute of Higher Education, soon to become Dublin City University, which I had entered after ten years working as a compositor, eighteen months of unemployment, and another year working as a labourer.

That first story was about the Dublin Jewish community of 'Little Jerusalem', an area of Dublin centred on Clanbrassil Street, but which stretched in seven synagogues all the way from near the National Stadium on the South Circular Road to Adelaide Road. One of the synagogues was on Lennox Street, where I also lived. One 'Little Jerusalem' resident, Chaim Herzog, went on to become president of Israel, and returned to the area to open the Irish Jewish Museum.

The newspaper in which the story about my Jewish neighbours appeared in March 1987, and which earned me my first shekels as a working journalist, was the *Irish Press*. So from the start of my newspapers life, I had a special affection for it.

My entry into the world of print had actually begun much earlier. Before and after school I did a newspaper round for my mother, who worked in Doyle's newsagent shop in Charlemont Street. Here I could catch the first read of all the day's newspapers.

Customers were always happy to see me, as back then newspapers were eagerly awaited as a primary source for the news of the day, or rather, the news of yesterday.

My close association with the printed word continued when I jumped at the opportunity to escape the schoolroom to take up an apprenticeship I had been offered as a compositor with the European Printing Corporation in Coolock.

EPC was owned by Robert Maxwell, who was also proprietor of the *Daily Mirror* newspaper. For some time, two of us wrote for and produced an occasional in-house publication, which we grandly titled *The EPC Times*. Maxwell's company had a connection to another newspaper through a director, Major Tom McDowell, long-time chief executive of *The Irish Times*.

For the first six months in the hallowed halls of EPC, I was forbidden even to touch a live production page. First, I had to imbibe the practices and processes of print in the company training centre, where an iconic poster on a wall solemnly declared:

THIS IS A PRINTING-OFFICE
CROSSROADS OF CIVILIZATION
REFUGE OF ALL THE ARTS AGAINST THE
RAVAGES OF TIME
ARMOURY OF FEARLESS TRUTH AGAINST
WHISPERING RUMOUR
INCESSANT TRUMPET OF TRADE
FROM THIS PLACE WORDS MAY FLY ABROAD
NOT TO PERISH AS WAVES OF SOUND
NOT TO VARY WITH THE WRITER'S HAND
BUT FIXED IN TIME
HAVING BEEN VERIFIED BY PROOF
FRIEND, YOU STAND ON SACRED GROUND:
THIS IS A PRINTING-OFFICE

It was the 'Friend, you stand on Sacred ground' in particular that drew me in. From that day of initiation into the world of print I had a strong sense of being on holy ground, where the word became flesh, where the word was god.

I stood in awe of the journeymen compositors in EPC who had 'served their time' (completed their apprenticeships) to become esteemed practitioners of that ancient craft, bearers of its delicate skills and repositories of its dark artisan secrets. Our trade union, the Irish Graphical Society, was steeped in printing's centuries-old Dublin tradition and was dominated by members working in the three national newspapers, *The Irish Times*, the *Irish Independent* and the *Irish Press*. To work in a newspaper was seen by printers as the Holy Grail, where pay was by far the highest in the trade – and then there was the glamour of it.

In the years after qualifying as a journeyman, however, new technology began to incorporate compositors' skills and the trade as we knew it went into decline. I began studying after work at night in the College of Industrial Relations, formerly the Catholic Workers' College, which some at the time suggested was established by the Jesuits to save us proletarians from turning into godless communists. All untrue, though my interest in industrial relations later influenced my becoming involved as Father of the Chapel, or chief shop steward, for the Irish Graphical Society in EPC, and later as chapel officer in the *Irish Press*, and later again as Father of the Chapel in *The Irish Times* for the National Union of Journalists.

During the recession of 1983, EPC closed down and I had my first experience of the corrosive effects of unemployment. After fourteen years as a compositor, I spent the next eighteen months looking for any kind of work at all.

But as the tide goes out, so it comes back in, and I was next hired as a labourer in Telecom Éireann, laying underground pipes for telephone lines. My year of digging holes ended in 1986, and

I entered a portal to another world after being offered a place on the postgrad course in journalism in the National Institute of Higher Education, now Dublin City University. After exams and a placement in *The Irish Times*, I worked freelance, getting the call for an occasional day's work, or 'shift', as a reporter for *The Times*. These welcome shifts became more regular, as did shifts as a sub-editor in the *Press*, editing news stories and writing headlines for the next morning's publication.

In 1988 I was offered a staff job as a subeditor in the *Irish Press*, and immersed myself in the nightly adrenalin rush that was the *Press* newsroom. I also wrote the occasional feature story, such as 'The Life and Death of the King of the Road', about a well-known street character named Tommy Higgins who sat and sang every day while drinking across from the National Gallery, and who, as many others like him before and since, was found dead outdoors on a freezing November morning. Another story was 'Local hero', about a new pub on Wexford Street named Whelan's.

In the *Press* I would spend many mainly happy days as a small cog in the enormous machinery of the Burgh Quay behemoth, which every day produced two national newspapers and on Sundays, a third.

In its lively newsroom was a particularly gifted generation of *Press* reporters and feature writers, many of whom were or would go on to be household names. They sat at the Burgh Quay end of the room beneath huge windows that looked out across the River Liffey. Clattering away on their typewriters and working the phones after arriving back from markings, they produced the evening's first copy, which they passed down the room to news editors, who passed them on down to the senior subeditors, who sat across the room in a long row on the 'back desk', where they designed the page layouts before passing them on again to the chief subeditor, who skimmed them around the subs' desk to us 'down-table' subeditors.

Sitting around the *Irish Press* subs' desk in a square horseshoe shape in intimate association was a collection of the most eclectic and colourful characters that could possibly have been assembled. They included three poets, a playwright, a Joycean scholar, a few lawyers, and others from all social classes and disparate backgrounds who had chosen the newspaper life. At the helm was chief subeditor Sean Purcell. He had recently taken over from John Banville, who was destined for better things. Sean's deputy was Terence Killeen, who usually sat with his well-worn copy of *Ulysses* at hand, and talented assistant chief subeditors Catherine Osborn and Liam Scully, who worked the late shift and stood in when one of the other two was off.

Every evening the shift started quietly as we waited for the harried reporters to release their stories down the line. While our evening was beginning, for *Evening Press* colleagues it was ending. Sometimes the great Con Houlihan, who wrote beautifully about life through the medium of sport, would still be lumbering around. I recall one evening finding a huge paw on my head only to look up and see the giant Con with his other hand over his face, looking down at me and uttering his peculiar term of endearment, or blessing, 'Me little maggot'.

The fun on the down-table desk was fuelled by Sean Purcell's sparky humour; by the muffled barbs of bearded Dan Coen; the tales of the late gentle playwright, cartoonist and author of a history of the bicycle, Seamus McGonagle, about his nights in the bars of bohemian Fleet Street; garnished by passionate political points by poet Hugh McFadden; goaded by larger-than-life agent provocateur and perennial pressman Joe Walsh; with friendly reminders of transgressions on the feminist front by Therese Caherty and leftfield interjections from polymath John Brophy, whose talents ranged from calligraphy to flute playing, and of whom it was rarely said, 'I know exactly where you're coming from.' All of which was occasionally becalmed by Terence Killeen's judicious professorial interjections.

The entertaining cacophony of banter around the desk made most evenings hugely enjoyable occasions, especially so after the return from breaks in Mulligan's pub, when the desk could be transformed into a theatre, often of the absurd.

Late one night on the desk, Dan Coen suffered a heart attack. As he was being stretchered out, he glanced back at the desk and muttered in the typically black humour of Dublin journalism, 'The things I do for you fucking freelancers ...'. With him gone, there would be four extra weekly shifts available to them.

After a while on the desk, I took over the foreign pages from Seamus McGonagle. Over four frenetic nights each week, I copy-tasted mounds of computer printouts and photographs from the news agencies. From these I subbed and marked up all the stories and laid out the one or two foreign pages allotted to foreign that night. It was a very eventful time: the first Gulf War was in progress, apartheid was collapsing in South Africa, East Germany was falling apart, the war in Yugoslavia was raging and the Cold War was ending everywhere except Cuba.

Later, the subs' desk would be described by a representative of Ingersoll's, the *Press* management's US partners, as being 'inhabited by eccentrics and ungovernables' – a criticism taken by many with no little pride, having been sanctified with faint criticism by one of the *Irish Press* 'partners' who would go on to spend so much of their precious time and scarce *Press* finances at each other's throats in the Four Courts.

With the night closing in on the subs' desk, the tension mounted as minds became more focused and the mood turned to the serious matter of getting out a national newspaper. As the copy first trickled and then flowed down from the Liffey end, stress levels rose. Raised voices resounded around a newsroom shrouded in a fog of swirling cigarette smoke as stories were handed from reporters to the back desk to the subeditors and out to compositors in the next room, who shaped the typography and translated headlines, text and captions from our instructions scribbled on typewriter scrolls and A4 paper, and which would end up as the finished articles on pieces of bromide paper to be pasted up in pages on the stone by compositors. Copies of these made-up pages were photocopied and checked by subs, corrections made in a final flurry of frenzied activity before being finally released, and with them the tension, to the printers below, with Sean Purcell's loud imprimatur: 'Give it to the people.'

Relations between journalists and compositors were mostly good, but on occasion some compositors resented the instructions of the uppity journalists who had replaced them as aristocrats in the newspaper hierarchy. At such times of friction the partition dividing journalists from compositors could have marked the front line in a class war that occasionally broke out on the stone, where demarcation was king and where journalists were forbidden to put a finger on a piece of bromide on a page. As the pages were assembled every night on the stone, skirmishes could continue until 3 a.m. in an undeclared war between the former 'aristocrats of labour' and former 'gentlemen of the press'. Here, my background as a journeyman compositor turned journalist could be an advantage. In a sense, I could come out as bi-social.

Over the evening on the subs' desk, breaks from our labours wrestling with words and verbally with each other were taken nearby in Mulligan's pub in the company of the irrepressible Joe Walsh, peacemaker Liam Scully, elegant and erudite Enda O'Doherty, convivial Catherine Osborne, bright young cub Philip Hedderman, and urbane Maurice Healy, who had recently been granted asylum on our desk from the *Press*'s renowned sports department. 'Mull's' was our home-from-home for all our animated talk of the night's stories, for juicy office gossip and reviews of the previous night's drink-fuelled escapades after the paper had been put to bed.

Around the time the night shift was ending, the building would feel as if it were trembling as the thousands of copies of the first edition were being churned out by monstrous printing machines below. It was as if the whole shuddering edifice were giving birth, which in a sense it was, delivering our ruddy little baby, the *Irish Press*. Outside, Poolbeg Street was a hive of activity as scooters and vans arrived to pick up bundles of papers for delivery to newsagents and their paperboys and girls.

With the paper finally 'put to bed', and after Mulligan's had shut up shop, the search was on for somewhere to continue our conversations over a nightcap, a necessary evil to come down from the fevered excitement of the evening's work. Very often the venue was the Irish Times Club in Fleet Street, where assorted shady characters and lost souls of the Dublin twilight gathered in unlikely association.

That rich and rewarding life of work and play wouldn't last, however. The final years of the *Press* were troubled by controversial managerial decisions and by conflicted industrial relations, which all resulted in declining readership and revenues. Resultant losses led in turn to further conflict, and a spectral, sardonic dance of death began.

On the day before my forty-second birthday, twenty years ago, I left Bewley's Oriental Tea Emporium on Westmoreland Street, a popular press haunt, to work the late shift on Burgh Quay, when I noticed an *Evening Herald* billboard on a lamp post on the south-west corner of O'Connell Bridge.

'There's only one evening paper,' boasted the *Herald*, our rival from the Independent Newspaper Group. I suspected what it meant, and an old feeling of dread descended. I took down the offending billboard and carried it with me as I rushed across Westmoreland Street and D'Olier Street, down Hawkins Street and around the corner into Poolbeg Street, running up the back stairs of the *Press* office, past the printing works, through the composing room and into the crowded, hushed newsroom, where a chapel meeting was gathered in solemn session.

It was bad news on Burgh Quay. 'We're gone,' someone whispered as I joined the meeting. 'So I heard,' I replied, lifting up the *Herald* poster. The meeting was outraged by the poster: how could they crow about the loss of 600 jobs and the effect that would have on their families? We later had word from our colleagues at the *Indo*, who disassociated themselves from the offending billboard message.

For a while, many of us fought to find some way of keeping the *Press* titles alive. We worked on the *X-Press*, a homemade free-sheet, which we distributed while seeking donations from the public in small white plastic buckets. My daily newspaper stand was at the junction of North Earl Street and O'Connell Street, beside the statue of James Joyce. It was a particularly hot summer in 1995, and often I wore shorts on my stand, which allowed my inner paperboy to re-emerge and cry out variations on old themes, such as '*X-Press, X-Press,* read all about it!'

Messages of support from passers-by were many, as the *Press* had a long tradition of loyal support. For decades, the paper was a leading voice of nationalist Ireland. On the street, people stopped and talked of their long family connections to the paper. Such warm messages were comforting and welcome, although one *Press* man ruefully remarked, 'It's a pity enough of them didn't buy it.'

As part of our efforts to save the newspapers, one weekend I travelled with copies of the *X-Press* and my white plastic bucket from our Liberty Hall base to Belfast. There I was helped by Belfast friends I had known since attending the Donegal Gaeltacht in Gweedore on summer holidays from Synge Street. In Kelly's Cellars in Belfast city centre we met the *Press*'s northern correspondent, Anne Cadwallader, and began accepting donations. It was then on to Madden's public house nearby and to bars along the Falls Road and beyond to Andersonstown. The response was generous and sympathetic. Many people mentioned that the *Press* was the only national newspaper that supported the Northern peace process. By coincidence, in 1993 I had written an op ed story in the *Irish Press*, 'Clonard, this time the bells signal peace', arguing that the potential peace signals coming from Clonard Monastery via priests from Republicans were of particular significance and should be listened to.

During our time of protest, a small number of us also took part in a sit-in in the Burgh Quay newsroom. The camaraderie involved in this effort offered comfort, as did the vast public support garnered from the huge media attention it received. Generous local businesses delivered free food and drinks. A well-remembered highlight was the arrival on a bus in Poolbeg Street of Ireland soccer team manager Jack Charlton with a number of the team to lend their support, and a bottle of whiskey. Alas, I had been off alcohol since the beginning of the year.

Our occupation of Burgh Quay ended when we were instructed to do so by the NUJ leadership, who said that we would be better served in securing the titles' future if our protest ended. We didn't like the decision, but reluctantly accepted it. On our last emotion-filled night, each of us took turns to speak about what the sit-in meant to us. By early morning we were taking turns singing our songs and delivering recitations. And at the very end, I have a last happy memory of the newsroom, with a line of us meandering around the room while sitting in our four-wheeled chairs as the huge empty hall rang hollow with our laughter.

Next morning we trooped dejectedly down the stairs to awaiting reporters and photographers from other newspapers. Where once we had been a newspaper, now we were the news. 'Heroes all' lauded a sympathetic line the next day in the *Star* newspaper beside a photograph of our retreat down the back stairs into Poolbeg Street. But the feeling was one of defeat. It was gone. All was lost.

Of the 600 or so Press Group staff cut adrift in the scattering from Burgh Quay, some would make it to the *Irish Independent*, *The Irish Times*, RTÉ, the *Irish Sun* and the *Irish Daily Star*, but most ended up on the dole queues, and some didn't make it at all.

Mná na Press

Kate Shanahan
(Feature Writer, Irish Press, 1987–1995)

Though I did not know it then, I joined the Irish Press Group at a time in the late 1980s when Ireland was on the cusp of huge social change. Women working in print led much of the coverage of other women, but that did not mean that they were all feminists. There was, for example, a group of older women hacks, 'grand dames' of the city's newsrooms who remained confined to female beats like fashion and social columns. In person they exuded a mixture of chic confidence and cold-hearted charm, especially when dealing with younger female colleagues. One, addressing an ingénue as she sat waiting in a hotel lobby for a press conference, noted witheringly, 'Is that you, Nuala dear? I didn't recognise you; I thought you were the sofa.'

'Nuala's' weight and flowery dress were thus disposed of in one pithy sentence. The kind of woman journalist I had admired growing up, however, was a far different creature. The 'intrepid girl reporter' was the type of gal many of our mothers feared us becoming. When the writer Mary Kenny made one of her regular appearances on RTÉ television, my late mother always commented on her performance with the words, 'That one must be drunk,' so outlandish were her views on female emancipation. Indeed, when the selfsame Ms Kenny told her own mother that she wanted to be a journalist, she too was less than ecstatic at the notion of her daughter joining the grubby ranks of the Fourth Estate.

'Oh, darling,' she warned her, 'women journalists are awful, so cynical and such hard drinkers.' By the time I started work in the *Irish Press*, the era of radical feminism as epitomised by Kenny, who had been women's editor of the *Irish Press* in the 1970s, was long gone. It's a testimony to her legacy, though, that one evening in the 1990s I watched, open mouthed, as a section editor ran across the newsroom pursued by a female colleague, whose anger at a slight had been built up over the course of a few hours in a nearby hostelry. The elderly scribe beside me barely glanced up from his pages to mutter, 'She's good, but she's no Mary Kenny,' as the insulted one flew past in high dudgeon.

My female contemporaries may not have attracted as much controversy, but they were trailblazers in that they worked in news, politics, sports, features and editorial. So much so that, when out on a story, being asked, 'Are you the Girl from the *Press?*' seemed more a signifier of a grudging respect than a put-down. On occasion it even gave some protection. Once, in South Armagh, venturing into a local pub in mid afternoon looking for interviewees and facing a sub-zero reception committee, I used it myself.

'I'm the girl from the *Press*', I protested under hostile questioning. My friendly ploy worked well, a little too well. One of the men I'd interviewed about the peace process showed up at Burgh Quay weeks later to ask me out on a date. 'I have a baby at home,' I explained. 'Sure there's no harm in a child,' he replied, eventually conceding that the husband who came with him might prove a bit of an impediment.

In a strange way, though long associated with Fianna Fáil and de Valera, the Press Group, as I got to know it, seemed more analogous to an earlier era: it was what I'd always imagined pre-1916 Ireland to be like. In various corners of the large newsroom, Catholics, Protestants and Dissenters worked together, not so much in peace and harmony, but in a contrarian kinship. Everyone seemed to have written a book, or be in the process of writing a book, a play or a collection of poetry. No one really agreed with anyone else about anything, but if you pointed that out to them they all agreed that you had totally misjudged the situation. It took some time to realise that under the faint aura of conservatism that hung over the brown-stained mugs of tea and clusters of old newspapers lay an uncompromising rebel heart. And when I did discover it, along with everyone else who worked there, I fell hopelessly in love with the place and the people.

But on my first day in the newsroom, all of that remained to be discovered. Instead, I was puzzled by the number of middle-aged men who approached me throughout the day to inform me that I was 'missing an earring'. By the time mid afternoon came, and yet another helpful colleague pointed out that I had obviously lost some jewellery, my tolerance levels for the 'joke' at the new girl's expense had worn quite thin. I pointed out that the single large silver hoop hanging from my right earlobe was 'the fashion'.

'Well, if that's the fashion, then I'm coming to work with the one shoe on tomorrow,' an older subeditor noted acerbically. It all seemed a far cry from the magazine (*Hot Press*) that I had just come from, where difference was not just tolerated but positively encouraged. In Burgh Quay, conversely, I felt the heavy weight of history on my shoulders. More than once I heard that 'Dev' would be 'spinning in his grave', or that the 'Post-Mistress in Donegal', the oft-used arbiter of newsworthiness, would find a story boring or, God forbid, so racy that she might pick up the phone to launch a complaint. But even if at times their comments bordered on the harsh, I soon realised that my colleagues' critiques stemmed from a culture where newspapers were considered to be a group effort, thus there was little patience for the travails of ego. One editor waiting impatiently on my copy recounted the story of how Brendan Behan arrived one day looking for money he said he was owed. 'He was at the back door, and word came down to him: no money until you file. So he tore a bit of paper off a bale of newspapers, took out the stub of a pencil and wrote a column on the spot.' Whether true or not, it certainly put any agonising over a turn of phrase into perspective.

In essence, there was more sexism outside of the *Press* than within. The senior FF politician who told me in the course of a political interview that a woman could never become Taoiseach as 'once a month she'd go mad' was merely expressing what the rest of his party were probably thinking. Women might be accepted in the workplace, but ingrained views were harder to dislodge. On late-night 'markings', for example, female hacks knew that there was a time to make your excuses and leave. Even supposed liberals could turn feral with the right mix of drink and pheromones. One colleague at a political dinner felt someone playing 'footsie' with her at the completely male table. She kicked back and looked around at her companions to see who would react. The foot's owner gave her a sly wink; the leading left-wing TD would have been her last suspect.

Patronising gestures aside, the 1980s and 1990s were not a good time for women in Ireland. It was as if the very heart of the country were being torn apart by a tsunami of first-person narratives. The Kerry babies' case, the X case, the Lavinia Kerwick rape case, the Kilkenny incest case and priests hiding their love children all held a mirror to a society where women were still second-class citizens. Inside the *Irish Press*, the same arguments that the public had outside were being echoed in newsroom debates. When I decided to write a book about those changes I was encouraged, and given unpaid leave, by my editors. Even though an earlier attempt to be involved in the Mary Robinson presidential bid had been shot down (I was told that I could be a journalist or a campaigner, but not both), my concerns were now considered legitimate ones for a reporter to explore.

It is a testimony to their dogged adherence to 'The Truth in the News' motto that was on the *Press* masthead that editors protected their staff from any and all outside pressures. In one or two cases that affected their promotion chances, but it also caused those who worked for them to be loyal, with an *esprit de corps* that transcended more trivial spats. When I was elected as the first ever female Father of Chapel (NUJ shop steward), or the Mother as I was known, I felt that searing sense of loyalty at first hand. Within a few short weeks of being elected I discovered that I was pregnant, and months of nausea and tiredness followed. The nadir came when, six months pregnant, a long day that began on the steps of the High Court led to tense union and management negotiations as we sought assurances on the protection of the staff pension fund. To have looked for a food break would have signalled weakness. It was 10 p.m. that night before the talks finally finished. I went home, tried to eat some food and promptly threw up. The thought that my colleagues could be left pensionless had overcome any physical distress I felt throughout the day, but the pressure had taken its toll. For weeks afterwards, grisly old newsmen, not known for their emotion, came up to admonish me to 'mind that baby' as they patted 'the bump' on their way past.

Becoming Mother of the Chapel also meant that the swirl of characters who came in and out of focus on late smoky nights in the newsroom became more human. They loved where they were and what they did; they did not want that to change. When a big story broke it was as if a charge of pure adrenaline surged through the air. Names were shouted across desks, leads checked, the tapping of fingers now outgunned by the ringing of phones. The lines of red-faced editors on the newsdesk, like grimacing gorgons, were never easily appeased. The three-sources rule for every story was rigidly adhered to, becoming a Sisyphean labour on occasion. This was when the 'family' came into its own, but also when any attempt at measured delivery of criticism flew out the window. 'I believe I'm being accused of bullying,' one section editor complained to me in my Mother of Chapel role. 'And all I did was tell him that he was a useless bastard who should be sacked for fucking gross incompetence and that his pages were fucking useless. I mean, c'mon, Kate, if you can't tell someone that, then I give up!'

The other women in the *Press*, the copy-takers, secretaries and administrative staff, were made of equally stern stuff, loyal to the core, but crossed at your peril. One told of how she'd taken umbrage in her youth at the manner in which her then boss, a former IRA man, had spoken to her, when she complained about his feet being on the desk she had just tidied. He took a revolver out of a nearby drawer and said: 'This says you'll do whatever I tell you to do, and I can speak to you however I like.' Mustering as much energy in her tiny frame as she could, she replied: 'You'll have to shoot me first to get me to do anything for you from now on.'

She grinned at the memory. 'I wasn't putting up with that, let me tell you,' she explained, as though being threatened with a gun at work was a mundane enough occurrence, but one that needed nipping in the bud.

When the *Press* closed, many of the women reporters continued to meet up on a regular basis. We called ourselves *Mná na Press*, a fitting tribute both to the doughty women who had gone before us and their place in our history. Most of us continued working as journalists, but even if our careers progressed professionally, something was always missing.

Post the 1995 closure, for example, I could not physically walk past the old Press Building, often taking laborious detours to avoid that part of the city. Too many ghosts and memories lay dormant there. I wanted to remember it as it once was, thriving with the heady mix of breaking news, gossip, the smell of ink and print wafting up from the presses in the bowels down below, full of characters who did not know they were characters. Most of all, though, I missed the person I had once been, notebook in hand, exhilarated at the feeling of being at the heart of a beating city, the 'girl from the *Press*', just one quote away from that front-page lead.

Con Houlihan: when a giant walked the Earth

Liam Mackey
(Football (soccer) Correspondent, *Sunday Press*)

Con Houlihan, the Castleisland colossus, cast such a gigantic shadow that it once temporarily obscured one of the most revered figures in English football history. The setting was the press box at Wembley on the occasion of the England v Ireland European Championship qualifier in 1991, a game fondly remembered for the fact that the visitors fairly battered the home side in a 1–1 draw to chalk up another of those celebrated moral victories of the Jack Charlton era.

The real standout moment of a memorable night for me, however, was not Niall Quinn's equalising goal, nor even Ray Houghton's wasted opportunity to give Ireland the victory they deserved. The incident I most vividly recall occurred at half-time. Sitting just in front of me in the press box was none other than the great England World Cup-winning captain, Bobby Moore, who was there doing analysis of the game for a radio station. But when an Irish supporter approached on an autograph-hunting mission, he had, literally, bigger quarry in mind. Thus it was that the most golden of all the boys of the summer of 1966 found himself having to squeeze back in his seat so that one star-struck fan could stretch his arm across him to get his match programme signed by Con Houlihan.

That trip to London was my first assignment as the newly installed football correspondent for the *Sunday Press* and, having

295

long worshipped Con from a distance, in truth I wasn't far from getting him to sign a programme myself. Like so many others, I had been a devoted reader of his *Evening Press* columns, a magical literary experience fashioned in the teeth of unforgiving deadlines and without which no sporting occasion, however big or small, could be deemed complete. From point-to-points to All-Irelands to World Cup Finals, the last word, and invariably the best word, belonged to Con.

They advise that you should be wary of meeting your heroes, but for this nervous newcomer on the full-time sports-reporting beat, Con could not have been kinder or more encouraging. For my part, his great generosity of spirit permitted an easy transition from awestruck fan to comrade-in-arms, although I would always remain acutely aware that it was a privilege, as well as a joy, to – as he might put it himself – toil beside him in the same vineyard for a number of years.

As numerous colleagues will attest, life on the road with Con was never dull. In Seville for a World Cup qualifier in 1992, he adopted his usual practice of setting up his command post in a congenial bar close to the media hotel. This one was a small family-run place with a big window looking out onto the street. No sooner had the first sighting of the legend within been confirmed than the little bar was fairly besieged by Irish fans who wanted to talk to, buy a drink for, or simply be seen in the same place as the great man. After just one night of booming business, the owners were so overcome by the surge in profits that, much to Con's embarrassment, they refused to let him put his hand in his pocket again for the remainder of our stay.

That same year we were in the Parken Stadium in Copenhagen when Con, never a man to be mistaken for a dedicated follower of fashion, unveiled one of his most spectacular sartorial improvisations. The conditions that night were positively Arctic, with freezing rain lashing those of us who were unfortunate enough to be in the exposed front row of the press box. To my right, *Irish Press* colleague Charlie Stuart was manfully trying to keep his phone and notebook dry under an increasingly soggy cardboard box, while to my left I saw that Con was fishing deep in his battered holdall for something, anything, with which to ward off the elements.

When I turned to look again, it was with a start. What Con had found was a white hotel towel, but one that, judging by its pattern of bloodstains, he had used that morning to mop up a shaving cut. With this eerie veil now draped over his head and his great craggy face peering out beneath, the effect was extraordinary and unforgettable, like a cross between Mount Rushmore and the Shroud of Turin.

That was the World Cup qualifying campaign that culminated in the infamous 'night in November' in Belfast when the two Irelands drew 1–1 in a poisonous atmosphere in Windsor Park. And it was also the occasion when, in our press overflow area, a disgruntled local reached through a cordon of RUC officers to deliver a blow to Con, who was, entirely unintentionally, slow in getting to his feet for the start of 'God Save the Queen'. 'Stand up, you Fenian bastard,' was the accompanying order. A very ugly scene, to be sure, and I recall writing afterwards that perhaps the only consolation was to ponder what must have gone through his assailant's mind as Con did indeed rise to his full height, first blocking out the floodlights and then the moon.

All ended well for Jack Charlton's team on the night, of course, with the result that we found ourselves touching down in JFK the following summer to commence coverage of the 1994 World Cup. Four of us from Burgh Quay were travelling together and thought it would be a smart idea to pool our resources and hire a cab in New York to take us all the way to the Irish team's hotel in Parsipanny,

New Jersey. We had barely crossed the Hudson, however, when it became clear that our friendly taxi driver had never been outside Manhattan in his life. After about two hours we were fantastically lost and negotiating hairpin bends as we rapidly gained altitude on the side of a mountain. Initial jollity had long since given way to sullen despair when we found ourselves passing a yellow and black road sign that warned of the presence of bears. At this point the oppressive silence in the cab was broken by that unmistakable Kerry brogue. 'I think I smell Canada,' said Con.

We eventually did reach our destination, and later made it more or less intact down to Orlando too, where I recall that even Con – a man who would often have a big stew on the boil at his home in Portobello – was taken aback by the size of American portions. Declining an offer to eat out one night, he explained that for lunch he'd been served a pizza 'the size of the wheel of a donkey cart.'

The shocking closure of the *Irish Press* in 1995 brought an abrupt end to our adventures, although not before a long, hot summer of industrial action during which Con, despite his heartbreak at what had happened, threw in his lot with the friends and colleagues he called his 'comrades on the barricades'. Three times a week, he wrote for our little fundraising paper, *The X-Press*, wonderful autobiographical pieces that were later collected in a book called *Windfalls*.

And it wasn't long, of course, before his talents were once again available to a wider audience in the *Sunday World* and the *Evening Herald*. When he broke his hip while crossing a road in Cheltenham ('I fell in Cheltenham, not at Cheltenham', he was at pains to point out) it might have been the beginning of a long, slow physical decline, but his mind stayed razor-sharp and, for the most part, his spirits remained undimmed. I have happy memories from those years of dropping in to see him in the little house in Portobello, with its paintings by young artists adorning the walls, books and papers and writing material piled high on the table, the gas fire on the go, a bottle of wine uncorked, and the big match on the telly.

There were undoubtedly darker days to come for Con as he endured a protracted hospitalisation. On my occasional visits to see him in St James's – never frequent enough, to my shame – I'd find myself thinking of the lines written by the great American songwriter Guy Clark: 'To me he's one of the heroes of this country, so why's he all dressed up like them old men?' Yet, Con being Con, he could still contrive to cheer up his visitors more than they could him. It was during one such visit, I recall, that he stated one of his objections to plans to name the Castleisland bypass after him. 'I don't even drive,' he pointed out, 'so they should be naming a bike-pass after me.'

And, remarkably, even when flat on his back, and with all of his eighty-six years finally catching up with him, he continued to dictate weekly newspaper columns on subjects as varied as sport, politics, history, music, cinema, poetry and prose.

Con's death on 4 August 2012 prompted an enormous outpouring of affection as well as grief. But some of his closest friends knew best how he should be properly commemorated. At the crematorium, a piece of music chosen by Con's cousin, the internationally renowned orchestra conductor Robert 'Bobby' Houlihan, was played. It was Gabriel Fauré's *In Paradisum*, which, in the quiet of Mount Jerome, was enough to give even this heathen rocker a fleeting sense of the divine. Indeed, the only wonder was that the sublime soundtrack didn't inspire us all to sprout wings and ascend through the roof in a heavenly shaft of light. Yet, it was precisely at this special moment that I happened to notice a couple of Con's pals slipping out of their seats and making for the door. When one of them caught my quizzical eye, he replied with a little boxing mime.

Ah, but of course: Katie Taylor was about to fight in her Olympic semi-final, and even the music of the spheres was going to have to play second fiddle to that. Needless to say, Con Houlihan would not only have understood: he would have approved. Or as Eoghan Corry, another Burgh Quay exile, memorably put it on *Tonight with Vincent Browne* later that night: 'If Con had been at his own funeral, he'd have left too.'

In the many tributes that were paid to him following his death, it was frequently said that Con Houlihan was one of the finest sportswriters of his generation. That is true, but I suggest it would be even truer to say that he was one of Ireland's finest writers, full stop. Con was deservedly honoured in his time with busts and plaques and statues and awards, but he once said that the accolade that mattered most to him was from a reader of his 'Tributaries' column in the *Evening Press*, who wrote in to say: 'You gave me my third-level education.'

For my part, it was also an education to know Con Houlihan – and an uproariously entertaining one at that. It is no exaggeration to say that the private man was as much loved as the public figure was universally revered – and maybe that's the highest tribute you can pay to any human being. The only consolation in his physical absence is that the great windfall of words lives on in print. And I envy all those who have yet to discover his timeless world.

As the man himself would always say: now read on.

A brush with Brush Shields and a flower from the Diceman

Sarah O'Hara
(Reporter and Subeditor, Irish Press, 1990–1995)

Inevitably, perhaps, the memories of working in the *Irish Press* are golden, but for me they come in fragments rather than in finished anecdotes. Fragments of image and sound, a few sentences and a few of the stories, those published and those unpublished.

Firstly come the images.

The huge window overlooking the Liffey, the river gleaming greenly now in memory, and the marvel at having such a seat, at such a wonderfully shabby, grand, pockmarked, scribble-stained wooden table, with such a grand view, right in the centre of the city.

The glass window box at the Poolbeg Street entrance, where the security guards always smiled, always ready for a quick chat on the way in; those strange tiled stairs (like the entrance to a public toilet, but in a good way); the several flights up; and getting lost once, stepping into the machine room, where the paper was printed, feeling I'd never get out. (The headline, so easy to imagine when working as a journalist: 'Freelance disappears, last seen going into Irish Press building'.)

And then, finally, the warm, wide, long room where everyone in the *Irish Press* and *Evening Press* worked. The trek from the door to the window, passing the caseroom guys, formerly typesetters, who did the paste-up overseen by subs. I always hoped that supervisor Tom Loughman was on so as to say: 'Hi, Tom, where's Dick and Harry?' (Dick was the editor of the *Evening Press*, and Harry Pidgeon another of the caseroom supervisors). Tom always grinned, as if he'd never heard me say that. The row of dumb terminals where anyone could sit and tap out an article.

The staff on sports and advertising, the men on the newsdesk (yes, they were men, then, in the 1990s; perhaps occasionally a woman might have slipped in, or perhaps she was just having a chat with a male editor) who always seemed strict and focused to me, and in the middle the picture editor, shuffling large, shiny, black-and-white photos. The two big reporters' tables, one for the evening and one for the daily, and then finally, at the end of the room, those lovely tables by the window where anyone could sit.

There are some visual details as well, the abundant hair of one of the *Irish Press* reporters and her easygoing manner, and the blondness (masculine) of an *Irish Press* editor. The 'girlie' posters that some caseroom guys had pasted up on lockers. Once there was a brief moment of extreme insecurity in comparing myself to these shapely models, all made up with lacquered hair and bikinis, but then consoled myself with a quick look at the guys who'd put the pics up. They were no models either.

And Des Crowley's coffee mug, like every other journalist's mug, with its quarter-inch caffeine granules coating the inside. My delighted disgust as I cleaned this mug for myself to have a boiled-up Nescafé (no free-trade, organic, Kenyan, Guatemalan, Colombian or Ethiopian in those days) on a week when I was filling in for Gerry Byrne on the *Sunday Press* business page. (Delight, because there was a sense of virtue involved in being, for once, 'the clean one'.) It took about ten minutes, as I remember, to get that mug maybe not completely clean, but clean enough.

Secondly, stride in the sentences.

'Hammer it out,' property editor Con Power said to me once at the beginning of my 1990s' stint in the IP. I had come back in to the

Press circa 1991 having been made redundant when the computer company, joined after a long stint in the public service, went bust. After working as a book editor for most of the 1980s I was a bit hesitant about 'hammering' anything 'out'. I was more used to going over other people's copy with a fine comb (the kind you use for lice, as we had so much more time in semi-state book publishing than in deadline-focused newspapers). It was good advice, although it took me a long time to get over the pernicketyness of copy-editing.

'An old shoe.' *Irish Press* editor Hugh Lambert describing Dublin as 'comfortable, like an old shoe.' In those days it was a shabby city, although all the more lovable for that (in memory), and where we worked, to the east of O'Connell Bridge, it was particularly shabby.

Old shoe was a good description of the *Press* atmosphere, which seemed to embrace everyone who came in with its warm comfort. There was a sense that you did not have to 'be' anything in particular, dress in a particular way, be 'good on the national question', and one never heard anyone complaining about someone because they were not liberal enough, or were too liberal. In a brief freelance stint in the early 1980s I remember standing in Mulligan's and giving out to a big, fat *Press* staffer who had a baby-feet badge on his lapel, and he just grinned. I grin too, now, remembering the goodwill under the differences of opinion.

'Anathema.' One of the caseroom guys made that pithy one-word comment about the prospect of the manual cut-and-paste layout of the paper disappearing as a result of new technology. He pronounced 'anathema' the way you would say *Anna Karenina*. Anna Thema. Just that one word, and the way he pronounced it, evoked a colourful Dublin sense of humour and that rock-solid common sense that took the hot air out of an issue without minimising its importance.

'I hope we get the weather you're expecting.' That was Dick O'Riordan making a joke about my clothes, and then quickly disappearing, although he could probably hear me laughing from about twenty feet away. It was the year I was fond of knee-length orange shorts. Extremely comfortable, and they seemed to feel right on St Patrick's Day, combined with a white T-shirt and a green cardigan.

'Are you reading your own story?' This was a question asked by one of the subs as I walked down Poolbeg Street, poring over the latest *Irish Press* edition. I must have looked surprised because she smiled: 'Reporters are always reading their own stories!' Well … yeah! There was after all the curiosity as to whether your byline was in bold caps, or bold u/lc (upper and lower-case letters combined), or in roman (caps or u/lc), and then wondering about that: there never seemed to be any logic to it. Naturally, one also worried about whether the story seemed okay, if an error had slipped in, or if it could have been punchier.

The other reason for looking was to see it as an independent outsider. I always remember the surprise on reading a news feature commissioned by John Garvey for the editorial page of the *Irish Press*. It was on the Censorship Board, and seeing it anew, on the day of publication, I could not help but notice a new insight: the Board was so committed to censorship that its members did not even let each other know which way they were voting!

On that day I realised the advantage of doing a straightforward reporting job. By not editing or filtering because of a particular opinion, you can show more than you realise at the time.

Here was the light-shedding sentence from the feature: 'Given that it is a secret ballot, members don't know how colleagues voted, although decisions generally are unanimous.' ('Secrets of the Censor's Office', *Irish Press*, 17 October 1992.)

Then there was the sentence of quick advice, probably standing up on the way out of the room from one of the *Evening Pres* reporters, now a columnist with Another Paper. 'It always looks as if you're a good writer if you use short sentences!' he said with a grin, enjoying the benefits of brevity. (The master of short sentences was of course Con Houlihan, much loved, and an epic in his own lifetime.)

Thirdly, then, are the pieces written, and the bits of things that 'disappeared' from an item once submitted. From interviews with politicians' children doing exams the comments of a Fine Gael TD's son were omitted, as were the comments of a 'Stickie' from a round-up on politicians distressed at losing their seats. (The *Irish Press* was, after all, a Fianna Fáil paper.) On abortion opinions, the quotes of Joyce Whelehan, wife of Harry, the then Attorney General, never saw the blurry blackness of *Irish Press* print. Neither did two stories submitted on spec: an interview with young gay people, and one on the semi-mystical visionary sensibilities of John Moriarty, known in those days before he got his first book published and became a media figure as 'the gardener philosopher'.

I include these only for completeness, and to indicate the background and character of the 1990s, because when you're a journalist, and you don't make the decisions, you accept that, and the focus is always on the next story, and the one after that.

John Garvey often asked me to review plays, although I was never officially 'drama critic', and when I came across them in the Irish newspaper archive (freely available online at public libraries) I could see there'd been fun in writing them. I always wrote for the person I'd been told was the *Irish Press* target audience: a postmistress in Donegal. I imagined her to be alert, curious and kindly, with little interest in being 'literary' for the sake of it. So for *Lady Windermere's Fan* by Oscar Wilde at the Gaiety, the postmistress might have read: 'It's difficult to play the part of a good woman when, like Martin Murphy's foppish Lord Darlington, most of us prefer to distinguish between the charming and the tedious rather than good and bad.'

(I cringe now, reading that sentence, wondering why I didn't write 'between the charming and the tedious rather than the good and the bad.' Maybe I did and it was changed on the subs' desk, or maybe I spent ten minutes or so wondering whether to include or exclude the definite article before going for exclusion! As reporters, we were expected not to sweat the petty stuff! Good advice, in general, methinks.)

And for *Brownbread* by Roddy Doyle at the Olympia, there was: 'What happens when you kidnap a bishop? And you're a schoolkid and your parents are away and you don't want to get the carpets dirty and the local garda and a plainclothes detective are outside with walkie talkies?'

We had many scandals during those years, but they have all been repeated in this century, in differing forms, depending on which 'gods' we have decided to follow slavishly. In those days, as now, there was hypocrisy and abuse of powerful positions, financial finagling and inner circles, and some offenders getting off but not others. Nowadays, coming across one of the lighter stories that emerged from the scandal of Bishop Casey being a father, in a biological as well as spiritual sense, I cannot help but smile. The story, based on an interview with a former Dominican, begins: 'Seminarians are warned that the love of a good woman is a major risk to their chastity ...'.

David Rice, author of *Shattered Vows*, is quoted (by me) as saying: 'We were often told it was the good woman who was the danger, not the bad woman, because her sheer goodness would attract you and make you let your guard down.' Mr Rice also said: 'You meet a very lovely innocent youngster and she'd be no threat and she'd be the one the priest would fall for, and I think that is what happened with Annie Murphy. She was a lovely, innocent person.'

Then there was a very minor scandal, which probably no one remembers. I didn't remember it myself until coming across it in the online archive. It was published on Tuesday 7 July 1992, and based on a call to the Telecom Éireann accounts department about my phone bill. The headline is, appropriately, scandalised: 'Year-old phone calls shock' by Sarah O'Hara (in bold caps).

'Telecom Éireann is billing customers for calls made up to a year ago and some callers are facing bills hundreds of pounds higher than their normal phone bills as a result.'

There is an obligingly outraged comment from Caroline Gill of the Consumers Association, 'accus[ing] the State body of abusing their monopoly position' and referring to 'this unacceptable business practice'. Ah yes, those were the days!

To be able to get a 'shock horror' story published because you had a problem with a phone bill ... oh, but come back, Telecom, all is forgiven.

To have the chance to chat with rocker Brush Shields about his rural life, explaining this (to the Donegal postmistress):

'There are two goats, three or four ponies and a pet cow [on his farm, on the Meath/Kildare border]. The cow isn't going anywhere, he says mysteriously, a possible reference to the slaughterhouse. It's not for milking either: it's a virgin cow so it hasn't begat another cow. It thinks it's a donkey and the donkey thinks it's a cow.'

To hear the views of those who are different to oneself. Of Judge Rory O'Hanlon, for example, after he had been fired from the Law Reform Commission for 'controversial' opinions on abortion (he was subsequently paid damages). He told me:

'... the much-denigrated old values contribute to happiness. Modern ideas of self-fulfilment involve complete freedom of action to behave any way they want to on sexual morality. When you take away all restraint, it is like a spoilt child allowed to do anything they want to. The old-style Catholic traditional way of life helped people to live with peace of mind, even in the face of trials and adversity.' That was his opinion, and the *Irish Press* published it in detail, without editorialising it.

To talk with that well-known Grafton Street figure of the 1990s, the Diceman, about his love of flowers! That was Thom McGinty, mime artist and friendly Scotsman. In an era when gay was definitely not 'in', McGinty was definitely 'out'.

Perhaps he and Judge O'Hanlon would have had some interesting discussions. However, the story was about flowers and not sexual morality. It was published in the *Evening Press* as news (a human interest story, no doubt), and McGinty was pleased, and gave me a beautiful, long-stemmed, scented, suggestively droopy, flowering plant. It was a talking point when I had to bring it to my next reporting gig, a hang-out for recovering alcoholics in Dún Laoghaire.

Ah yes, those were the days!

Memories of my dad, and all that jazz

David Diebold
(Copyboy and Feature Writer, *Irish Press* and
Evening Press, 1988–1989)

I grew up in a world of paper and ink, in a house where sheaves of smudged copy paper, swiped from the *Irish Press* newsroom, yellowed all around us. We'd rolls of the stuff, doubled up with carbon paper sandwiched between, and I learned how to crank it into the roller of my dad's typewriter before I could even ride a bicycle. I longed to be able to mimic the mechanical clatter he made on that thing as he pounded out word after word with such speed and force that you could run your fingers over the underside of each sheet and feel the sharp bumps that the letters punched through. I remember the ding as the carriage reached the end of a line and the noise of the return as he swiped it across with one thick, hairy arm. Watching him as he thundered through a book review or jazz column, writing seemed such a visceral act, so suited to the terrifying, mythical place where he worked every day; a place, it seemed to me at that young age, of gods and monsters, and giants of men.

He'd taken me there once, and I'd seen the wild-eyed people plucking cigarettes from their mouths to pummel stories into shape with their fists, or tear reams of them from where they spilled from the mouths of machines, or snatch them up and skewer them on spikes. I remember the smell of ink and metal, of cigarettes and rancid paper – a newspaper office in the days of hot metal was something you could almost taste in your mouth.

It was also an indescribably exciting place for a young boy to visit, and I remember how special I felt, how privileged, when a man sitting astride a hulking machine that rattled and wheezed and smoked dropped a fat slug of metal into my hands with my name cast in it. I turned it over and over, clutching it until it cooled. My name in type. What a feeling. 'Don't lose that, now,' he growled. 'T'anks,' my dad told the man, which made me cringe because, with his American accent, it sounded like he was putting it on. 'Any time, Bob,' the man coughed, waving him away.

This was the bewildering world where my father spent most of every day for twenty-five years, a noisy maze of paper and desks, battered typewriters and Teletext machines, filthy walls and cabinets pasted with curling yellow cuttings or slivers of bromide and typography. When he brought me out of a door and onto a catwalk looking down to where a blur of the latest edition rumbled by off massive presses, I recall being so overpowered by a sense of place my head reeled. The next time I would stand at that exact spot would be as a copyboy many years later, watching my first ever published article roll off. When my dad took me back up to the office on that first trip, someone leaned down and examined me with their red, varicose face and bristly eyebrows, so close that I winced at the powerful smell of pub. 'Will this lad be following in his daddy's footsteps then?' I was sure it was me he was asking, not that I had the first clue what he was talking about, but it was my dad who answered: 'Oh, I think he can do a lot better than that,' he said.

But I couldn't have imagined ever doing 'better' than my dad, or what such a thing even meant. His world and the characters in it that we'd so often overhear him talking about as years went by, the friends, lunatics, misfits and fistfights, the great writers, egos and heroic drinkers, all the extraordinary and uproarious stories contained in that big black glass box on Burgh Quay through the 1970s and early 1980s, were larger than life itself. Gods, monsters and giants. How could anyone be bigger or better than that?

Dad once described a man he worked with who would glide silently into the office wearing what seemed to be nothing other than a shiny black plastic mac as though his feet weren't touching the ground, a man he duly nicknamed 'Blimp'. Another, blind drunk and hungry, once tore the head off a fish with his teeth then ate the rest raw, was called 'Yum Yum'. Others, drunk by 10 a.m., would clamber over office tables or hurl a typewriter or phone in fury. Someone doused himself in petrol; another colleague offered him a light. A brawl out the back on Poolbeg Street over a bet was settled by a sub who chewed up and swallowed the money. Men roared, red-faced in Mulligan's, or collapsed asleep, face-first onto the bar, wages stashed between kegs. Men bashed galleys of lead on the stone into editions to make dirty black print that flew off shrieking presses, making floors tremble, along mucky rails and into bundles to be carried off by kamikaze moped riders to the very ends of the city.

And yet I like to think my dad, Bob, fitted in rather well with this gallery of rogues and eccentrics that I pictured. He'd been a waist gunner, aged only twenty, on a B17 Flying Fortress for the final months of World War Two, notching up twenty-four bombing missions before being busted down the ranks for disappearing off on the tear for three days. As war in Europe ended and he waited to find out whether he'd be shipped off to the Pacific theatre of operations, he supplemented his income selling cigarettes and winning at poker, then fell to playing tenor sax in an off-duty dance band that ended up touring Europe and North Africa in a C47.

311

Bob began working in daily papers at the age of twenty-four, doing just about every job from writing to subediting and photography on titles from Chicago to Los Angeles, all while moonlighting as a jazz player at clubs, once even accompanying jazz legend Louis Armstrong on piano. He moved us to Ireland only after the race riots, gangs and assassinations finally sickened him to the point of leaving, in particular Martin Luther King, whom he interviewed just weeks before the man was shot dead. King told Bob that it wasn't so much a question of 'if' he would be shot, but 'when'. A little over eight weeks later, Bob was in the newsroom when a young trainee snapper, annoyingly persistent about getting some photos of Bobby Kennedy while the presidential hopeful was in town, was finally told to buzz off to the nearby Ambassador Hotel and do it. Boris Yaro's harrowing images of Bobby, dead on the hotel floor, would go down in history.

We arrived in Ireland, a ragtag family of bewildered Californians, to rainy, low-rise Dublin, under its pall of exhaust fumes, where Dad set about researching a historical novel about Dermot MacMurrough, and we were soon the unlikely custodians of a small cliff-top house overlooking the beach where *Saving Private Ryan* would one day be filmed. We lived there for a year. The book couldn't find a publisher. 'Probably too much sex in it,' my dad said later. He took to writing a few travel features for the *LA Times*, once travelling around with a photographer and tourism rep for a big piece for one of the supplements. A commissioning editor heard back from the photographer that Dad didn't seem to be writing much in the way of notes, so he fired off a letter saying: 'I hope you're not going to do some sort of hack job on this.' Dad was furious. Hack job? He wrote back: 'Only that I'm committed to the deadline at this point, I'd tell you to go and fuck yourself!' Apparently, the guy stumbled into the office of Dad's old boss, shocked, and whispering hoarsely: 'Who is this Bob Diebold anyway? He just … he just told me to go fuck myself.'

Two years of rejection slips for the novel followed, during which Dad picked up news shifts at RTÉ, commuting between Montrose and south Wexford every day in a tiny, beat-up old Hillman that was once overtaken by one of its own rear wheels. It was around this time, I remember, that he said he began 'automatic writing': contacting a spirit guide named Michael by using a method of scribbling until words formed in handwriting that seemed like someone else's. This spirit guide supposedly said that Dad was the reincarnation of a washerwoman named Mary Kelly. Did Bob really believe this? He could tell us some strange things sometimes, like that a cricket umpire's job was to tickle the back of the neck of the batsman with a feather to remind him to swing the bat, that sort of thing, then he'd just sort of walk away, jangling his change and whistling. He'd a devilish sense of humour when the mood struck him. He once lodged a piece of pipe into a sea blowhole in the cliff outside our house in Wexford, so that when the wind blew the sea spray at high tide that night the howl became a shriek. Next day, all the old farmers propping up the bar in the local pub were talking nervously. Who had heard the Banshee?

Wicked humour or not, we'd still visit graveyards on our travels around the countryside, and Dad would send me off to look for a grave. 'Which grave?' I'd say. His grave, of course, Mary Kelly's grave. I asked him, many years later, if he'd ever tried contacting the dead through his typewriter rather than automatic handwriting. 'Once,' he said, quite seriously. 'Did it work?' I asked. He told me the typewriter spat out the words: 'Old Jim died of gut gas,' so he hurled the thing on the floor like it was a spider and never tried again.

This was the father who left us every morning in a pall of fresh aftershave and coffee fumes, trundling off to Dalkey station in his red Daff, a god, a monster, a giant in a blue Dutch fisherman's hat, with a black umbrella and shoulder bag with nothing in it but a cheap detective novel. It almost all didn't happen, however. We'd gone back to the States after the last rejection slip, and him back to his old job in the *LA Times*. This lasted mere months, until one day he just turned his car around right in the middle of the highway and drove back to announce to us that we were returning to Ireland. That's where he wanted to live forever. Our things probably hadn't even made it back to us yet through the Panama Canal. He contacted Sean McCann, features editor, who went to editor Sean Ward on the *Evening Press*, who promised him subediting shifts on the desk. It was all a far cry from the modern, paternalistic organisation of the *LA Times* he was used to. On his first day, he was correcting and marking up pages of copy, handing them back to the chief sub-editor and asking for more, until he was doing twice and three times more work than anyone around him. Someone pulled him aside. 'What the hell do you think you're doing?' they said. 'Slow down, for Jaysus' sake. You're makin' us all look bad.' He was advised to take the union-mandated 'fresh air breaks' every hour or so, which, curiously, seemed mostly to take place at the bar of smoky Mulligan's next door.

This was where he disappeared to on the train for twenty-five years, in among these various egos, eccentrics, alcoholics and geniuses, until his retirement. He got back into playing piano with jazz bands when a dispute at the *Press* in the early 1980s resulted in a lockout. If you reported for work during a lockout, you were entitled to your pay. All he had to do was show up and sign in and the day was his. The rest of the time was devoted to gigging. At one point during the dispute he got back up to three or four gigs on the go. His reputation among Dublin musicians began to grow as he started arranging music for various bands and gigging as far away as Wexford, and Cork, where he went on to play the world-famous jazz festival with a bebop group called Jazzology, headed by singer Bob Whelan.

He brought me in to where he worked just that once, when I disappeared with him into that yawning mouth at the back on Poolbeg Street, past chain-smoking delivery boys and up all those grimy stairs. I went home with my little personalised lead slug, the sound of presses still ringing in my ears, a sheaf of copy paper stashed inside that day's *Evening Press*. For months after, I used the paper to make little folded newspapers of my own that I'd deliver to the houses on our street. After Bob retired I got a job as a copyboy on the *Irish Press*, then moved to Tele-ads at night, where I could sit in on the subs' desk from time to time. My first article was published by John Boland in the *Evening Press* features section, my second by Frances O'Rourke in the *Sunday Press*. Each time I'd clamber out onto that gangway and watch the issue start up on the presses and build up to a blur. I remember getting ink on my good pullover. It never came out. Years and years I wore that jumper with that smudge of ink on it. Dad retired before I got into newspapers as a bona fide writer, rising to assistant editor before cashing in my chips after fourteen years. 'Heh heh. Followed in his old man's footsteps,' he wheezed when I told him, his eyes glittering with what I think was mischievousness. I suppose I did follow in those giant footsteps somehow – I certainly worked with my share of monsters – but I'm certain I was never once better than him.

At Bob's memorial his old jazz mates played a few tunes. It was a quiet affair up at the Killiney Castle Hotel. We'd been instructed to 'keep it family', but I decided to ask along a few of his old *Press* colleagues anyway. John Boland, Pat Chatten and Frank Coughlan were there. Some months later I was going through some of Dad's old things. I didn't take much, a few books, some old photos, but some of my most treasured possessions are now never far from where I sit these days to write: an old hardback *Oxford English Dictionary* inscribed by the old man, with some *Evening Press* typography notes and font sizes on the battered inside cover; an old typewriter that I keep propped up in the bookshelf so that I can see right into its inky guts; and Bob's Irish Press Limited identity card, which reads: 'Robert A. Diebold, E.P. subeditor', and is signed with a squiggle, 'Bob'.

Bollickings are part of the job

Therese Caherty
(News Subeditor, *Irish Press*)

There were few mobile phones at the time, no Twitter or Facebook, hardly any email. When I finally made it to Poolbeg Street to get the full story on the *Irish Press* lock-in, comedian Brendan O'Carroll was ahead of me, trailed by TV cameras, brandishing the last edition of the daily, shouting: 'Give us the answers to yesterday's crossword – that's all I came for!'

Fellow freelance Mary O'Carroll called to me from a window above: 'Pleeeease … bring duvets. There's nothing soft in here to lie on.' Someone else asked for magic markers – don't ask, I can't remember. A few of each were duly delivered to the back door I'd walked through five years previously to my first news shift.

On 25 May 1995, I was freelancing on the finance desk of *The Irish Times*. And when word of Colm Rapple's sacking came through, that's where I was – in a state of disbelief. It wasn't just about the industrial dispute. A few hours earlier I had phoned the *Irish Press* HR department to turn down a slot on Sean Purcell's subediting team.

Conditions at Burgh Quay, never the best in my time, had worsened. 'Ingersoll, Ingersoll, wherefore art thou?' ran the graffiti on the doors of the *Press*'s lift (not a machine for the faint-hearted). It was a calamitous union. A senior *Press* journalist was blunt when I told him I'd got what I wanted. 'Stay where you are,' he said. 'Freelance shifts on *The Times* are more reliable than anything you'll get here.' I took note. Was ever a hack so prescient? Not that it was all about me....

Back in 1990, everyone knew the *Press* was in trouble, but the lift's slogan suggested that help was in the offing. When Enda O'Doherty urged me to send in a CV to Purcell, I did so with little hope. But then Purcell's deputy, Terence Killeen, rang. As I climbed those stairs with their dust-furred walls to my first shift, I got the smell of ink, noted the waxen pallor of the nightworkers, the peculiar smog that hung over the newsroom with its various sections slotting together in ways known only to the initiated. I was an instant addict.

Dan Coen trained me in. Puffing on his Major, he glanced at my red pen, the only thing I'd brought, and asked: 'Are you new to this?' Exposed before I'd even read a word! I had my own PC, and through former employers Attic Press and Printwell Co-operative I was familiar with onscreen work. So when he reached for his ragged pencil case to introduce me to the tools of the trade, gasping wasn't in it:

1. Dressmaker pins to keep the sheets of a story together;
2. A Pritt Stick for the original cut-and-paste job;
3. A metal ems ruler for layout and for tearing copy cleanly;
4. A sharpener for all the pencils, including the non-repro ones used on layout sheets;
5. An india rubber;
6. Tippex; and
7. Teabags for refreshment.

By the next shift, I'd sourced the lot – along with emergency supplies. Dan then defined me: 'You're a downtable sub. That's your top table, that's the back desk, that's sport, and down there? That's news.'

He explained that forty words made an inch; 'two fat pars' were needed for each element in a string of bolds; each line in a head was a deck; if copy was short, it was 'shy'; too long, it was 'over'; he explained the difference between an em and en dash; he offered a radical redefinition of widows and orphans; he explained a 'wob' (white on black) and a 'blob' (bullet point); the spike, for discarded copy, was the thin needle of solder sitting in front of Purcell.

I devoured it all, and invested in a new library, which serves to this day: *The Oxford Dictionary for Editors and Writers*; Harold Evans's *Essential English* (or *Newsman's English* as it was titled then); Strunk and White's *The Elements of Style*.

He pointed towards the raft of manual typewriters I'd noticed on my way in with their great rolls of carbon copy paper – if anything needed retyping, that was the place to do it. And indeed it was, as I found out on the night when Willie Rock, chief sub for the Sunday, marched me over there after I'd tried to help out a well-known columnist by completely rewriting his copy. 'The hallmark of a true sub is knowing when not to edit,' he said, standing over me as I retyped the original article. Thank you, Willie!

Such justifiable humiliation didn't end there. Purcell erupted one night, red in the face (he wasn't alone), with: 'Who the hell wrote this?' The headline – 'Garda head gets new body' – was me giving expression to the outright barbarous! Purcell hadn't time for niceties. I sucked it up, and found that plain and simple did the trick. But there was fun with headlines, such as the memorable offering from Joe Walsh that never made it: 'Bang, bang you're deaf' (for soldiers claiming compensation for hearing loss). And the anonymously authored one that did: 'Dead sheep found in ditch'. National news at its best.

Over on D'Olier Street, things were different. There, the subs competed for headline of the month with winners and losers published in the daily along with the authors. Some entries had multiple signatures. Burgh Quay responded with a long drawn-out 'Jaysus!' Poor industrial relations, frequent walkouts and chronic underfunding meant that the obvious – two people or more working on a headline – was unthinkable.

Coen kept referring to the caseroom. 'You'll be out on the stone soon enough,' he said. If the newsroom was known territory, the caseroom was that part of the map marked 'Here be dragons'. From a distance, the compositors didn't so much talk as breathe fire.

For a young woman, fresh out of a feminist publishing house and a lefty printing co-operative, it was a dizzyingly un-PC all-male preserve, the paste-up area an extensive collage of dodgy images of women (eventually removed after NUJ freelance rep Alva McSharry complained). 'Don't touch the galleys or the layouts,' went the safety instructions as I headed in, 'keep your hands behind your back at all times and stand well clear!' Sound advice. And of course, once there, many of the printers helped me out of a hole more often than I care to remember. One was a *Star Trek* fan – a true blue Trekkie. He lent me what I thought didn't exist – *Star Trek* books – regaled me with tales of Trekkie conventions and revealed that the T in Captain Jim Kirk's name stood for Tiberius – men in the Kirk family took the names of Roman emperors. Sorry, there was nothing about the Kirk women. It was a happy night when we worked the stone together.

In contrast, my introduction to the D'Olier Street caseroom started to the strains of Beethoven. On entry, the spotless, airy and music-laden room was a shock after Burgh Quay's clatter and shabby chic. The rules of engagement were the same, though, and the exchanges no less robust. I stood well clear with hands behind my back. Alas, no Trekkies. But many of the IT comps had been apprenticed to the IP and recalled its heyday. They expressed concern about the conditions under which their colleagues laboured.

No one said it, but I assumed there was a hierarchy on the desk: big stories for the most experienced subs. Seems sensible, right?

Not a chance. On my second or third shift, Michael Farrell finished typing an article and Purcell flung it my way with a mark-up. I froze. *What was he thinking?* Michael was one of his senior subs, an author, an established journalist outside the *Press* and a highly respected political activist. Plus, his name was a familiar newsroom cry. Anything contentious to do with the North, and John Garvey would bark: 'Where's Farrell? Check it with Farrell.' If he wasn't on shift: 'Call Farrell.' With no other option, I set to, determined to avoid a repeat of 'Garda heads and bodies'.

The desk, in fact the *Irish Press* itself, was a great leveller, and Purcell simply the best boss. Fair, kind and uncompromisingly direct, he ran a tight ship with his wayward band and didn't suffer fools – he hasn't changed! Under his command newcomers learned to respect copy, not fear it; to sense when to leave well enough alone and reshape only when necessary and without fanfare. We took pride in our work, although I quickly realised that then, as now, subs were poorly rated.

A (deluded!) senior reporter once told me that he'd never had his copy touched by one of us and had it improved. Another described us as a bunch of failed writers. Someone else asked at a news meeting if we actually understood what we were reading. And so on. Bollickings were part and parcel of the job – infrequent, but to be expected. Awareness was key: you could defend yourself only if you knew what you were doing and why you were doing it. Important lessons – learned in Burgh Quay.

When on-screen subbing arrived in the form of the Harris system, it devastated the pencil cases along with some of their owners. The changeover was anything but seamless as many struggled with the idea, not just the demands, of technology. The H&J command (hyphenate and justify), a sub's final action before releasing the piece to print, became a plaintive catch cry: 'Just H&J it and we'll all be fine!'

It is hard to believe today that we didn't have dedicated workstations. Lone terminals were scattered about Burgh Quay, and we frequently had to wander off-site to queue to sub our stories.

During the final battle, freelance and permanent staff did everything they possibly could to save the titles. True solidarity. But the men in suits weren't having it, and so the battle was lost. Still, the memories live on:

- Peigin Doyle, Lucille Redmond and me racing in from the *RTÉ Guide* to take our stations.
- The great heap that was Con Houlihan spread out across the sports desk, surrounded by corrected printouts.
- Rita O'Hare in solidarity on a rickety platform outside the back door, crying: 'Great to see you back on the barricades, Gerry O'Hare.'
- Michael Farrell at a union meeting, one foot on a chair, arm on raised knee, saying: 'If you let management treat freelances badly, they'll be after you next. Protect the weakest and you protect everyone.'
- During the afternoon switchover, the casual chats with the evening paper's Fionnuala Mulcahy and Jack Hanna that turned into lasting friendship.
- Emmanuel Kehoe and his Saturday impressions – particularly of the whistling primate, as he called him, Cardinal Cahal Daly.
- On 25 June 1990 during the World Cup marathon against Romania, Sean Purcell, sitting at an empty subs' desk (every man and woman of us at the newsroom telly), addressing no one in particular: 'How the fuck am I gonna get a paper out?' Packie Bonner saved the day on the pitch and in the newsroom.
- NUJ freelance rep Alva McSherry, confounded by her first undertaking on our behalf: softer toilet paper please.

- Enda O'Doherty staring at a colleague after his long run into work: 'I can understand someone running out of work; but why would you run into work?'
- The men's loo cordoned off with ticker tape after a part of it fell away during heavy rain and revealed asbestos.
- The journalist waiting to be interviewed for a promotion who was told: 'No, there's only interviews for scooter jobs today – is that what you're looking for?'

In the front door and out the back

Louise Ní Chríodáin
(Reporter, *Sunday Press* and *Irish Press*, 1989–2005)

There is a smell that my memory can still conjure up twenty years after I last set foot in the Irish Press Building – an acrid odour of ink and metal, an assault on the nostrils and the back of your throat, and strongest as you walked across the iron gantry above the printing presses.

There were two ways to access the *Irish Press* newsroom: via the front door on Burgh Quay, through the public office, past the well-groomed and smiling front-of-house staff; or the shabbier entrance from Poolbeg Street, up the steps that led, past the security guard in his cubbyhole above the pavement, to more stairs and then across that gantry.

One of the rare times I ever entered via the front door on Burgh Quay was for my first freelance shift on the *Irish Press*. I had supplied court copy as a stringer for the *Evening Press*, but in the autumn of 1989 this was my first 'shift'. Fresh from an 'overnight' at the *Evening Herald* – four stories in the four hours from 9 a.m. to 1 p.m. – I was delayed by a zealous security guard unable to get an answer from the busy newsdesk to check my credentials. I was late for the 2 p.m. start by a few minutes. Yet, despite the rollicking administered by then news editor Dermot McIntyre, as soon as I finally stood before him I knew within minutes that this was where I wanted to work.

I cannot remember the first story I was given to follow up, or even the first copy I filed, but I do recall being enthralled by my surroundings. There was a constant pinging as typewriter carriages

324

were returned, the sound of pages being ripped off machines as stories were finished, and shouts and slagging from desk to desk and down the length of the massive room, past the subeditors and sports reporters and into the caseroom, where the pages of the paper were 'made-up'. A chattering row of copy-takers echoed the words of stringers and reporters from around the country, and someone even appeared carrying stories just off 'the wires'. This was a living, breathing, national newsroom. I had cut my journalistic teeth in local papers, but this felt like arriving 'home' – although there were no family connections to the *Irish Press* that I knew of, and it had never been the 'paper of choice' in our Dublin house.

I made only a couple more appearances as a freelance in Middle Abbey Street. I knew that my future lay within the less lucrative but far more welcoming environs of Burgh Quay. For the first two years I moved downstairs to the calmer waters of the *Sunday Press* as a full-time freelance. A young reporter couldn't have asked for a better apprenticeship or better teachers, but my favourite working day of the week was Saturday, when we moved upstairs into the newsroom and caseroom to put the week's paper to bed, and to cover breaking news until the 2 a.m. deadline for the city edition.

By early 1992 I was a staff reporter with the *Irish Press*, entitled to a seat – if there was one free – at a designated cluster of desks. These lay between the rows of tables that made up the news and picture desks of the two daily papers, and the window desks overlooking Burgh Quay reserved for correspondents and feature staff. Overseeing us all was news editor Ray Burke – a calm pilot in every storm – but we were also watched over and minded by the sources of all newsroom knowledge and advice, administrators Miss Betty (Hooks) and Flo Gibson.

Like so many other journalists over the decades, I had a love-hate relationship with that grubby, untidy, often raucous room. We all complained about the lack of air, the heat, the cold, the broken chairs, the lack of chairs, the wires that dangled and tangled over every desk, the cigarette butts lined up on the computers (when we finally got computers), and the scarcity and lack of speed of those computers! It was not a place I would ever have chosen to live. Yet as May 1995 drew to a close, that is what I did.

Photographs and video footage of the union meeting that began on Thursday 25 May 1995, following the sacking of the late Colm Rapple, show a newsroom packed with grim-faced editorial staff from every paper and department. We had come to the brink before, but this felt too much like an orchestrated push by the management over the precipice. As the meeting was adjourned and resumed, workers came and went, keeping an ongoing presence in the building to show our availability for work and for negotiations.

The meeting continued into Friday, when the management announced that non-editorial workers were being laid off and ordered all journalists to leave the premises. More than 100 NUJ members responded by signing up for a roster to make sure that the building was occupied around the clock, and the first edition of *The X-Press*, a newspaper from the journalists inside the building, was published.

It was then that the outpourings of generosity and goodwill began. Food, drink, cigarettes, even games and books started to arrive from local publicans and shop owners, fellow journalists, politicians and other well-wishers. This would continue and even increase in the days that followed, and we were constantly overwhelmed by people's generosity and kindness. However, what resonated most were the ongoing messages, telephone calls and gifts from readers across the country; readers who had never met us, or would ever meet us, but who wanted us to know they supported us.

Friday night blurred into Saturday morning, and people came and went, going home to sleep or change clothes, or out to the shops or pub. There was speculation that the doors were going to be locked, but when the shutters finally did come down thirty of of us remained in the newsroom, many of us still there from the night before. There was no question of us leaving. We sent out for clothes, sleeping bags and toothbrushes.

We were a very mixed bag – reporters from every department, feature writers, subeditors, photographers, freelancers, even assistant news editor Gerry O'Hare and deputy picture editor Pat Keegan. However, despite our relatively junior status, Paulette O'Connor and I were the only union officers left in the building, becoming the link to the chapel committee on the outside and the go-to for all suggestions, queries, requests and gripes on the inside.

To be accurate, Paulette and I were really only one officer. We had recently been persuaded to run for the role of 'Equality Officer', but only if we could take the position on a jobshare basis so we could divide attendance at committee meetings! Ironically, we would spend much time in the following months attending meetings and hearings and discussions and court cases. Under the rock-solid stewardship of Father of the Chapel, Ronan Quinlan, we would go on successfully to petition for the appointment of an examiner, but we were also forced to fight a decision by the Department of Social Welfare not to grant journalists unemployment benefit, and to fundraise for workers during the months they received no welfare payments. There were also other battles to be waged, including the extraction of mortgage protection insurance from the Irish Nationwide Building Society. Nothing comes easy for workers when a company closes, and dignity is quickly abandoned. My lowest moment in the months that followed would be addressing a chapel meeting to tell men and women who had written for and run three national newspapers, some for almost four decades, how best to extract money to feed your family and pay your bills from a Community Welfare Officer.

But all that was in the future. What was happening inside the Burgh Quay offices over those May days in 1995 mirrored what had always made the Press Group of newspapers special: camaraderie in the face of adversity. A sometimes volatile mix of opinionated personalities and temperaments and talent put aside differences and arguments to pull together on whatever needed to be done.

Ray Cullen and Tony Gavin took on the role of official photographers, while Pat Cashman borrowed a video camera from Bermingham's camera shop and documented the occupation for *RTÉ News*. Everyone found a role for themselves, from sweeping the floor and sorting food supplies to producing the *X-Press*. The paper's computer system was shut down on Saturday to prevent the *X-Press* being produced. However, that first occupation edition had actually been pieced together by graphic artist Julian Kindness using a separate Mac. His colleague Karen Doyle, who remained inside and became one of the last to leave the building, continued to produce the pages of the *X-Press* to send out for printing, until the penny finally dropped and a manager was sent in on Monday to dismantle her computer, but alternative arrangements were soon made.

Base camp was set up in the newsroom, with regular gatherings for news bulletins around the television and radio at the night-town desk (day-town if you worked for the *Evening Press*). This was home to a panel of buttons that could speed dial almost every garda station in the country, and two massive 'mobile' phones that, despite being permanently charged, gave about a minute's call-time if taken on assignment. In more normal circumstances it was the semi-permanent habitat of Myles McEntee, night-town reporter and the barometer of the seasons within the *Irish Press*. Myles heralded the arrival of winter by the addition of socks to his work uniform of white T-shirt, jeans and sandals.

The security guard's station above Poolbeg Street was where much of the action happened. A constant stream of food, drink, clean clothes and other necessities came through the window, and this is where we took turns to 'hang out' and talk to friends and family. The always-obliging security guards called up with messages and to herald waiting visitors. When word spread of the arrival of a politician, or 'celebrities', we all raced to the 'back canteen' on the floor above to stand on tables and peer out of the tiny windows that opened out onto the street.

In quieter times we explored offices and staircases and rooms we had never seen before, wearing headlamps to navigate at night, and braved cold showers in cubicles decorated with inky handprints in the machine room, deep in the bowels of the building.

There were mysteries – nobody was leaving the building, yet fresh supplies of pens continued to vanish! And there were meetings to keep everyone briefed on what was happening outside and inside. In keeping with the spirit of union democracy, these meetings were often interminable, as occupiers took the opportunity to air their opinions and concerns. Dave Kenny reminded me recently that on one particular occasion I sat patiently as everyone vented – a talent I have long since lost – before I finally lost that patience and announced that I wasn't 'bloody Oprah!'

Sleeping arrangements varied in their location and success. Gerry O'Hare managed to rest, without incident or accident, on what could only be described as a shelf in the caseroom canteen. Some occupiers slept on top of desks, but most opted to bed down in the *Sunday Press* office, or any other office that offered a thin mattress of scratchy, static-creating carpet tiles. However, the hard floors and desks quickly turned even the most gregarious resident wits into morning grouches. I can recall at least one lilo that deflated during the night, and a blow-up bed that took Dave Lawlor, and a number of others, hours to blow up. Philip Nolan, however, took the prize for most organised occupier with a camp bed, duvet, pillow, bedside lamp and even a Nintendo Gameboy for some bedtime entertainment!

The closest I ever came to being the editor of a national newspaper was when I withdrew to sleep in Hugh Lambert's office. Gentleman that he always was, he would not have begrudged me a solo sanctuary from the fug of smoke, food and beer fumes in the newsroom, and the possibility of wandering rodents that haunted less spruce surroundings.

None of us, however, got more than a few hours' sleep any night. There was too much to be done, or talked about. Meanwhile, the phones rang incessantly, and there was a constant humming and fizzing from the fluorescent lighting. There was even a fire alarm test at 5 a.m. The management also took other steps to ensure that we didn't get too comfortable. Hot water was turned off and, after a group of us appeared on the 6 o'clock news unfurling a banner on the roof, we were quickly barred from accessing the roof for fresh air for 'health and safety' reasons.

Each night we stood on tables and hung out of windows to be serenaded and entertained by colleagues emerging from Mulligan's, Chris Dooley's composition 'Minimum Wage' and deputy news editor Richard Moore's energetic punk version of 'Nancy Spain' being particular crowd favourites. On the final night we staged an epic chariot race on the newsroom's wheeled chairs. Who won? I can't remember, but I laughed until I cried. Despite the occasional tensions and discomfort and worries about the future, I don't think I've ever laughed so much as I did in those few days. If you were going to live in a building for five days and four nights, this was a good bunch to do it with.

But we weren't playing. We were too conscious of what was going on outside, and the implications for all 600 of the *Irish Press* workers. Many of these weren't happy with the continuing occupation, but we stayed inside because we knew the importance of keeping a story alive.

One of the recurring roles of a reporter in the Ireland of the early 1990s was to catalogue the ongoing job losses and factory closures around the country. For every high-profile Digital, there was the gradual decimation of once-vibrant workplaces like AT Cross in Ballinasloe, and the devastating loss to local communities and towns of companies like Larbaun in Westport. I had covered far too many stories of companies that had shut down, companies that were forgotten within days once they left the news, except by the people left jobless and their families.

Others will disagree, but looking back with the benefit of hindsight I'm even more convinced that if we hadn't remained in the Irish Press Building there would have been no *X-Press* newspaper, no Labour Court hearings, no examinership process, no bid to start up the papers again. We didn't succeed in the end. The *Press* newspapers are gone, but twenty years on I'm still proud to say that we tried to keep them alive.

Back in Burgh Quay in May 1995 our numbers dwindled slowly as people needed to return to families and other commitments. I had no children, no commitments, but I had the support of my husband, Bryan O'Brien, a former group photographer. He had reluctantly seized the opportunity to take up a job at Independent Newspapers over a year before, as the future of the *Press* looked increasingly uncertain, and we struggled under the weight of a massive mortgage – around 16 per cent in 1993!

By Monday, eighteen people remained in Burgh Quay. The problem wasn't getting people to stay; it was getting people to leave. It took hours to persuade everyone around to the union's position that we needed to leave on Tuesday afternoon so that talks could be held in the Labour Court. Many of the eighteen weren't convinced that vacating the building was the right thing to do. And though I had been persuading everyone out, I hated leaving too.

The arrangement was that we would leave the building once a rally from outside the Dáil had made its way to the back door. Charged with a heady mixture of emotion and exhaustion, we waited in the back canteen, our eyes welling up when we heard the drums and saw the crowds snake onto Poolbeg Street. Inhaling ink and metal, the eighteen of us made our way out together, above the printing presses for the last time. The shutter was pulled up and we trailed out to a roll-call of our names, the last workers to leave. We left behind an empty building and an unfillable void, for as one of our number later wrote, 'we had taken her soul with us.'

I still have the piece of paper with that roll-call of names typed the night before we left. 'The Long Haulers' are the journalists who had remained inside for most of the occupation. 'The Bunker List' is the order in which the final eighteen left the building.

The Long Haulers:

Charlie Weston
David Lawlor
Tony Gavin
Pat Chatten
Peigin Doyle
Caoimhe McCabe
Sean McCarthaigh
Michael Morris

The Bunker List:

Louise Ní Chríodáin
Paulette O'Connor
Pat Keegan
Ray Cullen
Caroline Lynch
Philip Nolan
Mary O'Carroll
Gerry O'Hare
Aoife Mac Eoin
Enda Sheppard
Dave Kenny
Yvonne Judge
Liam Mackey
Donagh Diamond

The newspaper owner who took the piss. Literally.

Chris Dooley
(News Reporter/Agriculture Correspondent, 1982–1995)

I never met the late newspaper publisher Hugh McLaughlin, but I owe him an enormous debt of gratitude. In 1982, with the successful launches of the *Sunday World* and *Sunday Tribune* newspapers behind him, McLaughlin made his boldest move to date, establishing the first Irish tabloid daily.

Unlike his previous ventures, the *Daily News* was not a success, folding after just eighteen issues. I remember hearing the story of the repossession men arriving one day, while the paper was still in production, to remove the unpaid-for urinals from the men's toilets, an episode that the staff perceived as a bad sign.

I was just out of third-level education at the time, having spent two years studying journalism at the College of Commerce in Rathmines, Dublin – now DIT Aungier Street. The *Daily News* was offering good rates of pay, but only to established journalists; my fresh-faced fellow graduates and I had no chance of landing work there. But its arrival on the scene created an opening elsewhere: the new paper lured some of the *Irish Press*'s best reporters away from Burgh Quay, thereby creating vacancies in the *Press* newsroom.

I applied for a job and was duly called for interview, where I presented a falsely impressive body of work for the editors to examine. At that time a highlight of the Rathmines course was the summer, between first and second year, which students spent on work placement funded by the state training agency, ANCO.

ANCO paid the student journalist £35 a week, and the newspaper got an extra hand for free. In a large organisation you were liable to spend your time traipsing around after staff journalists and getting in their way as they tried to do their work. In the smaller provincial papers, however, such as the *Midland Tribune*, where I spent my summer in 1981, you were quickly put to work covering everything from District Court cases to council meetings to GAA club matches. Regardless of your level of ability, every word you wrote made it into print, many of them under banner front-page headlines such as, to take an actual example: 'Nenagh Junior Tennis Championships a great success'.

My interviewers, then, were presented with a bulky portfolio that disguised through quantity what it lacked in quality. Michael O'Kane (senior), the chief news editor, cast a sceptical eye over my work and asked me some searching questions that threatened to expose my true inexperience, but he was somewhat ambushed by the editor, Tim Pat Coogan, who flicked through the inordinate pile of photocopies of my stories and declared me to be an astonishingly productive journalist for my tender age of nineteen.

For a few moments Tim Pat and Michael sparred over my true worth. 'He's great, isn't he?' said Tim Pat. 'Look at this, another lead story …'.

'Well, yes,' countered Michael, 'but he hasn't got much experience, and we're interviewing a lot of people.'

'Ah, but he's very good all the same,' Tim Pat parried.

The result, I think, was a draw. I was too young and inexperienced to be offered a staff job, but there was freelance work going in the newsroom, and I was offered casual shifts.

The routine that followed involved my fellow five or six newsroom freelances – several of them fellow graduates from the class of 1982 in Rathmines – and me, calling the newsdesk each morning to enquire if there was any work that day. More often than not you would be assigned to cover a case in the Four Courts.

Whether by accident or design, the *Press* newsdesk had hit on an ingenious way of inducting its young journalists into the world of court reporting. Until you got established and knew your way around, you were advised to go to such-and-such a courtroom and ask for the resident journalist from the *Irish Independent*, which had a staff reporter assigned to each court. Unsurprisingly, a couple of *Indo* reporters did not willingly accept this new, unpaid-for supervising role, and left you to your own devices. But others could not resist taking under their wing these lost souls, just out of college and fearful of never making the grade, and showing them the ropes.

There was much more, however, to this policy of letting us loose among the lawyers and judges on Inns Quay. Our editors back in the office knew that if you could cut it in the courts, you were up to the job. With or without the guidance of a more senior colleague from a rival paper, you could not survive as a court reporter without a good shorthand note, an ability to listen well and assemble facts coherently, and to write quickly. Your first report of the day had to be phoned in to the *Evening Press*, where a copy-taker would type it up as you dictated it, by 12.30 p.m. Accuracy was paramount: an error in your copy could see you landed with a contempt charge or even cause the collapse of a trial.

After several months on the courts beat we were allocated shifts in the newsroom, where our training went to another level. You were assigned stories and expected to deliver them without delay. Everything you wrote was challenged by your desk editor. 'Who told you that? Did you ring him yourself? Did you check it with anybody else?' Your copy had to be crisp and clean, and clichés were likely to land you in trouble. 'We don't do miracles here,'

Paul Muldowney, my duty editor, once snapped when I described a 'miraculous' escape from a car crash. I have never repeated the mistake.

If you lapsed into merely rehashing a press release or the details of a garda or fire brigade report without probing a little deeper, you were challenged. On an early morning shift in the *Evening Press* I once wrote up a perfectly adequate report about a city centre fire. All the important details were there, or so I thought. Paul Dunne, the news editor, knew better. 'Can you put in more about the fire, Chris?' he urged, his expression animated and his arms waving. 'Describe it to me. Were the flames big?'

Were the flames big? A simple question, the answering of which transformed a factual but pedestrian story into a vivid scene for the reader.

In those early days the open-plan newsroom was an intimidating place for a young journalist. It wasn't that the older hands weren't nice to you. Far from it; every one of them was courteous and generous. But they were so damned good at what they did and seemed so self-assured in the doing of it that all you could feel in response was the weight of your own shortcomings.

There were then, and are now, more stressful jobs than being a news reporter, but working for the *Evening Press* brought a peculiar kind of pressure on those involved. Starting at 8 a.m., the reporters on the evening paper worked the phones, calling government ministers at home, or the emergency services, or anybody at all in the know about the issues and events of the day, urgently seeking a 'line' that might make a lead story. As the 9.30 a.m. deadline approached, copyboys stood by as the reporter wrote a paragraph, ripped the paper containing it off the typewriter, and handed it over for delivery to the subeditors. By the time the copyboy returned, seconds later, the next paragraph had been written and was duly handed over.

I watched in awe reporters such as Michael Sharkey and Laurie Kilday in action, and found that my main ambition in life was to be as good a reporter as they were. I still consider that a noble ambition. I was soon working alongside them – and others such as Anne Flaherty, Aindreas McEntee, Stephen Collins, Fergal Keane, Ray Burke, Fergus Black, Clodagh Sheehy and Don Lavery – trying to match their standards.

Three decades later, I'm still trying.

Computer Ink

Fergal Kearns
(Messenger/Computer Department Operator/Siptu
Branch Secretary, 1982–1995)

First day, first hour.

'Who are you related to?'

'What?'

'You're here, so who do you know?'

'Ah, yeah, dispatch overseer is a mate of me Ma and Da's.'

Who you knew usually far outweighed what you knew. You learned early on that whole families, and generations of families, were employed by the *Press* (so inevitably a row with one person could mean you just gained yourself a whole dynasty of new enemies).

The next thing you learnt was:

'Don't put your …'

'Huh?'

'… hand on that.'

I looked down. I was just leaning against a table. My hand was black....

There was ink everywhere. Every surface, all the time. It was in the air. Even in sealed areas like the computer room. In later years, when I moved to the computer department, we had a regular cleaning routine, wiping tape and disk covers, and the cloths were always jet black afterwards. It can't have been healthy, but then again it seemed that most people smoked constantly, so you were probably fecked anyway. (Not to mention liver failure getting you before your lungs went, but that's a whole other topic).

Obviously, the most concentrated area for ink was the machine room. The toilets in the machine room contained huge vats of strong-smelling Swarfega, which was pretty good at removing ink (and your fingerprints). The banter down in this part of the house was ferocious, and sometimes positively lethal.

'Jaysus, there's some weight in that, I'm not liftin' that.'

'I'll get it.'

'Ah, thanks [Metal block is lifted with one hand]. Jaysus, you're one strong fucker!'

'Heh, why do ya think they call me Horse?'

'Oh, I always thought that was because of the state of your head.'[Man starts running followed by man with metal block still in hand].

My first role in the *Press* dealt in death. I worked as an advertising messenger in the front office on Burgh Quay on the evening shift. My job was to bring the death notices, which had been rung in by the undertakers of the land (and written up by hand), up to the caseroom for typesetting. We also had an arrangement with the *Indo* where we'd take notices for them and vice versa. So every hour, on the hour, from 6 to 11 p.m., I trekked from Burgh Quay to Princes Street with my book (for everything had to be signed for) and all these death notices.

One of the most important tasks for the rural undertaker was to ensure that their notice made the Country edition. One evening, one of the lads in the front office took a call just after 11 p.m., and therefore past the deadline for death notices for the Country edition. Next thing I know I get roared at to leg it up to the caseroom and pull one of the death notices. I arrived at the overseer's desk a sweating wreck and told him I needed to pull a death notice I had brought up earlier.

'Too late, it's already set.' I must have looked ashen because he went on to ask why.

'Because he's not flippin' dead!' I said. Apparently the undertaker was assured that the old man was a goner and decided it had to go in the Country edition, but then had to alert the *Press* to the fact that 'the deceased' was now 'sitting up in his bed having a drop of soup.' (It was not the first or the last time that happened.)

The IT department, always known as the computer department, began as a very small function in the early 1970s and slowly grew as technology advanced until it took a huge leap forward in 1985 with the adoption of computerised typesetting. The little-known commercial computing side played a crucial role in the production of the paper, the best-known and only appreciated example being the printing of the wage packets. The next most important thing was the printing of the labels for the many-sized bundles of newspapers parcelled up by the dispatch section. The operation was a little more sophisticated than you would imagine in that the labels had to be organised by route drop so as to guarantee the most efficient delivery of the papers by the many trucks, vans and bikes queued up in Poolbeg Street. There were different labels and route drops depending on the edition, and even the weather. 'Snow drops' were the labels produced for those occasions when extreme weather limited our ability to deliver to the more isolated newsagents. This kind of thinking was, I believe, a remnant of a time when the *Press* was a genuinely innovative newspaper (and acknowledged leader in things like distribution), but innovative thinking was on a downward slope by the time the 1980s came around.

The department also calculated the daily and weekly sales of the newspaper, often a source of inter-departmental friction.

[Circulation Rep] 'Those figures can't be right.'

[Computer Department] 'They're correct.'

[CR] 'You have to check them, they can't be right.'

[CD] 'They're correct.'

[CR] 'The circulation manager says that those figures are wrong. Your programmes must be doing something wrong, or your inputs …'.

[CD] 'Tell you what, you tell me what fucking figures you want "input" and I'll put them in there, ya b****x [slams phone].'

The problem of course was that sales were falling. Unfortunately for us all, the figures were correct.

One of the oddest nights of the year on which to work was Holy Thursday. As there was no paper on Good Friday the only people who worked were the watchmen and whoever was on in the computer department on the 4 to 11 p.m. shift. It was quite amazing to see the place so empty, and I'd always take a walk around to soak up the silence (until about 7 p.m., when the watchman and I deemed it safe to bolt up the place and go for a pint).

The opposite of that was the moment just before the editions began to roll off the presses. The place was so alive. I never tired of the sights and sounds of the machine room. Even towards the end I still got a thrill walking out on the mezzanine floor, waiting for the buzzers to signal the slow start to the presses and looking down as they slowly gathered speed until the noise enveloped you.

The *Press* was full of trade unions, and we were all in one. In addition to the major unions like the Transport Union (the ITGWU, later SIPTU, which had three branches), the NUJ and the IPU, there were also unions for the more specialised printers, for the fitters, electricians and at one stage carpenters (no, I've no idea either). This naturally led to rivalries between them, though these were always put aside for the regular face-offs with the management. The management was regularly served notice of industrial action, and the staff could have papered their houses with protective notices. Suffice it to say that the *Press* deserves its very own case study in industrial relations.

To many of us, the most important union of all was the Credit Union. The Irish Press Credit Union, founded and managed by the staff, was hugely popular with all. 'Going over to Danny' (and later Ann-Marie) was simply notification that you were going for a loan. Danny believed we all lived in mansions given the amount of 'home improvement' loan requests made to his office. The Credit Union helped save many a holiday (and marriage), and continues in its 'subsumed' form as part of IndoGroup Credit Union to this day.

The *Irish Press* was my first job and my second home (and second family) for over ten years, and here, twenty years on, I still bloody miss it. I'll finish with one of my favourite *Press* stories.

Cutline. The break from 9.30 p.m. to 9.50 p.m. every night elicited an exodus from the office to Mulligan's and the White Horse. The pints were of course standing ready to go with the second being pulled almost directly after the arrival of our thirsty heroes. The rule, however, was that you were back at your desk at 9.50, no ifs or buts. On one particular evening one of the printers arrived back a couple of minutes after the requisite time and was pounced on by an overseer.

Not on, not on at all.

The gentleman looked the overseer directly in the eye and said: 'I'd like to see you drink four fuckin' pints in twenty minutes.'

Locking horns over Stagg with the gardaí

Richard Balls
(Freelance News Reporter, 1992–1995)

The phone rang in the *Evening Press* newsroom. Síle Yeats picked it up. 'Yes, Richard Balls is here. That's right, he wrote that story. Do you want to speak to him?' A pause. 'No, I can't confirm whether or not he's English. And why do you want to know that?' Looking aghast, she put the phone down.

'He said he's going to be in the audience on *Questions & Answers* and say that you are English and the Emmet Stagg story is an example of English tabloid journalism being imported to Ireland.' I don't remember now if that caller got his chance on the RTÉ show. However, I recall Progressive Democrats TD Pat Cox on the same programme calling for the 'rat' in the gardaí who leaked the story to be publicly outed. The fury was not at the politician, it seemed, but those behind the story.

As satisfying as it was to break a big political story, it proved an uncomfortable time. I was, after all, an outsider: an Englishman and mad Norwich City supporter living in Dublin with no Irish connections whatsoever. My revelation on the front page of the *Sunday Press* on 6 March 1994 was that an unnamed prominent politician had been stopped by the gardaí on several occasions associating with rent boys in the Phoenix Park. The scoop was not that the politician in question was gay, but rather that his nocturnal activities had become an issue for police trying to stop the park becoming a pickup joint for male prostitutes and their cruising

343

clients. By failing to heed previous warnings, he was putting himself at personal risk, something underlined by the fact that he had been mugged near the park late at night some years earlier. This was clearly a matter of public interest.

The first edition of the *Sunday World* had run a similar piece the same night (a curious coincidence, for which I have my own theory), but the story was seen as something of a departure for the *Sunday Press*, and I was quizzed live on air by Pat Kenny the following morning on RTÉ's breakfast show. Even within the Burgh Quay newsroom, reactions were mixed. Some were uncomfortable about the nature of the story, and one reporter told me they saw it as anti-gay.

Long after Stagg was forced out into the open by his own party and the public furore died down, the story haunted me. Like other reporters, I desperately began seeking work in the aftermath of the closure of the *Press*, and after putting in a few phone calls I was offered a shift at a Dublin-based newspaper. All went well, and a story with my byline appeared in that weekend's edition. But when I called the following week to see if I could come in again, the news editor had some bad news. The editor had been away when I had been in the office, and had then instructed the desk never to employ me again. The reason? The Emmet Stagg affair.

At a job interview at the *Sunday Tribune* the following year, I was asked by one of the panel how I could justify the Stagg story.

I had arrived in Ireland in the spring of 1990. I knew no one, but I did have somewhere to stay and a six-month contract with the embryonic *Dublin Tribune*. My patch was the west city, taking in the Phoenix Park, among other places. Editor Michael 'Mickser' Hand revelled in introducing me to people. 'This is Richard Balls. He has come over from England, doesn't know anyone in the country, and he's living in Mount Pleasant Square for £20 a week.' My contract was ended abruptly amid financial cutbacks, and I could have climbed back on the ferry and gone home, but I loved every minute of Dublin life in the 1990s and decided to stay put. I went on to work as a journalist in Dublin for nine years, working for a dozen titles in the city, including the *Evening Herald*, the *Irish Independent* and *The Irish Times*. However, the happiest and most exciting period of all was the three years I spent at Burgh Quay.

Sure, as an Englishman and a freelance, I was always going to be an outsider. 'You're an Ingersoll spy, Balls. That's what you are,' veteran *Sunday Press* reporter John Kelly would frequently say accusingly, but always with a faint smile at the corner of his mouth. Some staff journalists liked to be disdainful of 'hired hands'. However, in the cramped quarters of the *Sunday Press*, overlooking the River Liffey, I felt a camaraderie and common respect. Editor Michael Keane's door was most often open, and he was genuinely friendly. Andy Bushe, the news editor with the Nike slogan 'Just Do It' on his in-tray, was hugely supportive, probably the best mentor I ever had. From the subeditors in their corner to the graphic design team hidden away in a makeshift space, a friendly face could always be found. Mulligan's in Poolbeg Street was simply an extension of the office, a place to download and share the events of the day.

There was, of course, a serious side to the job, especially for someone writing about Dublin's criminal underworld. I used a pseudonym for at least one piece about Martin Cahill, aka 'The General' (November 1993). An exclusive at around the same time about the kidnapping of NIB chief Jim Lacey even led to me being interrogated by the gardaí. Two detectives turned up unannounced in reception wanting to speak to me. I went with them to a nearby pub where they demanded I reveal my garda sources. I refused, and the incident was subsequently reported in *The Phoenix*. 'Needless to say, the hack, who is already apprehensive about The General discovering his own identity, was not anxious to assist the two detectives with this particular line of enquiry,' it reported under the headline: 'Gardaí Interrogate Hack'.

These were exciting times. I was in my twenties and had only been a journalist for around six years. Moreover, these were turbulent and unsettling times for Ireland. The Bishop Casey scandal, allegations of sex abuse against prominent clerics and the killing of a young woman, child and a priest by Brendan O'Donnell were just some of the stories I covered for the *Sunday* and *Evening Press*. I genuinely looked forward to Saturday night shifts during those years.

I was blissfully unaware of the closure of the *Irish Press* when it happened in the summer of 1995. The first I heard of it was when *Evening Press* reporter Damien McHugh phoned his wife as we were on our way back from a junket in northern France. Only when we picked up a paper on our arrival back in Ireland did we get the full story. The *Irish Press* had been closed, and our colleagues were staging a sit-in protest at Burgh Quay. My friend and flatmate, Enda Sheppard, was one of them. I remember to this day how surreal it felt as I gathered clothes, a towel, soap and shampoo and headed down to the rear entrance of Burgh Quay to hand the bag to him through a hatch.

I'm not sure now, but it may have been the same day that Jack Charlton and the Republic of Ireland football team pulled up in a coach behind the Press Building in a generous and public show of solidarity with the staff. They signed footballs and other items, which were later sold to raise money for those losing their jobs.

Inside the building, the visit was reported in the *X-Press* paper being produced by the protesters. I played my own small part in the campaign to save the papers by standing in the rain on Burgh Quay selling copies of the *X-Press* and busking on Grafton Street with subeditor Dave Kenny. I also helped with the fundraising concert staged at The Olympia Theatre, shadowing one of my musical heroes, the late great John Martyn.

My time in Ireland was full of ups and downs, but I emerged from it with lifelong friends and some extraordinary memories. Of all the news organisations I worked with in the 1990s, the *Irish Press* was the only one that felt like a family.

The sound of news being written

Aileen O'Meara
(News Reporter/Analysis Writer, 1986–1987)

It was 1986 and I'd got a foot in the freelance door of the *Irish Press*, months after graduating with a master's in journalism from what was then NIHE in Glasnevin. It was a one-year programme in only its third year, and a qualification that didn't quite impress the hardened hacks and editors in the *Irish Press* newsroom.

News features editor John Spain gave me the foothold and the break I needed, bringing me in to write fast-turnaround news analysis of the stories of the day, with a prominent byline inside the paper and a chance to work the phones. I also landed a few front-page news stories that were picked up by *RTÉ News*, and the next news reporter job was mine. The only trouble was that I didn't exactly have great shorthand, and I'd failed to mention that I couldn't drive.

The seasoned hacks were right that having a master's diploma didn't automatically make you a great reporter. I was useless at court reporting (yes, the shorthand) and sports. The master's in journalism didn't teach the art of standing at small, local GAA matches with a knowledgeable neighbour who could give you the key points and the accurate scores for the local paper. And 'How in God's Holy Name did you think you were going to get anywhere if you couldn't even drive for feck's sake?' to quote an exasperated *Sunday Press* news editor one Saturday evening when he discovered that the desk reporter couldn't take one of the pool of cars out the back because she didn't have a clue how to drive it.

But I kept the head down and watched the experts at work, and I learnt on the job. I watched reporters like Maol Muire Tynan and Stephen Collins work the doors of neighbours to get titbits of vital detail to build up a two-page spread the day of the Raglan House gas explosion in Sandymount. I learnt how to observe, to see telling detail, to chat to guards, shopkeepers and locals for stories that ranged from front-page giant headlines of Dublin suburban carjackings for the City edition of the *Evening Press*, to drownings of Derry fishermen for the *Irish Press*, and getting my first ever helicopter ride with Garret Fitzgerald during the 1987 general election campaign.

I realised the importance of working your contacts and minding them for leads and steers, and I learnt how to write clear, sharp and concise opening paragraphs – the trademark of *Irish Press* writing. It was a great newsroom in which to learn, and there was lots of encouragement.

I watched reporters like Tim Hastings work the phones to build up an impressive industrial relations brief. I learnt the art of holding back some details of a news story for a quiet Sunday evening from desk editor Philip Molloy. All around me I saw the value of the regular phone calls to the guards, the fire brigade and contacts for the early start on what might be a lead later on that evening.

And I won't ever forget the cacophony of sound that was the newsroom in full throttle in the hour before the *Irish Press* first edition deadline, a sound now only a memory for those of us who worked in the pre-technology environment. When the rows of those huge manual typewriters were all going at full blast, the sound was deafening and exhilarating. Pure concentration on the faces of reporters, subeditors and copy-takers alike meant that this noise was no distraction.

Up to the late 1980s, reporters in the *Irish Press* typed their stories on typewriters at long rows of tables placed at right angles to the news and picture desks. The manual typewriters had deep keyboards, and prominent and noisy carriage-return handles, and the copy was typed onto rolls of carbonated paper, with the slug at the top and the 'ends' at the bottom. The top copy was placed in the basket at the end of the table, and the carbon or black held back as a record.

When the story was a lead, and being written up to the deadline, a reporter had the unenviable experience of having the copy torn off by an impatient editor paragraph by paragraph, with a subeditor shouting for copy as the deadline fast approached. I may not have been able to drive then, or even manage the fast shorthand of my fellow reporters, but the fast and accurate typing skills I'd learnt to get a job as an office typist when I left college stood me in good stead on days like that.

The Irish Press Group was a huge employer and an influential trendsetter, but it seemed to me that it was always looking over its shoulder at the *Independent* across the river, and was very conscious of its heritage. But it was slow to change and to adapt. Even as I got my first reporting job there, it was clear to me that the future was uncertain, with talk of a tabloid size and new investors being required.

So, when the *Sunday Tribune* came asking, I took the leap to the smaller but innovative weekly paper edited by Vincent Browne, even though I'd only been a staff reporter for a year.

Already, by 1987, Browne and his small team were producing the kind of lengthy interviews, detailed analyses and photo-centred layout that made the *Press* titles seem old-fashioned, even though their circulations were still enormous and influential.

And up on Baggot Street there was no cacophony of manual typewriters rushing to deadline. In this brave new world, new technology had already been embraced. Hello the future.

Zarouk, Earthlings! Greetings from your old friend, Zodo

Sean Mannion
(Copyboy/Subeditor/Assistant Features Editor/Assistant
Editor, *Irish Press*, 1976–1995)

I have been asked to give a comprehensive analysis of the editorial dynamic and strategic policies that drove the *Irish Press* features department in the 1980s.

No, I haven't. I've been asked to write about Zodo.

If you are thirty-five or younger, let me introduce you. Zodo was a space creature that landed on Burgh Quay around 1985. Small, with big eyes, a baby face and a tail, he hailed from the planet Daros. He was allowed leave his mothership, the Zepo Moa, in his little craft, and venture around our country for an indeterminate period. He spoke a language whose words mostly began with the letter Z. 'Zabanga' meant great. 'Zarouk' was not polite.

Zodo was a homely, innocent, friendly alien, conceived by yours truly and drawn by Paddy Malone, a freelance illustrator who did cartoons and illustrations for the *Irish Press* generally. Paddy had also drawn Feichín Francach, a rat whose life and adventures were recounted in Irish and who was admired and followed for the faint absurdity of his character as much as anything else. Zodo himself, even in the 1980s, felt like a cartoon-style throwback to the 1960s and perhaps further. But the 1980s liked him.

A tentative narration of his adventures first appeared in strip form at the bottom of a page. We invited children to write to Zodo and invite him to visit their town or county. They did, and he did. So if Jimmy Walsh aged eight from Carlow had asked Zodo to his garden birthday party, Zodo was there. But he got into dreadful scrapes, crash-landing into a hens' coop after hitting a clothes line. The tale ended merrily with Zodo and the young earthlings having a ball. When we became more sophisticated and received photographs from Zodo fans, we drew their character into the adventures.

We decided to test the waters further. The Zodo Club was founded and an application form published regularly. Cut out three banners of the *Irish Press* and send them to us and you would receive a membership card and badge. Zodo T-shirts were also made and used for competitions.

The club took off. Here, thirty years later, I would like to thank those in the computer department who inputted the entries and gave me sheafs of names and addresses each week. I also blame depopulation of my brain cells for not recalling who sent out the membership packs, but please make yourself known.

The Zodo letters column grew and showed Zodo's popularity. The strip was enlarged to two columns vertical, encompassing story, illustrations and children's letters, and now appeared three times weekly. During Zodo's time, colour was introduced to the group's newspapers, so Zodo landing in Letterkenny or Cahirciveen was now in colour. From time to time it was full colour, but we hit on black and blue only, which just required one blue overlay. I recall caseroom overseer Harry Pidgeon's painstaking efforts at ensuring the registration was right.

Zodo changed things completely for me with printers, clerical staff and journalists. The world divided into two camps: those who slagged and laughed but were on Zodo's side (the bigger camp), and those who slagged and ridiculed the enterprise. Upstairs in the computer department the applications continued to flow in. I remember being presented with a duplicate book of sheafs with addresses from 16,000 children who had applied to Zodo's club.

Another hit was the pen pal section. Children could tick a box in the application form if they wanted a pen pal. Most did, so we dived into the database. I went home, and on my new Amstrad paired Johnny (eight) from Donegal with Liam (eight) from Kerry. We tried to link members as far away as possible from each other to enhance the cultural experience. We paired boys with girls and had no complaints. The only complaints involved pen pals not writing to each other. We provided replacements. We had set off our members on a new course, but we had no way of monitoring the success of this. Maybe people made long friendships. Who knows?

Competitions threw up fascinating findings. Members from Kerry behaved as normal and as anonymously as any other region in the day-to-day business of the Zodo Club. But if there was a competition and prizes at stake, there was a sudden surge of interest from the Kingdom. Their entries almost equalled a third of the total. If you want an insight into what drives Kerry to win All-Irelands, I saw it in microcosm. I recall the Prendervilles in Kerry being a frequent letter-writing family.

Of course, Zodo peaked. He had a few good years, and the *Irish Press* had, in the meantime, a new editor and editorial personnel. The Zepo Moa summoned him back.

And his legacy? Those 16,000 Zodo Club members would now be approaching their forties, married with families, appearing before bank enquiries or retired from All-Ireland-winning Kerry teams. To all of you 16,000, Zodo says hello!

The News in Brief

Pansies don't get the lead story: you have to have an eye for the ladies

Dermott Hayes
(Feature Writer/Diarist/Finance Reporter)

Working in the Press Group was all about three things, I was told: news, news and news. A simple concept you might think, but from my perspective, as a freelance in the early 1980s, a latecomer and a graduate with a background in academia, it took a little study, a lot of manoeuvring and a neck like a jockey's bollocks. Get the story. Get the job done. No one stood on ceremony in Burgh Quay: if you could deliver the goods on time, you were in.

Three experiences stick out in my mind. The first was my entry into the mysterious world of stone editing. As an occasional feature writer, rock critic and occasional financial reporter, a daily story pitch was routine. One afternoon I was in the newsroom when someone from features announced the unexpected absence of the features' 'stone sub'. Being on a deadline, and anxious not to lose any of their allotted time or space, they asked, 'Can you stone sub?'

'Of course,' I replied.

One minute later I was in the stone room reading hot metal upside down and back to front, the crumpled page 'blacks' melting visibly in my sweaty paw. Happily, I got the job done, and from there went on to stone sub features pages in the tabloid days, as well as doing layouts and subbing of the property pages from Con Power.

The *Sunday Press* allowed even more scope. One week finance editor Brian O'Connor was away, so I was drafted in to put his page together. That same week the newsroom was dogged by staff holidays and untimely illnesses and the Bhagwan Shree Rajneesh was hiding out in Limerick. So, having finished my work on the finance page, I was dispatched to Limerick post haste. There I quickly found out that 'the saffron guru' had taken an entire floor of Jury's Hotel that was heavily guarded. Undeterred, I found a little hippy shop, bought an orange T-shirt and matching jeans, and then a bouquet of pansies. Unfortunately, my ruse didn't work and I didn't gain entry to the inner sanctum.

My next move was to have a pint in the bar of the hotel, where I met a reporter from BBC Radio Four. We soon spotted two glamorous young women who, the barman tipped us, were the flight attendants on the Bhagwan's private jet. In a flash we followed them to the Shannon Shamrock Hotel swimming pool, and soon got the goods on the guru. I rang the story in and it made the front page.

My last story comes from my days working in the *Irish Press* diary as a stand-in for Michael Sheridan. Mick often took a week off in December. One morning I had a list of events to cover that included a charity appearance by the Sam Maguire Cup in UCD, followed by a book launch in the Shelbourne, and finally, the highlight of the day, the launch of the latest Middleton whiskey in the Whiskey Corner in Smithfield.

Being a three-year veteran of this event, I knew the form: get everything done before you get there. So my pockets were stuffed with press releases, decorated with questions, quips and quotes. It was a cold day, I remember, so cold that a glass of high-quality whiskey was more than welcome. The only problem was they gave you samples of the three previous years' products before you got to the latest. They then gave you a bottle of whiskey. Outside there was a blizzard blowing. I got a taxi on Ormonde Quay at 3.10 p.m. and arrived at Burgh Quay at 5.05 p.m. There was less than an hour between me and my deadline, so I marched into the newsroom, shaking snow from my collar, a bottle of whiskey clutched under my arm.

The first person I met was Hugh Lambert, who, assessing the scenario, settled me down at a desk, fed a roll into the typewriter in front of me and then fetched a mug of scalding hot black coffee. 'Do you have everything, Dermott?' he asked. 'Yessssh,' I slurred, flopping a flurry of crumpled notes on the desk. Satisfied, he walked away.

I got the job done with five minutes to spare.

The haven of 'chancers' that gave me my novel approach to life

Muriel Bolger
(Reporter/Feature Writer, 1987–1995)

It may be twenty years since the doors closed on Burgh Quay, but for me they had opened a whole new world away from domesticity and the humdrum of family life, and a very unexpected marriage break-up that saw me having to go out to work.

I found myself in Niall Connolly's smoke-filled office applying for some work experience in 1987. This was a requirement of a course I had managed to get on, an ANCO course called 'Women into Writing'. (Does anyone remember ANCO?) It was a six-month course introducing us to aspects of publishing and related topics and was aimed at redressing the imbalance of men and women in publishing at the time.

I was a total rookie whose entire portfolio consisted of a handful of pieces published previously by Noeleen Dowling and the late and wonderful Sean McCann. After spending a week in the features department of the evening paper I was allowed do a day a week there for the next few months. There was no space for an extra chair at the features desk, so I could only go in on Thursdays when Noeleen was off, and through the haze from John Boland's half-smoked cigarettes I learned from the best.

1988 heralded Dublin's millennium celebrations and a further stint of work experience in the *Irish Press*, for a month this time.

Here it was Gerry O'Hare who pointed me in the right direction, something he often reminds me of, and he appointed Helen Quinn to hold my hand. She did, and with great good humour too.

It was a heady experience, being allowed to sit in the newsroom, type my stories and see my name in print as I followed Carmencita Hederman, then Mayor of Dublin, to countless events. They even paid me!

The whole Burgh Quay experience was unforgettable, stepping into a whole new world of enormous typewriters that noisily went clickety-clack, the smell of printer's ink, overflowing wastepaper baskets, coffee cup rings on the tables, the hum when the printing press started up, and the manic but intoxicating frenzy of a busy newsroom with phones ringing continuously.

The kaleidoscope of characters I met there – chancers (like me), alcoholics, brilliant writers, wits and raconteurs – guaranteed that life was never dull. Someone always had a yarn to spin. There was fun and laughter, but they could be serious too. They were very professional.

Michael O'Kane senior encouraged me to keep freelancing for them when the six months were over, and I never looked back.

When Dick O'Riordan sent me on my first press trip, my double life began. One was five-star luxury and Michelin dining, camel and helicopter rides, secluded beaches and glitzy cruises and a career as a travel writer. I cruised the Med, the Caribbean, the North Sea and went through the Panama Canal, and wrote about the different destinations. My other life saw me juggling with mortgage repayments and raising three opinionated teenagers – things Eoghan Corry frequently got me to write about in the weekly 'First Person' column that he gave me.

In the features department, my brief was to interview incoming authors on their book tours. Consequently, many a wonderful hour or two was spent drinking tea in the Shelbourne, the Merrion and

Westbury hotels, chatting to the likes of Douglas Kennedy, Nelson de Mille, Sue Townsend, Ken Follett, Polly Devlin and Jilly Cooper. Others, like Frank Delaney, Barbara Taylor Bradford, Jeffrey Archer and Robert Ludlum, merited lunches – long, memorable lunches. I didn't realise then that one day I'd be on the other side of the fence, the interviewee rather than the interviewer.

In between, I penned brochures for mattresses, home insulation and the cities of Ireland. I wrote about food and finance, pets and pests, and for garden centres and property companies. I even wrote for a magazine for truckers!

As I sit here beginning novel number six, I find myself pondering on the enormous difference walking through those doors in Poolbeg Street, up the stairs and along the metal walkway into the unknown, has made to my life. It changed it dramatically. It paid my bills and filled my days with interesting people and places, new achievements and, most precious of all, with wonderful friends with whom I've been able to share it.

I still miss it.

How to keep the head down...

Tom Reddy
(News Reporter, 1982–1985)

Claude Cockburn once wrote that the best thing about being a journalist is spending other people's money. Unfortunately, the *Press* wasn't a big spender, but fortunately I got to see all corners of the country, I had great fun and great colleagues, and it was a wonderful time with magic memories.

I recall one slow Tuesday morning in the *Evening Press* newsroom. The 'day-town' box reporter had turned up an unremarkable story from the routine calls to garda stations in the city and around the country. However, it was the splash for the first edition.

Three rows of desks ran perpendicular to the newsdesk. I was at the reporters' desks in the middle; the photographers were in front of me, features behind me. We were shooting the breeze when Gerry O'Hare threw down this challenge to the four other reporters and me: get through the shift without writing a story. It was nothing short of heresy. News editor Dermot McIntyre was at his desk, head down, busily drawing up a list of potential story leads. Ominous, we thought. Dermot is best remembered by me as the news editor who would shout at reporters: 'Don't take your coat off!' as we arrived on shift as dawn broke and were immediately redirected to a crime scene or disaster. (I also remember his habit of vanishing from the newsroom after the first edition went to bed to buy fruit in Moore Street.) This particular morning, Dermot bustled over to our desks, which were strewn with battered typewriters, copy paper and cigarette ash.

'Gerry, hi.' His strong Donegal accent singled out our redoubtable travel correspondent. 'Here's a travel story ...'.

'You won't believe this, Dermot. You won't believe this,' said Gerry.

The salmon rose to the lure.

'This fellow ...' he said, pointing to me accusingly, 'this fellow doesn't know how hard you had it as a reporter before you came to Dublin. He just doesn't believe it!'

Dermot was standing still and looking at me. His clutch of news leads written on torn copy paper forgotten.

'Tell him about how you cycled to cover District Court cases on your bike. How much was it, five bob a week in Donegal?'

And Dermot did, as Gerry stood behind him pointing and grinning at me as I learned about journalism in Donegal a generation earlier. I eventually felt I'd made those journeys.

Needless to say, Gerry won the bet and I was the only one who got a handful of leads to follow up.

Sickness, it's all in the mind

Des Nix
(News Reporter, *Irish Press, Evening Press*, 1973–1981,
News Feature Writer, *Sunday Press*, 1981–1995)

Burgh Quay was a veritable Boys' Town in the summer of 1973. Experienced journalists were leaving – sixteen in eighteen months – for better pay elsewhere, ego enhancement in RTÉ maybe, or to practise the dark art of public relations. They were replaced mostly by young, single male recruits from provincial papers. At the end of a shift we had no wives or mammies to go home to; we went to Mulligan's instead.

On an adventurous journey, where the road travelled was never the same as the day before, Mulligan's could be a dangerous crossroads. *Evening Press* staff would repair there in mid afternoon to be joined by *Irish Press* hacks on their 5–6 p.m. 'tea' break. Sometimes, the edges blurred. Such as the early evening Kieran Patton rang his news editor from Mulligan's coin-box phone, and was heard to declare: 'George, I'm psychologically unprepared for work.'

Poor Kieran died too soon to meet his oft-proclaimed promise to win the Nobel Prize for Literature, but he left the legacy of a debate that still persists – that not being in the right frame of mind for work was the same as being at home in bed with the flu, a point he continued to pursue that evening until closing time. He went to Iran after....

First things first

Travel editor Gerry O'Hare, because of a previous career in logistics, assumed leadership of the Sacramento Seven, a crack team of journos sent to the US in 1991 on Operation SII. We were to break the code of this complicated new newspaper computer system and bring it all back home to the troops on Burgh Quay.

Gerry always got straight down to the fundamentals. On day two in California, he rang *Irish Press* headquarters to proclaim that we couldn't possibly live there on just $60 pocket money a day. They upped it to $100. Then the first Gulf War broke out and all the good ol' boys began turning up at the training centre in full combat mode, ready to head on over there and take out Saddam themselves.

Our much-loved sports sub, Shane Flynn, God rest him, ever a champion of the underdog, took to throwing his coat on the crowded canteen floor and prostrating himself in prayer in the direction of his estimation of Mecca's whereabouts.

O'Hare took the initiative straight away. He rang *Irish Press* headquarters, soliciting danger money for his men because of our new location – in the middle of a 'War Zone'. It didn't wash. We had to stand him down.

The Last Word

On Saturday, the *Sunday Press* team would descend on the subs' desk to do their business close by the caseroom. The Saturday copyboys were a diverse lot, but invariably the student sons of some employee or other, trying to make a few bob to indulge whatever vice was current in the halls of academe.

'Sean,' editor Vincent Jennings summoned, handing some hot copy to his young Mercury. 'Ask the caseroom overseer to get that on now.'

The overseer was Mr B., a Northerner known to be partial to the odd drop and possessed of an impressive range of entertaining expletives. This evening he was wassailing in his perch at the bridgehead.

'Mr Jennings said you were to get that on fast,' said the young acolyte.

'Oh, did he now?' says Mr B., effecting an unsteady semicircle in his eyrie. 'Well, you can tell Mr Jennings from me that I said he can go and fuck himself.'

Whereupon our obedient servant returned to his editor, proclaiming with an accuracy that would have advanced the reputation of a far more seasoned scholar: 'Mr B. says to tell you you can go and fuck yourself.'

We don't know where he is now, but wherever, nobody, but nobody, is messing with that boy's buzz.

Ballet blues during Desert Storm

Maura O'Kiely
(Feature Writer and Columnist, *Evening Press*, 1988–1991)

Nina Tully walked into her ballet studio, where I was waiting to interview her for the *Evening Press*, and headed over to the barre. Although she now needed to use a walking stick, her reflection in the wall-sized mirror reflected a lifetime's dedication to good posture.

As principal of the Merrion School of Ballet in Ballsbridge, Tully had taught several generations of schoolgirls (and some boys), and was known for her single-minded dedication to classical ballet. I don't remember why features editor John Boland sent me along. Tully's teaching days were over, but perhaps it was because Operation Desert Storm was dominating the news and there would be no harm in reminding readers that a gentler world also existed.

Throughout the interview, Tully was the epitome of old-school decorum. Ever the teacher, she corrected mispronunciations and prompted questions about the realities of aspiring to be a professional dancer that I hadn't thought to ask ('Yes, body proportion does matter') and outlined the importance of discipline and poise. I remember that she made the most elegant gestures with her hands as she spoke.

Tully was personable, but there was also a steeliness that left you in no doubt that only the very foolish would have neglected to practise their arabesques and pirouettes between classes. She walked me around the studio, reminiscing about her fifty years as a teacher, precise in her recollections of past glories and successful former students. She referenced the great ballets and the most famous ballerinas. She was keen to emphasise how 'barre' was spelt.

Later, she gave me cake and tea and offered sherry. She said that the house we were in was her family home and that she lived there with her sister. She was outraged when I told her that a teacher had long ago told me not to even think of keeping up ballet as I was 'like a young pony'. 'I'm sure you would have been splendid,' Tully said gamely.

She asked me to post her a copy of the newspaper when the article was published, and steered me to the front door, where we said our goodbyes. 'Be kind to me,' she called from the doorway.

Of course I was kind to her. She was perfection. I probably went over the top with the superlatives. The piece was published. The opening line read: 'Nina Tully wanks into the room and heads for the bar'.

I didn't send her a copy.

Rocke and rolling back the years

William Rocke
(Assistant News Editor, *Sunday Press*, 1966–1995)

Looking back at my career as a journalist, I still feel rather proud that I was one of the few who actually wrote my way into the late, lamented *Sunday Press*. Even during my schooldays at St Andrew's National School in Dublin's Pearse Street, I always had a penchant for reading and writing, haunting my local library from an early age. Nobody else in my family had a literary bent, so I don't know where it came from.

I left school at fifteen, worked as a junior clerk for twelve years, and when that job folded became a freelance writer and began selling news stories and feature articles to newspapers and magazines, both in Ireland and occasionally the UK.

I also had a natural ability as a subeditor, and during that learning period did casual nights on the *Irish Press* newsdesk. I thought the rate then (26*s*. 6*d*. per shift) was fantastic! Whenever a permanent journalist's job became vacant in the group I was among the first to apply. Called for an interview, I'd face a trio of solemn-faced men: Bill Redmond, Colm Traynor and Conor O'Brien. I was invariably rejected when Bill discovered that I hadn't attended college and didn't have shorthand.

While casual subediting on the *Irish Press* I answered an ad for a subeditor's position on the *Belfast Telegraph*. I applied and got the job, even though I was short on experience. The *Telegraph* was an excellent newspaper with higher standards than any I had worked in, and I learned a lot there. That was late 1964.

I married my wife, Phyllis, the following summer, and we lived in Belfast until 1966 when the *Sunday Press* advertised for 'an experienced all-round journalist'. I applied and came to Dublin for an interview with the mild-mannered editor, Mr Carty. He had apparently seen action with the Old IRA in Belfast, and was more interested in what it was now like for a Catholic to live up there. Mr Carty skipped over my skills (or lack of them) as a journalist. I got the job.

Within a few short months of working with the *Sunday Press* I was being told to deputise as news editor to the late Gerry Fox, who, at that time, was frequently ill. It often meant editor Vincent Jennings asking me to compile an on-the-spot news list for our weekly conference. I'd often spend several weeks manning the newsdesk, deputising for Gerry – less than six months after I had been turned down flatly for a permanent job on the *Irish Press*. I must have been a fast learner.

It was a sad day indeed when the *Press* closed its doors. The feeling still abounds that we journalists provided a tired management with the opportunity to close down its loss-making, strike-purged newspapers.

It may well be. Now, on the twentieth anniversary of its closure, I still miss the camaraderie of the newsroom, the roar of the printing presses, the smell of the ink – and that man Con Houlihan.

Man, if the years could be rolled back, I'd still want to be a journalist!